Creative Teaching
of
Science
in the
Elementary School

2nd edition

ALBERT PILTZ
United States Office of Education

ROBERT SUND
University of Northern Colorado

Allyn and Bacon, Inc.
Boston, London, Sydney

To teachers everywhere—
striving to teach science creatively

Library of Congress Catalog Card Number: 73–90255

Printed in the United States of America

ISBN 0–205–04278–3
Second printing ... April, 1977

Dr. Piltz is a professional employee in the United States Office of Education. No official support or endorsement by the Office of Education is intended nor should be inferred.

Handwritten library markings:
LB
1585
P5
.1977

Alanar 7.95 (handwritten)
5-23-78 (handwritten)

CONTENTS

Foreword   vii

Preface   ix

CHAPTER I: Creativity in the Sciences   1

Science: A Creative Discipline   1
Superstitions of the Past and Science   2
Science as a Creative Force Expands Horizons   3
Scientific Creativity Defined   4
Characteristics of Creative Scientists   7
The Role of Instrumentation   10
Creativity and Science Education   11
Summary   12
Questions   13

CHAPTER II: The Schools and Creative Science   14

Influence of the Scholastic Tradition   14
Humans Have Multiple Talents   15
Intelligence and Creativity Do Not Always Correlate   18
Why Has Creativity Not Been Encouraged?   20
Teachers May Not Recognize Creative Individuals   22
Overstructuring Restricts Creative Possibilities   23
Developing Creative Enterprises   26
The "Big Bang" Teacher   35
Administrators Have Not Encouraged Teaching
    for Creativity   36
Summary   36
Questions   37

CHAPTER III: Working Creatively with Children
    in Science   39

Piaget's Four Stages of Cognitive Development   39
Summary of Piaget's Four Stages of Cognitive
    Development   42

Contents

Cognitive Evolution Varies with the Child   43
Implications of Piaget's Theory   44
Importance of Enriching Youthful Experiences   45
Setting the Stage for Creative Learning in Science   51
An Instructional Theory for Creative Development   55
Teachers May Stimulate or Inhibit Creative Ability   57
Stimulating by Questioning   61
Motivation and Problem Solving   64
Fostering the Creative Process   66
Summary   67
Questions   68

CHAPTER IV: Fostering a Creative Science Program   69

Home as the Spark Center for Creativity   69
*The Community: Provider of Centers for Creative Work
   and Social Responsibility*   74
Creative Teaching of Environmental Education   75
*Selected Sources of Environmental-Conservation
   Education Materials*   88
Wilderness Areas   89
Drug Education in the Elementary Grades   91
Scientists and Engineers Help   94
The Local Library   95
The Science Museum   96
The School: Magnifier of Creative Talent   97
How to Make Creative Learning of Science Exciting   97
Guiding Creative Development   100
Summary   112
Questions   113

CHAPTER V: Significant Factors for Creative Teaching   116

The Creative Teacher   116
The Physical Environment   121
Summary   126
Questions   128

CHAPTER VI: National Studies Programs—The
   Concern for Creativity in Curriculum Reform   129

*The National Revolution in Science Curriculum
   Reform*   129
Elementary Science Study (ESS)   132
*Science—A Process Approach (AAAS Commission
   on Science Education)*   148

Science Curriculum Improvement Study (SCIS)   156
Adapting Science Materials for the Blind (ASMB)   168
*Minnesota Mathematics and Science Teaching
    Project (MINNEMAST)*   172
*The Elementary Science Project (ESP)
    (Howard University)*   177
*Conceptually Oriented Program in Elementary
    Science (COPES)*   178
*Individualized Science (Formerly Individually
    Prescribed Instruction in Science—IPI Science)*   186
Science for the Seventies (SFTS)   192
*Model Educational Program in Ecology, Kindergarten
    Through Adult Education*   195
*Project In-step (In-service Teacher Education
    Program)*   201
*All Elementary Curriculum Materials Can Be Made
    More Creative*   206
Summary   206
Questions   207

**CHAPTER VII: Improving Curriculum Projects—The
Concern for Creativity in Curriculum Reform**   208

Elementary Science Textbook Revision   208
On Using Your Science Textbook   209
*Criteria for Selecting and Evaluating Science
    Textbooks*   210
*The Science Supervisor Should Encourage Teachers
    To Be More Creative*   218
*Trends in Elementary Science Teaching of a Past
    Decade—Have They Been Realized?*   218
*A Suggested Evaluation of Curriculum Materials
    for Creativity*   219
Designing a Science Curriculum for Creativity   220
*How an Elementary School Administrator Can
    Contribute to Creative Activity in Science*   221
Summary   223
Questions   223

CHAPTER VIII: Examples of Creative Science Activity   225

Principles of Creative Teaching   226
Rules to Follow in Stimulating Creative Work   227
Inquiry Discussions: A Special Technique   227
Inventing or Improvising   235
Counterintuitive or Discrepant Events   238

Contents

Pictorial Riddles   246
How Would You Draw Diagrams to Show . . . ?   261
How Would You Relate Words?   261
Brainstorming   263
Environmental Activities for Involvement Outside Class   263
Systems Analysis Approach   264
Preparing a Science Folder   266
Stories to Stimulate Creativity   266
Writing a Play Illustrating Scientific Discovery   267
Make and Collect Cartoons Depicting Scientific
   Principles   267
Make Stick Figures Indicating Some Science Concept   267
Prepare Science Collages   268
Identify Hidden Objects   268
Creatively Fill the Spaces   269
Additional Creative Suggestions   270
Use of a Grid to Force Creative Production   270
How to Use Experiments Creatively   271
Guide Children Toward Discovering Open-ended
   Possibilities in an Experiment   273
Steps to Follow in Helping Students Experiment   275
Changing a Cookbook Experiment to Make It More
   Creative   275
Demonstration as a Means of Discovery   279
Procedure for Selecting and Presenting a Creative
   Demonstration   281
Examples of Creative Demonstration Lessons   282
Summary   289
Suggested Activities to Increase Understanding of
   Information Given in This Chapter   290

CHAPTER IX: Conclusion   291

Selected Bibliography   297

Index   305

FOREWORD

In the Foreword of the first editions of the Creative Teaching series, E. Paul Torrance expressed a concern that many exciting, meaningful and potentially important ideas have died because no one has translated them into practical methods and that this could be the fate of the creative movement. Fortunately, this concern has not been realized. In the past ten years educational literature has been flooded with reports of research studies, theories and experimental programs which focus on the creative development of each child as a goal in modern education.

Including the development of creativity in each child as an educational objective is a staggering challenge for all school personnel. Its calls for the invention of new materials and tools, the development of new time schedules and new patterns of organization, a new approach to child study, the invention of new testing methods, the devising of unique evaluation processes and the creation of new textbooks and teaching procedures. And most of all the task calls for a commitment and dedication on the part of many people to take risks, to make choices and decisions, to push their own creative potential to new limits.

This has been done! In the past ten years the creative spark has caught fire. Thousands of people in all walks of life have found in the creative movement, self-realization and the challenge of making life meaningful for others. The educational scene in America has become peppered with experimental projects in the development of creative thinking.

No movement in education has swept the world as the creative movement has. The need for creative people across the globe today is tremendous. Developing the creative potential of each child has become an educational objective even unto the far corners of the world. The authors of the Creative Teaching series hope these volumes will contribute in some bold measure to producing the changes in teaching methods in the elementary school necessary to realize this objective.

James A. Smith
Oswego, New York

PREFACE

At no time in the history of education has the need for creative teaching of science been greater. The impact of science and technology on our environment, together with population growth and its accompanying pressures, has placed an overwhelming burden on our ecosystems. Accelerated change, new life styles and subcultures, the overall quality of life, are indices of the great challenge before us.

This book is addressed to the creative aspects of science teaching. It is replete with suggestions on developing and nurturing children's creative potential in the sciences. It outlines modifications of standard teaching methods to make them more creative, and gives examples of experiments, demonstrations, pictorial riddles, inquiring discussions, and counterintuitive activities. Various elementary science curriculum projects are analyzed and reviewed from a creative standpoint, and suggestions are made for developing creative criteria for evaluating elementary science texts. Environmental and drug education are discussed in the context of creative science programs.

First and most important, scientific literacy is a major objective in science education; our best educational effort is required to help the child understand science (now integral to our culture), in relation to himself, his society, and his natural environment. There is an urgency today for science education to engage in solving problems of human living. Corrective action on the environmental condition requires a scientific understanding of the nature of ecology and environmental systems, coupled with social responsibility. Science today is more important than ever—not only as a means of sanitizing the environment and contributing to the "good life," but also because of its very nature, it stands for the forces of reason against irrationality. Science education of the 70s needs modernized curricula and a particularly creative style of teaching on all levels of instruction, for goals consistent with the needs of the time.

Research in modern psychology has revealed that the development of creative ability in the young may be far more important than has been believed. There are critical periods in a child's life when the creative potential must be released or it will lie dormant, never to manifest itself fully in the life of the individual. This book endeavors to make teachers more aware of this point and offers suggestions for providing more creative science instruction, perhaps to ignite a spark in the young so they may live the excitement of science achievement. Because science is investigative by nature, it offers bountiful opportunities for both teacher and pupils to unleash their abilities to cope with the challenge of the times. If in some way we help teachers achieve this end, the authors will have attained their purpose.

ALBERT PILTZ
ROBERT SUND

CHAPTER I

Creativity in the Sciences

When Sir Humphrey Davy described his student Michael Faraday as his greatest discovery, he told us who teach that our greatest contributions may well be made when we help release the potentiality to create that exists in all our students. The good teacher encourages creativity through expressing interest, providing facilities, guidance and inspiration to his pupils.

GLENN O. BLOUGH

SCIENCE: A CREATIVE DISCIPLINE

A page from the history of the advancement of mankind is a page from the history of science. The influence of science in modern life is so powerful that it stimulates and colors all phases of human development. Science has moved out of the laboratory into the living room of man; it has become a discipline integral to his survival in the present and his progress in the future.

There is no field of human knowledge that affords a greater outlet for creative activity than science; its very nature and structure demand innovation and encourage original thought and action. While from its inception applied science (or technology) has solved many of mankind's problems, it has at the same time introduced new universal problems. And it may well require the scientist's imagination and know-how to help us understand the relationship of modern technology to our own lives.

The scientist has specially acquired the skills for developing new ideas, models, and products. The ground over which the scientist moves is usually unexplored and requires new approaches. Science, if it can be personified, asks only that it be used to help man unearth nature's secrets and lead him to a better understanding of his natural and industrial environment.

SUPERSTITIONS OF THE PAST AND SCIENCE

In its widest sense, superstition includes all those beliefs which have no scientific basis or factual support. We fear what we do not understand. Primitive man was mystified and terrified by such natural phenomena as fire, lightning, thunder, even seasonal changes: a comet flashing through the sky was a frightening aspect of nature. Even today, the widespread existence of superstitious belief among primitive peoples proves how common to all men these feelings are. This erroneous perception is the first of the causes of superstition. A primitive man hears an echo, sees a mirage, or dreams a dream; not knowing the reason for these things, he develops fears and fantasies about the unknown.

Another basis for superstition is that throughout the ages truth has been corrupted by oral tradition. (The story of the Flood may, as we know, have some factual basis.) And a third reason lies in man's own deep instincts and emotions, which help to foster false beliefs and superstitions. His fear of death led man to such burial practices as binding the body of the deceased to keep the spirits from escaping. His desire to appease the gods led to the use of charms—carrying a fetish or an amulet, or beating a tom-tom. Curiosity about the future led man to the study of the stars and to astrology—and eventually to the science of astronomy.

Both inanimate objects and animals held special fascination for primitive man, who believe that they were inhabited by spirits. In order to explain to himself the reason for the presence of these spirits, man concluded that these were either the spirits of deceased humans or of the lesser deities.

Primitive man thought that some diseases were caused by the entrance into the body of an evil spirit, which had to be driven out to effect a cure. This exorcism was the function of the priest, magician, or medicine man of the tribe—and undoubtedly many ill people suffered more from the treatment than from the disease.

During the Middle Ages, several fearful epidemics swept Europe as fast as a rat could travel. Today we know that all of these plagues are both contagious and controllable; but at that time they were supposed to have been caused by evil spirits, bad air, hot winds, or fog. Yet prior to then, during Greece's Golden Age, Hippocrates had already laid the foundations of a science of medicine based upon experience, observation, and reason. And after centuries of groping, some glimpses of scientific medical truth began to appear. Modern medical science, as we know, has made great strides in removing the shackles of the past and pushing aside the boundaries of the future.

Many of the customs and superstitions of the past persist today because their causes have never ceased to be operative. Those people who are ignorant and untrained in scientific methods of thinking tend to draw conclusions from one occurrence or from coincidence. Thus the inability to draw a correct connection between cause and effect tends to keep superstition alive even today. In addition, an incorrect observation may become the basis for an incorrect generalization, and a reliance upon memory rather than upon fact accounts for many misconceptions. Superstition and misconception are of such ancient origin that many of them have become heritages of the race.

It is true that intelligent modern people are more accustomed to think in terms of natural causes. Nevertheless, there are still many events of which science knows little, and these will continue to be associated with mysticism until science understands them.

Superstition seems to go hand in hand with ignorance and poverty. Not until man is able to destroy the conditions under which it develops and the environment in which it grows will superstition be eliminated.

SCIENCE AS A CREATIVE FORCE EXPANDS HORIZONS

The birth of science may well have caused the death of superstition in the foreseeable future. The enemy is slowly retreating before man's developing knowledge and his understanding of the forces that threaten and subjugate him.

Science has had to earn its way to acceptance. This has not always been easy; taboos, superstitious customs, and cultural implants have fought the use of science as a creative tool. But scientific processes at work have dispelled many past fallacies, unsupportable hypotheses, and unfounded beliefs. Today there is scarcely one area of life that does not evidence the creativity of science. Our food, our air-conditioning and heating systems, our medical advances, and, most important, our present move out into space—all these and many other expanding horizons have been made possible only through science as a creative force used for the benefit of mankind.

The evolution of science has necessitated changes in thinking and psychological behavior. We have had to move from a simple pragmatic attitude toward life to one based on empiricism and logic as well. We are also aware that science has presented us with a Pandora's box, which, if opened without care, could result, not only in the denigration of science, but in total calamity as well. But, creatively handled, science's potential for good can be realized.

SCIENTIFIC CREATIVITY DEFINED

There are two pathways to the use of science as a creative tool—the standard, orthodox method and the more exciting unorthodox, unique approach.

How do we define scientific creativity? The products and processes of science are deeply embedded in the matrix of creativity; however, what science is in its modern context must be clearly understood. Perhaps we can understand science as a discipline

FIGURE 1-1. *Science is people searching, children investigating, inquiring, and seeking verifiable knowledge. (SCIS Photo)*

better if we know what scientists do. Dr. Paul Blackwood[1] has devised this working definition:

A working definition of science is helpful in giving clues as to what may properly be included in the study of science. The following tentative definition has the virtue of including enough ingredients to reflect the breadth and richness of science. *Science is man's relentless search for verifiable patterns, concepts, descriptions, or explanations of phenomena in the universe.*

In this definition, we see that man is in the picture. Science is an enterprise, an activity of people. Science is people searching. It is men, women, and children investigating, inquiring, and seeking verifiable knowledge. It is relentless, a continuous, never-ending attempt to find more accurate descriptions of things and events and to seek reasonable explanations of these events. The search leads to new discoveries, to new insights about unifying patterns, to concepts, to understandings, and to new knowledge. Many of these observations, descriptions, and explanations have been recorded by scientists and are available for use by other people as they attempt to extend their knowledge and understanding of the natural environment. This recorded knowledge, about which people can communicate, is an important part of science.

A definition of science like that discussed above has been eschewed by some scientists on the grounds that you can define science better in terms of what scientists do. It seems simple to say, "Science is what scientists do." But to understand this statement requires an analysis of what it is that men and women do when they are being scientists. Let us then, in our exploration of what science is, look briefly at three of the basic things that scientists do.

a. *Scientists make descriptions.* What is in the universe? How many? How much? How long? How frequently? Where? When? Under what circumstances? Answers to such questions are descriptions.

Astronomers use telescopes, cameras, and instruments of other kinds. They use mathematics and their minds to try to get a picture of our universe and how the bodies in space are interrelated. Geologists study rock structures, formations of the earth, and changes in its surface. The study requires careful observation and accurate reporting. Physicists attempt to find out how energy flows from one material to another and what happens to the materials.

1. P. E. Blackwood, "Science Teaching in the Elementary School," *Science and Children*, vol. 2, no. 1 (September 1964).

Thus, scientists attempt to describe what is, how things are, what things are like, how they change, and how they interrelate. Improved descriptions of things and events in our universe enable scientists to discover unity within vast diversity. Methods that have proven practical in discovering the elements of unity within diversity and in getting "check-up-able" knowledge we sometimes call scientific methods. As other people use these methods, they are able to verify what someone else has observed.

b. *Scientists make explanations.* In a sense, scientists attempt to tell "why" certain events and phenomena occur the way they do. This usually involves observing carefully how things interact with each other. What are the interrelationships? What precedes what? What follows what? Under what conditions do certain phenomena occur? Making explanations usually involves showing the connections between events or phenomena.

In a way, an explanation is a very careful description. For example, to explain why water evaporates from an open dish requires knowledge about the physical structure of water, about the nature of molecular action, about the capacity of air to hold water molecules, the behavior of water molecules when heat energy is increased, and the like. Scientists are detectives attempting to put descriptions together in ways that help us understand events. In this way, they make explanations.

c. *Scientists make predictions.* In order to make knowledge more widely applicable and to extend our confidence in its validity, it must be tested in many situations. Extending our knowledge to new situations involves prediction. We have observed that water will evaporate from a dish on a window sill. We predict that it will evaporate also if placed on a warm radiator. We test to see. If it does, then our prediction is correct.

Scientists are continually testing to see if principles that apply in one situation will apply in another. Making use of a concept of generalizations or law in a situation which has not yet been tested involves prediction. Scientists have not been on the moon.[2] Yet numerous predictions of what it is like there have been made and may be proven true. Actually, the acceptance of certain predictions as fact enables planning for the moon launch to proceed with confidence. Making predictions is an important part of what scientists do.

---

2. Since Dr. Blackwood wrote his definition, man has been to the moon several times. The generalizations and predictions were most accurate and facilitated the successful moon missions.

In making descriptions, explanations, and predictions, scientists use their minds; they use ideas of their own and ideas of others as tools for testing and gaining knowledge. They use many resources to get valid answers to their questions or solutions to their problems. They may invent new tools with which to observe or to check phenomena more accurately. Thus, scientists do many things in relation to making valid descriptions, explanations and predictions.

CHARACTERISTICS OF CREATIVE SCIENTISTS

Throughout history there have been men whose creativity in their respective scientific fields was outstanding—Galileo, Copernicus, Pasteur, Marconi, Edison, and Oppenheimer, for example. All of them produced lasting benefits, either for man's personal needs or in helping him utilize his environment better. What is so distinctive about these men? Perhaps it is that they *used* creativity to *produce* something creative. As Eisner says, "The product gives some indications of who will be called creative."[3]

And yet there are many scientists who labor long years and whose works are appreciated only after their deaths. Eisner also says that creativity "must be a product of the judgment. . . . It is some produce or act which is judged as creative by others." Consequently, both timing and the opinion of others have a bearing on creativity.

In judging creativity in the sciences, we find that there are certain essential parameters; two of these, originality and esthetics, appear to come into existence simultaneously. For example, when Leeuwenhoek developed the first microscope, he approached the problem of microviewing with both originality and imagination. While he knew that the lens could be used to magnify small objects, he presented the science of microscopy with an original structure by encasing the lens within a simple tube and using mirrored light so as to bring about an ordered magnification of the world in a drop of pond water. In addition, this simple apparatus was also a thing of unique design and esthetic proportion. Thus he demonstrated the two attributes of creativity in science—originality of concept and the development of a new product (original design). We might also add that Leeuwenhoek's microscope, as an instrument of research, has revolutionized the field of biology and the related sciences.

3. Elliot W. Eisner, *Think with Me About Creativity* (Dansville, New York: F. A. Owen Publishing Co., 1964).

Guilford[4] and his coworkers believed they could characterize the abilities necessary to creative thinking. Some of these include the following:

1. Ability to recognize problems.
2. Ability to produce novel ideas.
3. Ability to organize ideas.
4. Ability to evaluate.

Scientists do possess these traits and many more. Numerous studies have shown that scientists who made original contributions have a high degree of curiosity and awareness. (One eminent scientist has said that his eye was trained "to look at what everyone has looked at, but to see what no one else has seen.")

The scientist is resourceful; he is self-directed; he works with an open mind and an emotionality that could classify him as a missionary. Though creative people are not necessarily highly intelligent, the scientist does have high mental ability. He is articulate—particularly in asking the right kind of questions, although the answers are not always obtained in the conventional ways. The scientist has the vision to explore new pathways. And finally, the scientist is a positive person who knows who he is.

Pasteur, in nineteenth-century Paris, knew that both childbed fever and rabies were diseases. He reasoned that, instead of being accepted fatalistically as they then were, they should be recognized as challenges to be overcome. Pasteur's attitude reveals a characteristic common to scientists and possessing a dimension of creativity. He saw a problem and objectively assumed that it should be resolved.

Of course Pasteur's vision included much more than merely recognizing the problem. It encompassed another of the characteristics of creativity—the ability to produce a unique idea for dealing with the problem, in that point in time, for the positive good of man. Pasteur was able to determine the vector of disease as a bacterial agent. He gathered and organized information, and brought it to bear on the problem of developing a cure for the disease. His observations were based on experimentation and inquiry, which led him to the reconstruction of knowledge. This ability to organize and reconstruct from new findings is one of the more important elements of creativity in the sciences.

Insight and intuition, both characteristic of the scientist at work, are other sources of creativity. In scientific investigation,

4. J. P. Guilford, "The Structure of Intellect," *Psychological Bulletin*, vol. 53 (July 1956), pp. 267–293.

the problem is often identified and an hypothesis for solution pre-pared. This simple beginning may trigger a process of inquiry into basic definitions, suppositions, generalizations, principles, and relationships. After the solution is obtained, the creative process is manifest in the final steps—testing and evaluating the solution. An evaluation that considers the wide spectrum of the background elements for the scientific effort is usually one requir-ing as creative an approach as the process of solving the problem itself.

Over the years a determined effort has been made to define creativity in terms of personality. Traits that seem to characterize the creative scientist (as well as other creative individuals) have been identified. According to Eisner, the creative person possesses:

1. Emotional stability (certainly a most desirable trait when look-ing at a scientific problem in a creative, objective manner).
2. Sense of humor.
3. Character.
4. Wide range of interests.
5. Goal-directedness.
6. High academic achievement.

This list is based on research done by Getzels and Jackson, who, when testing children, compiled some interesting data from highly creative children.

Emotional stability should be emphasized as a most desirable trait. In science, the creative person often is nonconforming and out of step with the currents of time. Emotional stability will allow his creativeness to develop and to proceed without attendant neurosis.

The creative person in science follows Riesman's classification of inner-directedness—that is, he seeks inwardly for guidance on decisions and actions.[5] This quality requires a high degree of self-discipline and motivation.

Creative science flourishes best in an atmosphere that allows and permits challenge and does not hinder the thinking process. Of course, there have been exceptions. Many of the truly creative scientists survived hostility against the birth of new ideas, fought their greatest battles while in prison, and some, in their darkest hours, generated conceptual schemes that have shaped history and had a telling effect on the progress of mankind. Many house-hold names of today lived and died in their day in adversity.

5. David Riesman, *The Lonely Crowd* (New Haven: Yale University Press, 1950).

Copernicus was denounced as a blasphemer; Newton was forced to recant; Galileo was branded a heretic; and Darwin's theory of evolution brought the denunciation of the theologians down upon him.

Nevertheless, the great creative ideas of science have been most evident where there was a free environment with a minimum of pressure, stresses, and obstruction. The old maxim, "Where there is no vision, the people perish," has a direct application to the scientist. Science must have windows on the world which open to new vistas and allow for free entry and exit of ideas. Scientists must exercise freely in their environment, unhindered by prohibitions.

THE ROLE OF INSTRUMENTATION

Utility is implicit in the creative concept of science. A creative product must be a useful product. Fox says, "It must be useful in the broadest sense, including everything from a bit of equipment to a new concept in helping with the understanding or control of the environment."

What has been the creative significance of the development of the new instruments and equipment of modern science? It is this: These tools help scientific investigators use their senses to better advantage. Man has succeeded in developing tools that have enabled him to widen his horizons in incredible ways. Our only communication with our real world is through our five senses; but the telescope and the microscope have allowed us to see things we could not see with the naked eye. We are able to "see" stars toward the far reaches of the universe and to record cosmic phenomena that occurred billions of light years ago. The extension of sight through instruments has enabled us to visualize the structure of the atom and the microworld of the virus. Through radio telescopes, which stand ready to pick up sounds from the farthest galaxies, our sense of hearing has been miraculously extended through vast distances in space. Instrumentation has explored sounds through incredible distances in the ocean depths.

Our natural senses have been extended. But new senses have been created as well. We can now detect magnetic fields and minute amounts of radiation in and around the earth.

Perhaps the greatest advance in instrumentation is the electronic computer with its memory that can retrieve, record, and transmit man's many sensory impressions and solve his problems electronically. Without this enormously valuable tool, man would be hard put to utilize the results of the knowledge explosion. The American Institute of Physics alone publishes more than 25,000 pages of research reports each year.

At the present rate of research, the scientific knowledge acquired by the 1973 graduate will be inadequate by 1980; by 1985 much of it will be obsolete. In the nineteenth century our scientific knowledge doubled every fifty years; today it is doubling every ten, and the rate of increase is constantly accelerating.

The promise of the future is overwhelming. But we must remember that scientific progress will move unimpeded only if human values are used to engender broader human understanding and cooperation. To this end, man must exert his most creative efforts.

CREATIVITY AND SCIENCE EDUCATION

Since modern society is based principally on our great scientific progress, science has become a substantive part of the educational process today. Although a relative newcomer to the curriculum, science is now taught in almost every grade in every school in the United States and is well on the way to becoming a sequential program at all levels of instruction.

The ferment of change taking place in science curricula today is evidence of creativity in science education. The forces that are shaping science curricula, particularly in the elementary school, are powerful and pervasive. They show hope for the improvement of the instruction in ways that will release the creative potential of every child as he probes his physical and biological worlds in a society beset with problems.

These emerging changes are relatively new; they are not the result of our competition with other countries for superiority in science. Rather, they reflect a shifting focus on the objectives and values commonly held over the past thirty years for sustaining and improving the quality of man's existence.

What are some of the creative channels that are being provided in science education which will foster creative experience? For one thing, the learner in today's classroom will not spend his time regurgitating memorized answers to stereotyped questions. He will, instead, devote more of his time dealing with the nature and structure of science, and finding answers to problems that have relevance to the better understanding of his world.

We know that creative science is more than new knowledge. It is also a way of thinking and acting which demands that pupils learn to identify problems and seek their solution. For this they must understand basic principles and the process of science which encompasses the skill of observation, a questioning and exploring attitude, a knowledge of experimentation, the ability to work out relationships, the patience to test and retest, and the persistence to try again and again when their efforts fail.

The student who is working creatively in science will realize that, no matter how clearly the result of an experiment points to a conclusion, scientific problems are seldom answered conclusively. The concern of science education is the development of an inquiring mind and a respect for scholarship, for science is essentially a method of learning—a creative process—not a book of answers.

SUMMARY

There is no discipline or area of human endeavor that cannot furnish a mode for creative expression, but science can provide one of the most fertile fields of all for creative expression. Scientists are among the most creative persons in our society. Collectively, they represent a professional group whose activities make a significant difference to the lives of the whole human family. Although in the past, superstitions have impeded scientific progress and still persist in many forms today, science pervades our social, economic, political, and intellectual lives. Therefore, it is incumbent upon the beneficiaries of science to understand it and use it wisely. The modern definition of science has been broadened to include the work of the scientist and the creative aspects of his endeavors. Instrumentation has extended man's senses and was the precursor of many of the major "breakthroughs" in science. Science education is the means of developing a scientifically literate citizenry and training scientists and technicians for the multiple fields of science created by the explosion of knowledge. It is essential for the understanding of ecological and environmental systems for an increased awareness of the individual and his social responsibility.

QUESTIONS

1. What makes science a creative discipline?

2. What are some of the traits that the scientist has in common with other creative individuals who are recognized for their contributions to society?

3. How do superstition, misconceptions, fear, and false beliefs impede the work of the creative scientist?

4. What is the role of instrumentation in scientific advancement?

5. Is there a trend toward humanism in science today? Why?

6. It is said we are in an ecological crisis with regard to both human and environmental problems. Explain.

7. How has technological efforts to improve human life created hazards which endanger the human species? What other factors impact on the problem?

8. How will science education provide creative channels for children in the classroom?

CHAPTER II

The Schools
and Creative Science

There was a child went forth every day,
And the first object he looked upon, that object he became,
And that object became part of him for the day or a certain
*   part of the day,*
Or for many years or stretching cycles of years. . . .

WALT WHITMAN

INFLUENCE OF THE SCHOLASTIC TRADITION

For many reasons, schools and teachers generally have neither produced nor rewarded creative activity in science. The tendency to stress conformity in the school, the methods of instruction, and the fact that teachers have not used their skills have all contributed to the situation. Even today there is a thread of the scholastic tradition, dating from the thirteenth century, emphasizing the importance of the teacher as a reservoir of knowledge. This antiquated method of instruction directed the teacher to tell or read to the children, since books were then too expensive for each child to have. The teacher knew the answers and gave them when needed. Lecture and recitation dominated the approach to learning. Naturally, there was little chance of discovery and practically no chance for creative expression under such a method.

One outgrowth of the scholastic tradition was the emphasis upon the product rather than the processes of knowledge. It was assumed that if you learned the facts and rules of the body of knowledge you knew all there was to know about the subject. For example, if you learned the rules of logic you would be logical; or if you learned certain principles of design, color, and texture in art you could produce a good painting. Little concern was given to the fact that the activity of painting is a vital ingredient in the process of self-realization in art.

There is a simple explanation of why this overemphasis on product has continued. If you know the rules of policy of a discipline, you know considerably more than if you know just a few scattered facts. If you know the rules of grammar, you can obviously speak more correctly even though you may not necessarily be a more creative speaker. Knowledge of the rules helps to direct behavior in a more rational manner; but it may also restrict and diminish the problem-solving potential. Learning a series of rules, theories, laws, or principles without some involvement in how they were derived could stifle the imagination and limit their application.

The teaching approach that emphasizes *the product of knowledge* sets up a barrier to creative thinking. How can one experience the esthetic thrill of discovery or invention in science without living and feeling like a scientist? One can't learn the processes of science without being actively involved in science in a pragmatic and an intellectual way. Other disciplines, such as geography or history, may be described even superficially, and the learner may gain much. Music and art can give pleasure without the understanding of the individual, but science must be understood to be appreciated. Many teachers are not aware that science is a creative endeavor and this may be sorely reflected in their methods of teaching. In retrospect, look at your elementary school experiences. Where was your creative potential developed? How many teachers really tried to guide and encourage you to create in any subject, least of all in science? If you had been exposed to teachers who tried to set the environment to allow for creativity, would your teaching be different today? Have you stretched your own mind so that you are ready for the unexpected in your classes?

HUMANS HAVE MULTIPLE TALENTS

Over the last fifty years there has been a revolution in instruction that is still continuing. One major trend is the move away from the medieval teacher-centered concept to a modern student-centered approach.

Furthermore, there is an increasing awareness among educators that humans are a composite of a vast number of talents: academic, planning, forecasting, communication, social, musical, artistic, and others. It is the role of the teacher to facilitate the development of all these talents in as many ways as possible. Figure 2-1 shows some possible variations in the skills and knowledge of a student.

Dr. Calvin Taylor says: "If we limit ourselves merely to one talent, only 50% of the students will have a chance to be above average (the median). However, if we consider two talents, the percent above average in at least one of the two talents will be in the high 60s; for three talents, in the 70s; for four talents in the low 80s, etc. Across several talents, nearly 90% will be above average in at least one talent area; and almost all others will be nearly average in at least one of the talent areas. Therefore, almost all students are above average. From the same evidence,

FIGURE 2-1. *Multiple talent totem poles (Source: Calvin W. Taylor, "Be Talent Developers,"* Today's Education, *N.E.A. Journal (December 1968), p. 69.*

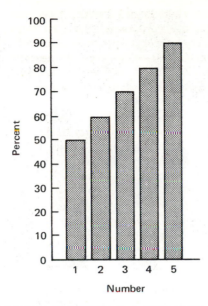

FIGURE 2-2. *Percentage of students in a class above average per number of talents*

about one-third of the students will be highly gifted in at least one of the multiple-talent areas."[1]

Compare for a moment two science classes. In one, three children are attempting to set up an aquarium; two others are trying to make a balance out of some sticks and boards; two girls are working on a mural showing different animals in dissimilar communities (the desert, grasslands, and coniferous forests); and two boys are trying to prepare a bog terrarium. Several groups of students are engaged in various activities to determine the conditions needed for seeds to sprout. There is real motivation as each of these groups tries to determine what will make its seeds sprout first. A few children are working on their projects for the forthcoming science fair. This classroom shows *diverse activities,* a certain supply of materials, and freedom for pupils to work out their problems with an inner direction and purpose. Some of the children work as individuals, others in groups, according to their problems or interests.

1. Calvin W. Taylor, "Nearly All Students Are Talented—Let's Reach Them!" *Utah Parent Teacher* (February 1969), pp. 9–10.

FIGURE 2-3. *Humans have over 120 talents. Which talents might this child be using and how is the teacher facilitating their development? (SCIS Photo)*

Contrast this with a science class where for a total program thirty children listen to the teacher read sections of the science lesson, ask questions about it, and then some pupils read part of the text. There are no aquaria nor terraria, no sprouting seeds, no models or murals or instructional materials. In fact, the room looks clean, neat, and sterile. This teacher isn't concerned about and probably isn't aware of the need to develop talents.

It is easy to see, however, that the first teacher maximizes the opportunities for students to develop diverse talents, and gives them many chances to be creative.

INTELLIGENCE AND CREATIVITY DO NOT ALWAYS CORRELATE

The research of the past decade has revealed that schools generally have emphasized the development of intellectual but not creative achievement. This has been partly due to the mistaken assumption that these two characteristics correlate relatively well. However, Dr. E. Paul Torrance, in studying the gifted, has found

that scores on creativity tests do not correlate particularly well with scores on I.Q. tests. He says: "No matter what measure of I.Q. is chosen we would exclude about 70% of our most creative children if I.Q. alone were used in identifying giftedness."[2]
This, he emphasizes, is true for all grades and any I.Q. test. In analyzing I.Q. tests, he found they emphasized mainly tasks requiring memory, cognition, and convergent thinking. Upon further study he found that high I.Q. is also considered more desirable in students and is better recognized by teachers than creativity. He says: "In general the high I.Q., lower-creativity pupils tend to be preferred by teachers to those high on *both* I.Q. and creativity."[3] Wallach and Hogan reported similar findings.[4] Although intelligence and creativity are not the same, Dr. Anne Roe found that the minimum intelligence required for creative production in science is decidedly higher than the average I.Q.[5]

Teachers have traditionally thought that if they concentrated on the high I.Q. student—the gifted—they would be giving their greatest attention to those with the greatest potential. Torrance's work, however, shows that this is far from true; it suggests one reason why teachers have not encouraged the creative child. In addition, an experiment was conducted in a science class in Salt Lake City, where students in the same class were compared under two systems of evaluation. The first part of the year they were rewarded mainly for academic achievement; the second part, for creative achievement. The outstanding students, those getting A's in the first part of the year, were not the ones who achieved in the second part.[6] Dr. Donald MacKennon, of the University of California, studied outstanding creative adults in our society. When looking at their school achievement, he found the majority received C's and B's rather than A's, clearly indicating the school did not evaluate on the basis of creative ability.[7] The National

2. Calvin Taylor and Frank Barron, *Scientific Creativity: Its Recognition and Development* (New York: John Wiley & Sons, Inc., 1963), p. 183.
3. Taylor and Barron, *Scientific Creativity*, p. 183.
4. Michael A. Wallach and Nathan Hogan, *Modes of Thinking—A Study of Creative-Intelligence Distinction* (New York: Rinehart and Winston, Inc., 1965), p. 6.
5. Anne Roe, "The Psychology of the Scientist," *Science*, 134 (August 18, 1961), pp. 56–59.
6. Calvin Taylor, "Creativity in Science Education," *News and Views*, vol. 7, no. 4 (December 1963), p. 1.
7. Donald MacKennon, "The Creative Individual," Broadcast #50250 V.E., Columbia Broadcasting System, University of California Explorer, unpublished (January 28, 1962).

Merit Scholarship Corporation, realizing academic achievement alone does not necessarily reveal the creative individual, has set aside special scholarships for students who have demonstrated creative ability even though their grades may not be outstanding.

WHY HAS CREATIVITY NOT BEEN ENCOURAGED?

Schools Have Overemphasized Verbal Skills

One reason why teachers and schools generally have not recognized and rewarded the creative child, particularly in science, may be the emphasis on verbal skills. Dr. Calvin Taylor, while doing research on creativity in young children, was struck by this possibility when he orally tested boys who had an outstanding degree of flexibility and inventiveness but had difficulty in writing and reading and, therefore, received low scores on written tests. Any teacher who has taught for any length of time probably has had similar experiences. We know of an intern teacher who was alert enough to recognize the same situation. He taught a unit on science to the fifth grade. During discussions and demonstrations one of the boys in class responded with good hypotheses as to what was going to happen in the demonstration and, at the conclusion of the demonstrations or experiments, had well-thought-out explanations. He certainly was above average in formulating hypotheses and drawing conclusions. However, when a test was administered this boy did poorly. The intern was frustrated and consulted with the master teacher. The master teacher told him she suspected the boy didn't read well and didn't want to take the test. Consequently, the intern asked if he could give the boy the same test orally and she encouraged him to do so. When this was done, the boy made only one minor mistake, indicating that poor reading ability was at the root of the problem. Students with interest in science may often demonstrate similar verbal problems. Dr. Anne Roe has cautioned teachers about students who seem to have an interest in science but poor verbal skills. She says:

> There can be another problem, especially in the very early grades, where the predominant emphasis of education is upon the development of verbal skills. The potential scientists are going to be of above average intelligence. Many of them, however, will have relatively lower verbal than nonverbal abilities.[8]

8. Roe, *The Psychology of the Scientist*, p. 133.

Dr. Finkelstein reports that when children are given pictorial tests and asked questions on audio tapes, many of them achieve much better than when given a written test. He says that many so-called science tests are really reading tests; the students often do know the science but fail the test because of poor verbal competence.[9]

Peer Pressures May Inhibit Creative Expression

Sociologists and psychologists have long pointed out that several group pressures for conformity are operating within the school. Dr. E. Paul Torrance, using creativity test scores and sociometric techniques, found that the peers of creative children do not generally rank them high in status. In summarizing a study of twenty-five groups of elementary school children he stated the following:

> Rather clear evidence of pressure against the most creative member of each group was found in all 25 groups studied. A majority (68%) of the most creative initiated more ideas than any other member of the group, just as they did in the test of creativity administered earlier. Few (24%) were seen by other group members as making the most valuable contribution to the group's performance. Boys tended to demonstrate and explain more principles than girls (significant at better than the .01 level). At the fifth-grade level, however, the girls initiated slightly more ideas than the boys, an accomplishment compatible with what appears to be a fairly general spurt in the development of creative thinking abilities in girls at the fifth-grade level.[10]

He also found that, particularly in the upper elementary grades, groups developed more techniques to control the creative individual. The creative child, in order to be accepted by his peers, soon learns to adapt in a number of ways, most of which hinder his creative development. Research of this nature on creativity and group dynamics clearly indicates another reason why the school has had difficulty in nurturing creative endeavor.

Teacher's Insecurity May Restrict Creativity

Another hindrance to the development of creative scientific ability in children is the fact that creative children may threaten a

9. Leonard B. Finkelstein and Donald D. Hammill, "A Reading-Free Science Test," *The Elementary School Journal* (October 1969), pp. 34–37.
10. Taylor and Barron, *Scientific Creativity*, p. 181.

teacher's feelings of security. Often a creative child asks questions and is enthusiastic about a scientific topic in which the teacher is very insecure, particularly if she believes she should "know the answers" to everything. The teacher's lack of training in the sciences often has given her such feelings of inferiority that when children present motivational opportunities for science activity she may be hesitant to develop them. Such an opportunity presented itself to a third-grade teacher when a boy ran into class with a spider he had trapped in a jar. He asked his teacher if he could raise it and make a home for it in class. The teacher, who knew nothing about spiders and actually feared them, told the boy the class was going to study stars during the science period. She also informed him that spiders were studied in a later grade and to take the spider out of the room and dispose of it. By reacting this way, the teacher failed to grasp the spark of enthusiasm in the child's mind. The child's immediate dynamic interest in spiders might have led to several possibilities of creative endeavor, not only on his part but the class's as well. The spider's presence could have aroused spontaneous questions which could have motivated the children to think and find answers. For example, she might have asked: What use are spiders? How should they be protected? What kind of a home does a spider require? How could we build a spider racetrack and have a spider race? How could we find out if spiders will race? What other insects could be raised in class? What kind of homes would they require? Many other question-problems would undoubtedly have arisen once the children began to investigate. Remember, some of the best learning is incidental learning.

TEACHERS MAY NOT RECOGNIZE CREATIVE INDIVIDUALS

Teachers may not be aware of the indications of creative ability as outlined in Figure 2-4.

Teachers have been inclined to control the above behavior by punishing the child; they have tended to treat the symptom rather than the cause of the misbehavior, thereby stifling the creative ability of many children.

Other blocks to the development of creative potential have been the teacher's emphasis on subject matter, overplanning, overuse of text books, and the use of gadgets. For example, programmed instruction has often emphasized academia at the expense of creative learning.

The Student May

Demonstrate deviating class behavior
Not want to follow the crowd
Refuse to accept superficial statements about science
Prefer to work alone at least up until fifth grade when peer pressures begin to grow stronger.
More likely act the clown
Become apathetic
Demonstrate inconsistent performance
Present more problems to the teacher if he or she doesn't have opportunities for creative release.

FIGURE 2.4.   *Indications of creative ability*

The academically oriented teacher may have difficulty relating to the child, she may become frustrated by the difference between what she believes the child should be able to grasp and what he actually seems to assimilate. This type of teacher generally mastered content, memorized a prodigious number of facts, and has been concerned with imparting this to her pupils. As a result, she has been dedicated to covering as much information as possible. This has meant stressing learning a body of knowledge, leaving the child little time to investigate, inquire, and create in science. Teachers of less ability on the other hand, have been more inclined to follow a course of study and maintain the status quo. Such teachers because of feelings of inadequacy, are not likely to teach creatively.

OVERSTRUCTURING RESTRICTS CREATIVE POSSIBILITIES

Overplanning has in some instances stifled the possibilities for creativity because in implementing her plan the teacher tends to restrict the freedom of her pupils. Overplanning is not in itself harmful, but a plan should be used with flexibility and judgment. When a situation such as the one with the spider mentioned above presents itself, it should be used no matter what is in the teacher's lesson. However, some teachers, particularly those who feel insecure, tend to follow a plan as though it were a recipe; they somehow think that if they don't add each ingredient in the order prescribed, they will never reach their objectives. It is good to have a plan and objective, but unfortunately no plan can predict how thirty or more personalities will react. Here is where the teacher

FIGURE 2-5. *Wise structuring includes not only the creative use of the textbook and classroom facilities but also that of the outdoors for discovery, questioning, and comparing. How has the teacher of these children designed the learning environment? (Photo by Lee Young-blood)*

uses his or her creative ability: implementing the unit by picking up cues from the children and reacting accordingly. Nothing can be more deadly in science teaching than for a teacher to go through a science lesson or activity in a monotonous, step-by-step manner, never deviating from the goal, no matter what the questions and interactions of the class.

The question of how much structure there should be in science teaching is open to controversy. The consensus is that there should be at least some structure and that the instruction must have purpose, not aimless play with science materials. It is thought, however, that the amount of organization and control by the teacher should be kept relatively low. Dr. J. Richard Suchman, in his inquiry studies, suggests a minimum of class structuring. He believes it should include some type of science activity which focuses the attention of the children, stimulates them to think, presents them with a problem, and gives them freedom to inquire. In a significant report he outlined his reason for becoming involved in Inquiry Training as follows:

> We have been trying to develop inquiry skills in elementary school children. This began back in 1957, when we were disturbed by the findings of some studies. One of these found that 97% of the questions asked in the classroom were asked by the teacher. Another one found that as children move from the first grade to the sixth grade, they become less empirical and base more hypotheses and tests of hypotheses on conclusion of authorities and less on their empirical operations.[11]

Research of this nature, indicating overstructuring of class activity by teachers, clearly suggests why science instruction in the elementary school has not been particularly successful in developing creative talent. Fortunately, today many teachers are aware of these data and have modified their teaching accordingly.

Overusing and relying on a textbook for instruction in science has probably been a major contributor to poor science instruction. Early science texts were written mainly in an expository manner; little attention was given to teaching science as a process, to inquiry, or to opportunities to be creative. Because of their poor science backgrounds, teachers have tended to rely almost exclusively upon the text as a source of science instruction. Occasionally they might bring a caterpillar into class for students to observe, or they might perform some other simple activity, but there has generally been little or no experimentation or opportunity for children to hypothesize or design experiments. In recent years some writers of science texts have endeavored to structure their books so that they offer more opportunities for discovery and inquiry. They still, however, are weak in offering creative oppor-

11. J. Richard Suchman, "The Illinois Studies in Inquiry Training," *Piaget Rediscovered*, A Report of the Conference on Cognitive Studies and Curriculum Development, School of Education, Cornell University, Ithaca, N.Y.

tunities. However, a teacher, if truly creative, can effectively re-cast a lesson suggested in a text to include some elements of creativity as indicated in Chapter VIII.

DEVELOPING CREATIVE ENTERPRISES

Dr. David Hawkins, past director of the Elementary Science Study, an elementary science project, has written an article having wide acceptance by science educators pleading for the reduction of overstructuring instruction. By overstructuring is meant that the teacher defines precisely what is to be learned and it is usually limited to academic processes only. A portion of this article is quoted below since it presents this view rather dramatically and has great implications for the development of creative enterprise.

MESSING ABOUT IN SCIENCE

—David Hawkins[12]

"Nice? It's the only thing," said Water Rat solemnly, as he leant forward for his stroke. "Believe me, my young friend, there is nothing—absolutely nothing—half so much worth doing as simply messing about in boats. Simply messing," he went on dreamily, "messing—about—in—boats—mess-ing—"

KENNETH GRAHAME,
The Wind in the Willows

. . . My outline is divided into three patterns or phases of school work in science. These phases are different from each other in the relations they induce between children, ma-terials of study, and teachers. Another way of putting it is that they differ in the way they make a classroom look and sound. My claim is that good science teaching moves from one phase to the other in a pattern which, though it will not follow mechanical rules or ever be twice the same, will

12. I would also like to acknowledge the assistance of Frances Hawkins, who has long practiced in preschool what I now wish to generalize over the entire elementary range.

evolve according to simple principles. There is no necessary order among these phases, and for this reason, I avoid calling them I, II, and III, and use instead some mnemonic signs which have, perhaps, a certain suggestiveness: ○, △, and □.

○ Phase. There is a time, much greater in amount than commonly allowed, which should be devoted to free and unguided exploratory work (call it play if you wish: I call it work). Children are given materials and equipment—things—and are allowed to construct, tests, probe, and experiment without superimposed questions or instructions. I call this ○ phase "Messing About," honoring the philosophy of the Water Rat, who absent-mindedly ran his boat into the bank, picked himself up, and went on without interrupting the joyous train of thought:

> "—about in boats—or with boats. . . . In or out of 'em, it doesn't matter. Nothing seems really to matter, that's the charm of it. Whether you get away, or whether you don't; whether you arrive at your destination or whether you reach somewhere else, or whether you never get anywhere at all, you're always busy, and you never do anything in particular; and when you've done it there's always something else to do, and you can do it if you like, but you'd much better not."

In some jargon, this kind of situation is called "unstructured," which is misleading; some doubters call it chaotic, which it need never be. "Unstructured" is misleading because there is always a kind of structure to what is presented in a class, as there was to the world of boats and the river, with its rushes and weeds and mud that smelled like plumcake. Structure in this sense is of the utmost importance, depending on the children, the teacher, and the backgrounds of all concerned.

Let me cite an example from my own recent experiences. Simple frames, each designed to support two or three weights on strings, were handed out one morning in a fifth grade class. There was one such frame for each pair of children. In two earlier trial classes, we had introduced the same equipment with a much more "structured" beginning, demonstrating the striking phenomenon of coupled pendula and raising questions about it before the laboratory work was allowed to begin. If there was guidance this time, however, it came only from the apparatus—a pendulum is to swing! In starting this way I, for one, naively assumed that a couple of hours of "Messing About" would suffice. After two hours, instead, we allowed two more and, in the end, a stretch of several weeks. In all this time, there was little or no evidence of boredom or confusion. Most of the questions we might have planned for came up unscheduled.

Why did we permit this length of time? First, because in our previous classes we had noticed that things went well when we veered toward "Messing About" and not as well when we held too tight a rein on what we wanted the children to do. It was clear that these children had had insufficient acquaintance with sheer phenomena of pendulum motion and needed to build an apperceptive background, against which a more analytical sort of knowledge could take form and make sense. Second, we allowed things to develop this way because we decided we were getting a new kind of feedback from the children and were eager to see where and by what paths their interests would evolve and carry them. We were rewarded with a higher level of involvement and a much greater diversity of experiments. Our role was only to move from spot to spot, being helpful but never consciously prompting or directing. In spite of—because of!—this lack of direction, these fifth-graders became very familiar with pendula. They varied the conditions of motion in many ways, exploring differences of length and amplitude, using different sorts of bobs, bobs in clusters, and strings, etc. And have you tried the underwater pendulum? They did! There were many sorts of discoveries made, but we let them slip by without much adult resonance, beyond our spontaneous and manifest enjoyment of the phenomena. So discoveries were made, noted, lost, and made again. I think this is why the slightly pontifical phrase "discovery method" bothers me. When learning is at the most fundamental level, as it is here, with all the abstractions of Newtonian mechanics just around the corner, don't rush! When the mind is evolving the abstractions which will lead to physical comprehension, all of us must cross the line between ignorance and insight many times before we truly understand. Little facts, "discoveries" without the growth of insight, are not what we should seek to harvest. Such facts are only seedlings and should sometimes be let alone to grow into. . . .

I have illustrated the phase of "Messing About" with a constrained and inherently very elegant topic from physics. In other fields, the pattern will be different in detail, but the essential justification is the same. "Messing About" with what can be found in pond water looks much more like the Water Rat's own chosen field of study. Here, the implicit structure is that of nature in a very different mood from what is manifest in the austerities of things like pendular motion or planet orbits. And here, the need for sheer acquaintance with the variety of things and phenomena is more obvious, before one can embark on any of the roads toward the big generalizations or the big open question of biology. Regardless of differences, there is a generic justification of "Messing About" that I would like, briefly, to touch upon.

Preschool Influences

This phrase is important, above all, because it carries over into school that which is the source of most of what children have already learned, the roads of their moral, intellectual, and esthetic development. If education were defined, for the moment, to include everything that children have learned since birth, everything that has come to them from living in the natural and the human world, then by any sensible measure what has come before age five or six would outweigh all the rest. When we narrow the scope of education to what goes on in schools, we throw out the method of that early and spectacular progress at our peril. We know that five-year-olds are very unequal in their mastery of this or that. We also know that their histories are responsible for most of this inequality, utterly masking the congenital differences except in special cases. This is the immediate fact confronting us as educators in a society committed, morally and now by sheer economic necessity, to universal education.

To continue the cultivation of earlier ways of learning, therefore; to find in school the good beginnings, the liberating involvements that will make the kindergarten seem a garden to the child and not a dry and frightening desert, this is a need that requires much emphasis on the style of work I have called ○, or "Messing About." Nor does the garden in this sense end with a child's first school year, or his tenth, as though one could then put away childish things. As time goes on, through a good mixture of this with other phases of work, "Messing About" evolves with the child and thus changes its quality. It becomes a way of working that is no longer childish, though it remains always childlike, the kind of self-disciplined probing and exploring that is the essence of creativity.

The variety of the learning—and of inhibition against learning—that children bring from home when school begins is great, even within the limited range of a common culture with common economic background (or, for that matter, within a single family). Admitting this, then if you cast your mind over the whole range of abilities and backgrounds that children bring to kindergarten, you see the folly of standardized and formalized beginnings. We are profoundly ignorant about the subtleties of learning but one principle ought to be asserted dogmatically: That there must be provided some continuity in the content, direction, and style of learning. Good schools begin with what children have in fact mastered, probe next to see what in fact they are learning, continue with what fact sustains their involvement.

△ Phase. When children are led along a common path, there are always the advanced ones and always the stragglers. Generalized over the years of school routine, this lends apparent support to the still widespread belief in some fixed inherent levels of "ability," and to the curious notions of "under-" and "over-achievement." Now, if you introduce a topic with a good deal of "Messing About," the variance does not decrease: it increases. From a conventional point of view, this means the situation gets worse, not better. But I say it gets better, not worse. If after such a beginning you pull in the reins and "get down to business," some children have happened to go your way already, and you will believe that you are leading these successfully. Others will have begun, however, to travel along quite different paths, and you have to tug hard to get them back on to yours. Through the eyes of these children you will see yourself as a dragger, not a leader. We saw this clearly in the pendulum class I referred to, the pendulum being a thing which seems deceptively simple but which raises many questions in no particular necessary order. So the path which each child chooses is his best path.

The result is obvious, but it took me time to see it. If you once let children evolve their own learning along paths of their choosing, you then must see it through and maintain the individuality of their work. You cannot begin that way and then say, in effect, "That was only a teaser," thus using your adult authority to devalue what the children themselves, in the meantime, have found most valuable. So if "Messing About" is to be followed by, or evolve into, a stage where work is more externally guided and disciplined, there must be at hand what I call "Multiply Programmed" material; material that contains written and pictorial guidance of some sort for the student, but which is designed for the greatest possible variety of topics, ordering of topics, etc., so that for almost any given way into a subject that a child may evolve on his own, there is material available which he will recognize as helping him farther along that very way. Heroic teachers have sometimes done this on their own, but it is obviously one of the places where designers of curriculum materials can be of enormous help, designing those materials with a rich variety of choices for teacher and child, and freeing the teacher from the role of "leader-dragger" along a single preconceived path, giving the teacher encouragement and real logistical help in diversifying the activities of a group. Such material includes good equipment, but above all, it suggests many beginnings, paths from the familiar into the unknown. We did not have this kind of material ready for the pendulum class I spoke about earlier, and still do not have it. I intend to work at it and hope others will.

It was a special day in the history of that pendulum class that brought home to me what was needed. My teaching partner was away (I had been the observer, she the teacher). To shift gears for what I saw as a more organized phase of our work, I announced that for a change we were all going to do the same experiment. I said it firmly and the children were, of course, obliging. Yet, I saw the immediate loss of interest in part of the class as soon as my experiment was proposed. It was designed to raise questions about the length of a pendulum, when the bob is multiple or odd-shaped. Some had come upon the germ of that question; others had had no reason to. As a college teacher I have tricks, and they worked here as well, so the class went well, in spite of the unequal readiness to look at "length." We hit common ground with rough blackboard pictures, many pendula shown hanging from a common support, differing in length and in the shape and size of bobs. Which ones will "swing together"? Because their eyes were full of real pendula, I think, they could see those blackboard pictures swinging! A colloquium evolved which harvested the crop of insights that had been sowed and cultivated in previous weeks. I was left with a hollow feeling, nevertheless. It went well where, and only where, the class found common ground. Whereas in "Messing About" all things had gone uniformly well. In staff discussion afterward, it became clear that we had skipped an essential phase of our work, the one I am now calling △ phase, or Multiply Programmed.

There is a common opinion, floating about, that a rich diversity of classroom work is possible only when a teacher has small classes. "Maybe you can do that, but you ought to try it in my class of 43!" I want to be the last person to belittle the importance of small classes. But in this particular case, the statement ought to be made that in a large class one cannot afford not to diversify children's work—or rather not to allow children to diversify, as they inevitably will, if given the chance. So-called "ability grouping" is a popular answer today, but it is no answer at all to real questions of motivation. Groups which are lumped as equivalent with respect to the usual measures are just as diverse in their tastes and spontaneous interests as unstratified groups! The complaint that in heterogeneous classes the bright ones are likely to be bored because things go too slowly for them ought to be met with another question: Does that mean that the slower students are not bored? When children have no autonomy in learning everyone is likely to be bored. In such situations the overworked teachers have to be "leader-draggers" always, playing the role of Fate in the old Roman proverb: "The Fates lead the willing; the unwilling they drag."

A Good Beginning

"Messing About" produces the early and indispensable autonomy and diversity. It is good—indispensable—for the opening game but not for the long middle game, where guidance is needed, needed to lead the willing! To illustrate once more from my example of the pendulum, I want to produce a thick set of cards—illustrated cards in a central file, or single sheets in plastic envelopes—to cover the following topics among others:

1. Relations of amplitude and period.
2. Relations of period and weight of bob.
3. How long is a pendulum (odd-shaped bobs)?
4. Coupled pendula compound pendula.
5. The decay of the motion (and the idea of half-life).
6. String pendula and stick pendula—comparisons.
7. Underwater pendula.
8. Arms and legs as pendula (dogs, people, and elephants).
9. Pendula of other kinds—springs, etc.
10. Bobs that drop sand for patterns and graphs.
11. Pendulum clocks.
12. Historical materials, with bibliography.
13. Cards relating to film loops available, in class or library.
14. Cross-index cards to other topics, such as falling bodies, inclined planes, etc.
15–75. Blank cards to be filled in by classes and teachers for others.

This is only an illustration; each area of elementary science will have its own style of Multiply Programmed materials. Of course, the ways of organizing these materials will depend on the subject. There should always be those blank cards, outnumbering the rest.

Careful!

There is one final warning. Such a file is properly a kind of programming—but it is not the base of rote or merely verbal learning, taking a child little step by little step through the adult maze. Each item is simple, pictorial, and it guides by suggesting further explorations, not by replacing them. The cards are only there to relieve the teacher from a heroic task. And they are only there because there are apparatus, film, library, and raw materials from which to improvise.

☐ Phase. In the class discussion I referred to about the meaning of length applied to pendulum, I was reverting back to the college-teacher habit of lecturing; I said it went very well in spite of the lack of Multiply Programmed background, one that would have taken more of the class through more of the basic pendulum topics. It was not, of course, a lecture in the formal sense. It was question-and-answer, with discussion between children as well. But still, I was guiding it and fishing for the good ideas that were ready to be born, and I was telling a few stories, for example, about Galileo. Others could do it better. I was a visitor, and am still only an amateur. I was successful then only because of the long build-up of latent insight, the kind of insight that the Water Rat had stored up from long afternoons of "Messing About" in boats. It was more than he could ever have been told, but it gave him much to tell. This is not all there is to learning, of course; but it is the magical part, and the part most often killed in school. The language is not yet that of the textbook, but with it even a dull-looking textbook can come alive. One boy thinks the length of a pendulum should be measured from the top to what he calls "the center of gravity." If they have not done a lot of work with balance materials, this phrase is for most children only the handle of an empty pitcher, or a handle without a pitcher at all. So I did not insist on the term. Incidentally, it is not quite correct physics anyway, as those will discover who work with the stick pendulum. Although different children had specialized differently in the way they worked with pendula, there were common elements, increasing with time, which would sustain a serious and extended class discussion. It is this pattern of discussion I want to emphasize by calling it a separate, ☐ phase. It includes lecturing, formal or informal. In the above situation, we were all quite ready for a short talk about Galileo, and ready to ponder the question whether there was any relation between the way unequal weights fall together and the way they swing together when hanging on strings of the same length. Here we were approaching a question—a rather deep one, not to be disposed of in fifteen minutes—of theory, going from the concrete perceptual to the abstract conceptual. I do not believe that such questions will come alive either through the early "Messing About" or through the Multiply Programmed work with guiding questions and instructions. I think they come primarily with discussion, argument, the full colloquium of children and teacher. Theorizing in a creative sense needs the content of experience and the logic of experimentation to support it. But these do not automatically lead to conscious abstract thought. Theory is square! □

We of the Elementary Science Study are probably identified in the minds of those acquainted with our work (and sometimes perhaps in our own minds with the advocacy of laboratory work and a free fairly ○ style of laboratory work at that. This may be right and justified by the fact that prevailing styles of science teaching are □ most of the time, much too much of the time. But what we criticize for being too much and too early, we must work to re-admit in its proper place).

I have put ○, △, and □ in that order, but I do not advocate any rigid order; such phases may be mixed in many ways and ordered in many ways. Out of the colloquium comes new "Messing About." Halfway along a programmed path, new phenomena are accidentally observed. In an earlier, more structured class, two girls were trying obediently to reproduce some phenomena of coupled pendula I had demonstrated. I heard one say, "Ours isn't working right." Of course, pendula never misbehave; it is not in their nature; they always do what comes naturally, and in this case, they were executing a curious dance of energy transference, promptly christened the "twist." It was a new phenomenon, which I had not seen before, nor had several physicists to whom, in my delight, I later showed it. Needless to say, this led to a good deal of "Messing About," right then and there.

What I have been concerned to say is only that there are, as I see it, three major phases of good science teaching; that no teaching is likely to be optimum which does not mix all three; and that the one most neglected is that which made the Water Rat go dreamy with joy when he talked about it. At a time when the pressures of prestige education are likely to push children to work like hungry laboratory rats in a maze, it is good to remember that their wild, watery cousin reminiscing about the joys of his life, uttered a profound truth about education.[13]

13. Reprinted with permission from *Science and Children*, vol. 2, no. 5 (February 1965). Copyright 1965 by the National Science Teachers Association, 1201 Sixteenth Street, N.W., Washington, D.C. 20036.
Dr. Hawkins, professor of philosophy and director of the Mountain View Center for Environmental Education at the University of Colorado, was formerly the director of ESI's Elementary Science Study, and remains a member of the ESS Steering Committee. He is the author of *The Language of Nature*, published by W. H. Freeman and Co.

Dr. Hawkins's suggestions for a teaching strategy allow for considerable student-centered instruction. One can argue with many of his ideas, but it seems reasonable if students are allowed time to "mess about," they will have greater opportunity for exploration and discovery, creativity and emergence of talent.

THE "BIG BANG" TEACHER

Some teachers who mainly use artificial devices to keep children occupied are sometimes referred to by educators as the "big bang" teachers. This is because the device-oriented teacher likes to set off explosions, crush a can by using air pressure, or perform some other dramatic demonstration. The purpose is to keep the children amused. There is nothing wrong with the demonstrations they choose; what is wrong is how and why they use them. The device-oriented teacher's instruction has been more theatrical than instructive. The use of a demonstration becomes the rationale of planning rather than an adjunct to it. As a result, the pupils have no chance to study and perform experiments in depth, to discover and inquire, to gain conceptual understanding of what goes on in the demonstrations, nor to design and test hypotheses related to them.

Teachers are human, and, because they are human, they naturally want to be accepted and liked by their pupils. To entertain is not undesirable providing it meets the criteria of sound instruction in creative science. For example, if a teacher were to use a demonstration illustrating the crushing of a can by air pressure some well framed questions would help evoke critical and creative thinking:

1. How do you feel about the can being crushed? Describe or draw your feelings.
2. What are all the reasons you can think of that might explain why the can was crushed?
3. If you wanted to crush the can further or with greater force, what would you do? Why?
4. If you wanted to speed up the rate at which the can was crushed, what would you do and why?
5. If you were to show what happened by diagrams or drawings what would you do?

Chapters III and VIII of this book contain suggestions on how this might be achieved.

ADMINISTRATORS HAVE NOT ENCOURAGED TEACHING FOR CREATIVITY

Both administrators and school policy have had a generally negative influence on the education of the creative child. Administrators have failed to encourage creativity for many of the same reasons that teachers have failed. Until recently, many administrators were not even aware of the problem of developing creative talents, and there are still some who do not know of the research in the field. Other problems have often preoccupied administrators. In some school districts, their time is so taken up with financial, operational, and community problems that they have little time to exert educational leadership. Due to the excessive demands on their time, some administrators have resisted innovation because of the added problems it would present. This type of administrator has tended to reward the teacher who represents the status quo and to discourage the experimental and creative teacher. What the traditional teacher has done to the creative child, the traditionally oriented administrator has done to the creative teacher. Many administrators have been very resistant to experimentation in their schools and to the testing of any new science curriculum materials; they may also have resisted ordering supplies and caring for them. Cost considerations have often allowed the use of outdated elementary science texts and have denied the purchase or use of supplementary science teaching aids. Because of their great influence, some administrators have had a tremendous effect in retarding progress in developing creative ability—particularly in science. Fortunately for the schools, more elementary school administrators are becoming increasingly concerned about the gifted and creative child in science and are endeavoring to improve the situation.

SUMMARY

This chapter has surveyed some of the factors that have tended to retard the development of the creative individual in science. The scholastic view of knowledge, with its emphasis on the product of knowledge as opposed to the process, has contributed to a poor understanding of the meaning of the scientific enterprise. The knowledge of science is its product; but the processes of science are revealed only by individuals who are actively involved in problem solving.

The processes of discovery and invention provide the creative aspects of scientific activity. But teachers have been predisposed to recognize and admire academic or intellectual achievement at the expense of creative achievement. This has been due in part to the lack of understanding of creativity and the mistaken notion that an intellectually outstanding person is also creatively outstanding. Dr. E. Paul Torrance has done extensive research with the creative child and has found that I.Q. does not correlate particularly with creative ability. In fact, on the basis of I.Q. alone about 70 percent of the most creative would be excluded in identifying gifted children. Teachers have tended to emphasize verbal skills, but the evidence, particularly in the lower elementary grades, shows that children with creative science potential have difficulty in verbal skills.

Peer groups, particularly in grades five and six, begin to exert influence on creative children to make them conform to group standards at the expense of individual differences. Teachers have also been more likely to reward conformity and to be disturbed by the somewhat deviant behavior of the creative child.

Other reasons for the schools not producing creative individuals in science have been the poor preparation of the teacher in science, the teacher's overemphasis on learning subject matter, overstructuring the class environment so that there is little chance for a child to react creatively, improper use of science textbooks, the use of artificial devices or gadgetry as opposed to an integrated pattern of instruction, and administrative resistance to innovation and curriculum developments.

QUESTIONS

1. Can you describe some teaching episodes you have seen which you think contributed to creative activity?

2. What do you think are the main reasons why creativity in science has not been encouraged? Why?

3. If you were to teach in a traditionally oriented school, how would you convince other teachers and administrators of the importance of creativity?

4. Knowing what you do about the verbal ability of children compared to their creative science potential, how would you evaluate them?

5. How would you use science textbooks in teaching science?

6. What role should a lesson plan play in science instruction?

7. How would you "structure" your teaching of science to provide flexibility and spontaneity for creative activity?

8. How would you use a demonstration to foster creativity?

9. How would a teacher with a multitalented approach differ in teaching methods used compared to a traditional instructor?

CHAPTER III

Working Creatively
with Children in Science

*Even in order to understand we have to invent, or, that is,
reinvent, because we can't start from the beginning again.
But I would say that anything is only understood to the extent that it is reinvented.*

JEAN PIAGET

Working creatively with children in science requires a well-
defined strategy that must take into account the physical and
mental development of the child, the learning environment, and
the selection of science-learning activities. All these factors play
essential roles in the creative process, are often interrelated, and
require skill of the teacher for judicious appraisal of the learner
and his needs.

PIAGET'S FOUR STAGES OF COGNITIVE DEVELOPMENT

The eminent Swiss psychologist, Jean Piaget, has shown that
children manifest different mental (cognitive) abilities as they
mature. Their minds evolve through a series of intellectual stages
as they progress from early childhood to adolescence. Piaget has
classified these into four main stages: sensory-motor (0–2 years);
preoperational (2–7 years); concrete operational (7–11 years);
and formal operational (11–15 years).

Sensory-Motor Stage

In the sensory-motor stage (0–2 years), the child is almost completely dependent upon the immediate environment for stimulation and merely reacts to it. He touches, feels, and slowly discovers mentally that objects have certain properties. As he progresses through this stage, he becomes able to recall the properties of objects without having to test them each time he sees them. By the age of two the child can imagine. He can remember and has learned the names of certain people, animals, objects, and some activities. Learning names enables him to use words as mental symbols to elaborate his concepts in the next stage of mental development.

Preoperational Stage

The preoperational stage (2–7 years) is called the intuitive stage because, as the child develops, he begins to sense the difference between an individual item and its class (singular and plural). For example, he knows the difference between "mother" and "women," "man" and "men," "father" and "man." However, he is not able to devise a classification scheme until the next stage of development. He may call an object large one time and small another, depending on what attracts him, because he centers his attention on one dimension of a problem. If water is poured from a tall vessel into a shorter, wider one, the child is apt to think the shorter vessel has less water in it. This happens because he centers on the height and not the width of the vessel. (The ability to center on height and width simultaneously does not occur until much later in the child's mental development.) The preoperational child is egocentric in that he cannot conceive of anyone's seeing or interpreting something other than the way he sees it. He has no understanding of chance or probability and cannot perform reversible mental operations. If you ask a child at this stage of development: "Did Daniel Boone kill animals?" The child will probably answer: "No." Then if he is asked: "Did Daniel Boone kill a mean fox?" The child is likely to say "Yes," with no apparent awareness of his illogic. This questioning might be continued by asking: "Is a fox an animal?" The child will say "Yes." The question about Daniel Boone killing animals may be repeated, and the child will probably still give the same answer "No." The preoperational child's thought processes go from fox to animal; he is incapable of reversing the process by going from animal to fox. Children of this period of development are also very animalistic in their explanations. They say such things as "The house doesn't like the cold," "The rocks are hurt when they fall," "The trees feel sad in winter."

Concrete Operational Stage

In the concrete operational stage (7–11 years), the child performs mental operations; he becomes more logical in his thought processes. However, these operations require the presence of objects for mental manipulations to occur. They are, therefore, concrete in origin. These mental operations are said to be stimulus-related because the child needs the stimulus of an object to bring to mind all the things he can do with it. He devises class and relation concepts, and can perform reversible mental operations. He conceptually organizes his environment through cognitive structures—organized ideas. Each new encounter does not require new extensive examinations. He can go beyond things and think of groups, make limited hypotheses, and mentally represent several related actions simultaneously in his mind. For example, if he pours water from a wide flat jar to a slender one he concentrates on both the width and height of the jars. The significant advance in this stage is that he studies the whole rather than being diverted by each individual property. He tends to think of all of the properties of an object as a group. By the end of this stage he is able to conserve matter, weight, and volume across transformation in its appearance.

Formal Operational Stage

The formal operational stage (11–15 years) is the period of development of abstract and reflexive thinking. At this age the child is able to think about his thinking. He can trace thought processes after having solved some scientific or mathematical problem. As a consequence, the child begins to think as an adult. He is able to represent his own mental operations by a series of symbols. He understands probability and thinks in terms of many possibilities rather than being limited by the facts before him. His thinking processes become more hypothetical and deductive. He formulates hypotheses as testable ideas in his *mind* and does not think of them necessarily as realities. Children in the earlier stages can construct hypotheses, but these are based on concrete entities testable in concrete terms. Because of the capacity for abstract thought, the formal operational child can discover principles and deduce from them hypotheses to be verified. He is capable of working simultaneously with abstract concepts and with actual objects, procedures, and situations. He is more at ease with abstract mathematical manipulations. He can deal not only with reality but also with the realm of possibilities and is generally logical in his thinking.

SUMMARY OF PIAGET'S FOUR STAGES OF COGNITIVE DEVELOPMENT

SENSORY-MOTOR (Ages 0–2)

1. Child develops thought through physical action.
2. Perceives and identifies objects and distinguishes mother and father from other adults late in the period.
3. Around ninth month develops object permanence—knows object exists even though it is not seen.
4. Learns the names of objects but doesn't really have language yet.
5. Uses some means to achieve certain ends—like pushes the door open to crawl from room to room.
6. Space—exists only immediately around him.
7. Time—is present.

PREOPERATIONAL (Ages 2–7)

1. Doesn't yet do operations such as ordering, seriating, adding, subtracting, one-to-one correspondence, reversibility, ascending a classification system.
2. Perception bound, he is fooled by appearance—i.e., a cupcake cut in half seems to him to be less cake than an uncut cupcake.
3. Egocentric—the way he sees it, is the way it is. The rules of the game are his rules. This egocentrism begins to change somewhat by age 4.
4. Develops language.
5. Animistic—gives inanimate objects animal characteristics and feelings.
6. Artificialistic—thinks lakes, mountains, moon, or sun are made by man.
7. Time—knows present, future, and past.
8. Space—broadened to include house, neighborhood.

CONCRETE OPERATIONAL (Ages 7–11)

1. Develops operational ability, i.e., seriation, reversibility, adding, subtracting, ordering, multiplying; classifies with class inclusion, ascending and descending hierarchies; measures, demonstrates advances in social interactive awareness.
2. Is concrete in his thinking—mainly reasons about things but has difficulty with abstractions and verbalizations.
3. Accepts ethics of authorities—father, teacher.
4. Conserves—substance, weight, and often volume.
5. Space—town, state, nation.
6. Time—weeks, month, years.

FORMAL OPERATIONAL (Ages 11–15)

1. Does hypothetical—deductive thinking.
2. Does propositional thinking, i.e., this or that is the cause, it's neither this or that, it may be this but not that, it may be that but not this.
3. Reflexive thinking—thinks about his thinking and evaluates his own thinking.
4. May think of and grasp theories.
5. Devises test and may control one variable at a time in an experiment.
6. Uses syllogistic and "if then" reasoning.
7. Realizes and constitutes ethics not by authority but consensus.
8. Space—includes universe.
9. Time—explains infinity.

COGNITIVE EVOLUTION VARIES WITH THE CHILD

The chronological age demarcations obtained by Piaget are not absolutes in terms of the individual child. They can vary, for instance, depending on the socioeconomic background of the child. The child from a high socioeconomic background may evolve through these stages more quickly than stipulated, while a child from a lower socioeconomic background may be slower. It has been our experience that this is particularly true for children in inner city ghetto schools. They are often behind in their development when compared with Piaget's time sequence.

This has been corroborated in the report on science achievement, *National Assessment of Educational Progress*, which states, "If the young American parents did not have the advantages of much education . . . or if he [the child] lives in the inner city . . . or if he is black . . . he, or she, as the case may be, knows less about science than the nation as a whole."[1]

Even in a classroom in which the children come from a homogeneous neighborhood and are approximately the same age, it is usual to find differences in cognitive development. For example, a grade teacher may have both preoperational and concrete operational children under her instruction.

Furthermore, stage development within the child himself may not necessarily be even. A pupil in transition from stage to stage may act as a concrete operational thinker in some situations and behave formal operational in others. Then too, though Piaget says that adolescents of 15 are formal operational, this does not mean that they are very proficient at thinking this way nor does it mean they will necessarily use this thinking ability under all circumstances.

A teacher should not be alarmed by these variations—that there are differences between human beings is nothing new. She should learn to recognize the different ways in which each child thinks, and in discussing ideas with him adjust her explanations accordingly.

The sequence of cognitive development always follows the Piaget progression but the rate may vary considerably. There have been no studies to show, for example, that a formal operative child skipped the concrete operational level but several studies indicate that many children do attain the levels at earlier or later ages than those shown.

IMPLICATIONS OF PIAGET'S THEORY

Piaget's research clearly implies the necessity of individualizing instruction in the sense that the learning environment is adapted to the child and not the reverse. Educational materials should be selected according to the cognitive level of the child. Frequent opportunities should be provided for children to "mess about" with materials, interact in groups, and have varied experiences that stimulate them to reason and think. When a teacher facilitates learning rather than totally directing it, a child is more likely to

1. *National Assessment of Educational Progress*, A Project of the Education Commission of the States, vol. 5, no. 1 (January–February 1972), Denver, Colorado, Sharon Sherman, ed.

develop his social talent, lessen his egocentricity, discover the multiple ways of looking at a problem, and become more creative and rational.

We believe there are two general principles derived from Piaget's work which must be abided by in trying to develop creative intelligence:

1. In the elementary school, children should be often involved in learning through physical (concrete) involvement. This is particularly true in science. They can learn best about magnets, sound, or seeds by being actively involved with them. Through such involvement they develop *mental actions* and *operations*. Piaget says the basis of all learning is experience. In this he includes both physical and mental experience.
2. Only the child himself can develop his cognitive abilities and creative potential—he cannot be told to order but must be involved in activities that give him opportunities to place things in order so that some day he will be able to order things in his mind without manipulating them physically.

IMPORTANCE OF ENRICHING YOUTHFUL EXPERIENCES

Piaget's work on the cognitive evolution of the mental stages of children from infancy to adolescence suggests several interesting questions relating to creativity:

1. How are creative abilities affected during progressive mental development?
2. Do children pass through hierarchies of creative development?
3. In what periods of development does creative ability need to be stimulated and nurtured more than others?
4. What precautions are necessary in trying to accelerate cognitive development so as not to strangle the manifestation of creative ability?

Although definitive answers to these questions are not possible at present because of a lack of research, there is sufficient evidence to indicate the importance of creative opportunities for children who manifest aptitude in science. Dr. E. Paul Torrance has stated that children at all levels in the elementary school are capable of creative responses. Recent research indicates that stimulation and activities for creative involvement are of the utmost importance, particularly in the early years of life.

Dr. Robert D. Hess has found in experimenting with rats that early experience is influential in determining later behavior. Dr. Hess took two groups of rats and blindfolded one from infancy. The other group was allowed to develop from infancy to three months without blindfolds and then blindfolded. Both of these groups were then allowed to run free in cages containing a number of objects. At the age of five months the two groups of rats were confronted with maze problems. The group that had been non-blindfolded until three months achieved significantly higher in solving maze problems.[2]

This study was followed by one similar in design. Dr. Hess divided two groups of rats from the same litter. He took one group home as pets. They were allowed to run about the house much of the time. The other group remained in the laboratory in cages. After several months, both groups of rats were confronted with maze problems. The performance of the pet rats was significantly higher than that of the laboratory rats. Other research from the fields of anatomy and physiology indicate that there are actually morphological and chemical differences between animals with enriched experiences and those from deprived backgrounds.[3]

Dr. Hess suggests that research of this nature indicates human genetic potential will not completely manifest itself unassisted. The individual must be raised in a stimulating environment for the potential to emerge. He goes on to emphasize that the stimulation should occur early in the child's development and that early deprivation may result in a permanent loss of mental ability. He stresses that "one of the primary purposes of elementary school education is the maximizing of mental capabilities by systematic stimulation and exercise of mental faculties.[4]

The Harvard Pre-School Project directed by Burton L. White has found that a lack of a stimulating environment, particularly between the tenth to eighteenth month, is very detrimental to the mental development of the child and may affect his I.Q. adversely.[5]

The implications of this research are of tremendous relevance to elementary school teachers. Because the early years are the important ones in shaping the lifelong cognitive and creative

2. Robert D. Hess, "The Latent Resources of the Child's Mind," *Journal of Research in Science Teaching* (1963), p. 21.
3. Edward L. Bennett et al., "Chemical and Anatomical Plasticity of the Brain," *Science*, 146 (October 30, 1964), pp. 610–619.
4. Hess, "The Latent Resources of the Child's Mind," p. 25.
5. Maya Pines, "A Child's Mind Is Shaped Before Age 2," *Life* (December 17, 1971), pp. 67–68.

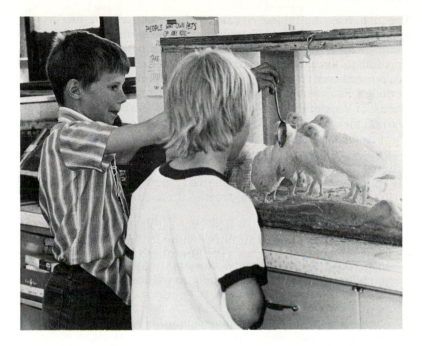

FIGURE 3-1. *How has the teacher of these children applied what we have learned about environment and its effect on individual potential? (Photo by Lee Youngblood)*

capacities of the individual, the value of the primary grade experiences and the elementary school teacher's contribution to the development or retardation of creative scientific ability are placed in a new and important perspective. Because what a teacher fails to do to enrich children's experiences may have permanent negative effects, the teacher has an even greater responsibility to engender a creative environment.

Further evidence substantiating the importance of enriching youthful experiences in science has often been recorded in the history of science. Galileo Galilei (1564–1642), the great Italian scientist, had early rich childhood experiences. It was he who developed the telescope, contributed to an understanding of the laws of motion, made the first crude thermometer, discovered the moons of Jupiter, and made many more contributions to science. Science historians credit him with contributing greatly to the acceptance of the empirical approach (the ideas that knowledge should be tested by experiment) to solving problems scientifically.

For this reason, Galileo is said to have caused an intellectual revolution. He contributed immensely to the marriage of mathematics with experimentation as a means of determining truth, as opposed to the pure deductive reason of the ancients. It should be remembered that the predominant philosophy of Galileo's period of history was authoritarian. Truth was to be found in the words of Aristotle, Galen, and Euclid, or derived by logic. The learned men of ancient Greece and Rome were considered the authorities up to the seventeenth century. The truth of the ancients was not to be disputed. Galileo's father, Vincenzo Galilei, however, differed from his contemporaries in his respect for the ancients. He was talented and educated in mathematics and music and had written and published several treaties. In one he said:

> It appears to me that they who in proof of any assertion rely simply on the weight of authority without adducting any argument in support of it, act very absurdly. I, on the contrary, wish to be allowed freely to question and freely to answer you without any sort of adulation, as well becomes those who are truly in search of truth.[6]

The father must have implanted into his young son this spirit of questioning and open-mindedness so characteristic of an inquiring mind. It is also known that Galileo (like another great scientist, Sir Isaac Newton) was creative in inventing numerous toys in his childhood. History does not tell us whether he was encouraged to do this, but we can certainly assume that the materials were provided for him.

Another scientist, Charles Darwin, the founder of the theory of evolution and an extensive investigator and writer in other areas of science, is also thought to have had a stimulating environment, especially during his early formative years. Charles's mother was a well-educated woman; she had been tutored by her many brothers and had traveled extensively. It is known that by the time of her death, when Charles was eight years old, he was an avid collector of birds, eggs, butterflies, beetles, and minerals, presumably with the consent if not the encouragement of his mother.[7] Erasmus Darwin, Charles's grandfather, was a brilliant man. He was a poet, doctor, and scientist, and had written a great deal about the problems of evolution. (These treatises and dis-

6. *Life of Galileo Galilei*, Scholar's Cabinet Library (Boston: William Clyde and Company, 1832), pp. 24–28.
7. Austin L. Porterfield, *Creative Factors in Scientific Research* (Durham, N.C.: Duke University Press, 1941), p. 172.

cussions on evolution, however, were based more on philosophy than on scientific investigation.) Charles's father was a wealthy and very capable physician. Although records of the influence these two gentlemen had on Charles is somewhat obscure, it can be presumed to have been extensive. It is known that Charles's father encouraged his son to study medicine and later approved of his voyage on "H.M.S. Beagle" to collect biological specimens and study natural history for five years.

The history of science is filled with biographies of men supporting the importance of experiencing early the investigative character of science. A recent study of the International Science Fair finalists has shown that most experienced interest in science between the ages of eight and fifteen, while many enjoyed such pursuits at an even earlier period of life (see Figure 3-2).

Dr. Richard P. Feynman, Nobel prize physicist, spoke on the importance of early childhood experiences in science, particularly those investigative in character, in an address before the National Science Teachers Association convention in New York in 1966. He said that when he was young his father assiduously captured his attention in scientific experiences. When young Feynman was in the high chair his father would stack blocks for him, red then white, and have his son continue the pattern. If the child didn't follow the proper alternating sequence of colored blocks, the father would take the block off the stack and let him begin again. When asked by his wife why he was doing this, Feynman's father replied that he was trying to teach his son patterns or recurrences in nature and matter.

Later, young Feynman's father would take him on walks in the woods and encourage him to investigate. Once the boy asked the name of a bird, and his father asked why he wanted to know the name, that to know the name of a bird was to know nothing about it. He told the boy: "Better you should know what the bird does, how it raises and cares for its young, how and why it migrates, and that this is a mystery to even the most learned of ornithologists." This lesson taught Dr. Feynman that although labels are important, ideas are far more so, and the emphasis should be on understanding ideas, not memorizing labels, which contributes little to understanding.

One day, undoubtedly because he had already learned the importance of observation and inquiry, young Feynman noticed that when he pulled a wagon the ball in it moved toward the back, but that when he stopped the wagon the ball slid forward. He asked his father why it did that. His father replied that nobody knew and then went on to tell him of other examples of inertia.

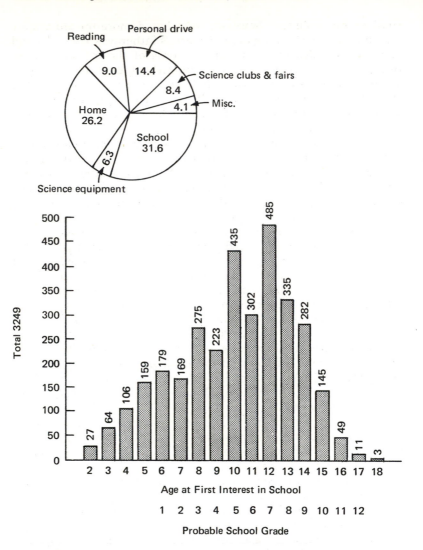

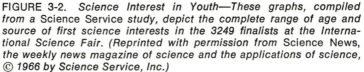

FIGURE 3-2. *Science Interest in Youth—These graphs, compiled from a Science Service study, depict the complete range of age and source of first science interests in the 3249 finalists at the International Science Fair. (Reprinted with permission from Science News, the weekly news magazine of science and the applications of science, © 1966 by Science Service, Inc.)*

Another time, on a hike, his father stated that all living things die to provide for the birth of other life. He described the wonderful balance in nature and outlined how life was limited by the raw materials nature provided. This discussion led to the study of decay. Young Feynman and his father collected decaying leaves, twigs and logs, and numerous fungi, and investigated the role of fungi and bacteria in returning nature's wealth to the soil.

The history of science amply demonstrates that parents and teachers can be instrumental in encouraging a creative spirit in youth that may follow them through life. With such a prospect, the value of the parents' contributions to the scientific enterprise may well surpass that of many teachers the child encounters in school.

SETTING THE STAGE FOR CREATIVE LEARNING IN SCIENCE

Freedom to Explore

Authorities tell us that a person cannot imagine that for which he has no basis in his experience. This holds true for creative

FIGURE 3-3. *Resource or interest centers can be set up in a corner with conventional classroom furniture. With motivating materials, simple instructions, and adequate reference sources, such centers facilitate discovery learning. (Photo from Los Angeles Unified Schools—A Model Educational Program in Ecology, ESEA Title III)*

endeavor. How many of us can think creatively in thermodynamics? The teacher must constantly widen the scope of a child's learning environment to provide for individual interests and abilities to develop, and to insure maximum opportunity for experience in many subject areas, which the child needs if he is to perform in a highly creative way. Since children learn in different ways, the greater the variety of instructional aids a teacher uses, the greater assurance she will have that more children will be helped in releasing their creative potential. After all, we know that children who are highly creative in one way are not always highly creative in others. Although some structure may be required in classroom instruction, provision should also be made for a setting where the child is allowed free exploration of exciting phenomena and where the rewards are not based on conformity but rather on the excitement of self-directed discovery. The environment should be one of permissiveness, where children are encouraged and feel free to venture new ideas, and where new ideas are held at a premium by both teacher and children.

Conditions That Hamper Creativity

In contrast, one can easily identify a science classroom that obstructs or impedes creative thinking. The conditions are rigid—emphasis is placed only on the "mistakes" or failures in a child's performance. Memorized learning takes preference over meaning derived from experience. Children are continually harassed to complete the work so that they can go on to the next assignment regardless of their present understanding. Discussion is held to a minimum and the only questions posed are those the teacher has ready answers for, and they are usually taken from a text. A science reference shelf is conspicuously absent, and enough room for the pupils to manipulate materials, explore, demonstrate, experiment, and carry out both individual and group investigations is not considered. There are no work tables or tools or construction materials for assembling simple projects. A "touch-and-try" section where the children can study plants and animals, foods, weather, water, soil, machines, electricity, heat, light, and sound is nowhere in view. No imaginative play corners, no quiz sections with electrical games, identifications, riddles, or picture puzzles are available. The room is also bereft of bulletin boards displaying the children's work; there are no museum features, such as dioramas, models, artifacts; and no equipment or materials so needed to carry on creative activity.

An Example of Creative Learning

There is no simple formula that insures creativity. Although a child should be secure in the classroom and free of anxieties related to his peers and teachers, the challenges of learning that come from confrontation and problem solving should be omnipresent. There is some evidence in research showing that highly creative people not only can tolerate perplexity but enjoy it as well. They do not seem disturbed at not getting immediate answers to questions. They can speculate on the answers and suggest alternate solutions to problems. They can suspend judgment until they have investigated a host of possibilities. The relevance of this in science is apparent since the structure of science as a discipline encourages hypothesizing and problem solving. The following activity in problem solving is illustrative.

While Jim was engaged in feeding fish in the classroom, he noticed a ring around the glass aquarium where the water level had receded. He asked the teacher where the water had gone. "What do you think happened to the water?" the teacher asked.

The children were given an opportunity to speculate (hypothesize) and to check or test their ideas and reject them if they were found to be invalid.

Several members of the class examined the bottom and sides of the aquarium with great care to see if the water had leaked out, but they discovered the outside was quite dry. Mary wondered if the fish drank the water. Bill thought the plants may have used some of it.

One by one their notions were disproved in the light of tested evidence. The inductive method was used where possible. Activities employing skills in investigation, experimentation, and reading were utilized. Elements for building scientific attitudes were introduced, among them careful observation, suspending judgment in drawing conclusions until sufficient evidence warranted it, understanding cause-and-effect relationships, respecting points of view that scientists hold, openmindedness, and intellectual honesty.

When Jim suggested that the water could have gone into the air, the group decided to experiment to test his idea (hypothesis).

The children were now investigating on a level commensurate with their interests and abilities and developing concepts about scientific method and content.

Proposals for ways of finding out—to experiment—were made

by the children. Materials to perform and experiment were carefully outlined by the class. This led to other problems, and more science information was required to effect a solution.

Having decided on procedure, the children selected two containers of identical size and composition, filled both with water, capping one (the control) but not the other (the test and single variable), so that results could be compared. When the children arrived at a conclusion, they generalized and related their finding to the two jars, not to the whole universe of jars. Later, the pupils filled several containers with water, leaving some open and capping others.

They learned about the nature and purpose of scientific experimentation. They learned the principles of evaporation and decided to test them further. Each time they experimented, controls were used.

The children then filled vessels of different shapes and sizes with water to discover whether surface area made a difference in the rate of evaporation. Later they tried alcohol and kerosene to see if dissimilar liquids had a different rate of evaporation. Then they tried to find out the effects of temperature and wind on the evaporation of liquids and drew conclusions after checking their data.

Application of the principle of evaporation was made by Jim, who remarked, "I know why mother hangs clothes out to dry on a warm windy day. Water evaporates more quickly when it is warm and windy outside." The materials used in the experiment were simple, easily obtainable, and appropriate to the solution of the problem.

As in the example above, the teacher in a creative learning environment acts as a catalyst among the best resources of the classroom, school, and community to bring about a variety of activities which have as their ultimate goal the release of the learners' creative potential. This suggests that the teacher herself must be creative, with competence in understanding materials, structured relations, graded difficulties, and psychological implications if she is to guide the learner in his development. Of the many important tools involved, inquiry and discovery have become integral to the creative process in science.

AN INSTRUCTIONAL THEORY FOR CREATIVE DEVELOPMENT

What Are the Discovery and Inquiry Approaches?

How should a teacher teach to nurture creative development? From the work of Piaget and Hawkins it has been evidenced that the discovery or inquiry approaches have advantages over traditional didactic teaching. The word discovery is used by psychologists and educators in different ways. However, there is general agreement among all of them that in these approaches children are told less, and allowed, through the mediation of their minds, to discover meaning. In the process, they may discover the meaning of some concept or principle or even an understanding of the structure of a discipline such as science. They may learn what "sciencing" is. Some educators use discovery and inquiry interchangeably while others differentiate between the two. Dr. Robert M. Gagné prefers to distinguish between them because he thinks it has functional value.[8] To him "discovery" is chiefly but not uniquely the purpose of science teaching in the elementary school. It mainly involves having children learn concepts and principles.

DISCOVERY

To Discover:	*Example:*
1. A concept	Cells
	Heat
	Air
2. A principle	When heated, metals expand
	Microorganisms may cause disease

Dr. Gagné believes "inquiry" differs in that it involves the higher sophisticated behaviors such as shown below:

8. Robert M. Gagné, "The Learning Requirements for Inquiry," *Readings in Science in the Elementary School* (New York: The Macmillan Co., 1971), pp. 420–423.

INQUIRY PROCESS

1. Originating a problem
2. Designing a relatively complex experiment
3. Formulating propositional or hypothetical deductive thinking
4. Evaluating experimental procedures
5. Developing scientific attitudes such as the desire to be truly objective, or to suspend judgment until sufficient data is collected.

Although there are elements of inquiry in learning activities on all levels, Dr. Gagné is convinced that inquiry teaching might best begin in the upper elementary grades and progress in sophistication through junior high, high school, and college levels. Discovery teaching forms the foundation of inquiry development, however, and Dr. Gagné states that one must be careful not to imply that there is no overlap among the kinds of capabilities acquired at each of the four "levels" of instruction which he describes in distinguishing between inquiry and discovery.

Why Teach by Discovery or Inquiry?

The unstructured, student-centered approach to discovery and inquiry clearly allows pupils a better opportunity to develop their talents. You only learn to think by having opportunities to think and you only learn to be creative by having chances to be creative. The teacher provides the environment and attempts to facilitate as much as possible creative thinking by the students. The instructional strategy may begin by providing students with some novel approach that motivates them to get involved. The learners are invited to investigate, given time to explore. Discussion follows where there is a free interchange of ideas, and all ideas are valued. This then may provide, depending upon the situation and the need felt by the instructor, to closure statements of what has been learned, i.e., concepts or principles of science.

"Covering" Versus Learning

A discovery or inquiry teacher is not so much interested in having students cover information, i.e., read a text, as he is in having them involved in investigating. Teachers have long thought that their main purpose was to cover, tell students facts, principles, and theories. They have made the mistaken assumption that to be made aware of something, the student has learned, and then modified his behavior. Nothing can be farther from the truth! How many individuals know cigarettes are harmful to their health? How many of these people have *internalized* this idea and modified their behavior as a result? Teachers aspire to changing behavior of the learner in some positive fashion and not in having minds cluttered with knowledge which does not contribute to the child's growth or enrichment. Teachers should be interested not in covering, but in uncovering by the learner. This seldom occurs without the active involvement of the individual. It does little good to tell the child how to be creative unless he becomes totally involved in creative activity and behaves as a creator. Only then is there visual evidence of internalization through performance.

The "covering type teacher" soars through the material and, unfortunately, is oblivious to the debris of lost talent in his wake. Discovery and inquiry, on the other hand, allows for greater manifestation of talent.

TEACHERS MAY STIMULATE OR INHIBIT CREATIVE ABILITY

As the child leaves the infant years where he has enjoyed a great deal of autonomy in the home and where he has tested a variety of materials—rattles, balls, toys, fur, water—through sensory-motor activity, he enters, in the late preschool or kindergarten years, an environment of experiences preplanned by either parent or teacher. The child soon learns the system of rewards based on obedience and conformity which unless modified through the wisdom of a creative teacher can act to inhibit his human potential. There is a growing awareness by teachers not to commit the errors illustrated in the poem by Helen Buckley, reprinted on a following page. They are realizing more frequently that children must have both internal and external freedom in order to grow in creative expression. An example of this is seen in Bill, who had always been a capable follower—always waiting for instructions. He was stimulated by a need for a device to help him in his play. The setting that provided external freedom was the classroom—a highly science-oriented, responsive environment. It was Bill's laboratory. There he did his work, his experimenting, and there he could find answers to his questions. The teacher, hoping to develop self-direction, resourcefulness, and responsibility in her charges, found Bill particularly receptive one day. Bill was confronted with a problem concerning the reflection of light, which he promptly brought to class. He had bought a small periscope but found that he needed a bigger one to use in his snowball fight, scheduled for Saturday (the fort he had built was quite high). He took the small periscope apart to find out how it was constructed. He had all of the materials with him for construction of a large one. The environment of the science workroom and the quiet encouragement of the teacher (Why not try it out?) gave the boy confidence in his ability to construct a large periscope. When he had completed the work, the boy not only had a larger periscope but a telescopic one as well. Bill's project gave him much information about the use of mirrors in reflecting light—but the significant thing for him was that he had constructed a periscope that made possible Saturday's victory! Furthermore, he had exercised his creative talent and developed self-confidence, which contributed to the building of his self concept.

Stimulating Creativity within the Forced Relationship

Helen Buckley has captured the essence of how a well-meaning teacher may in fact do disservice to creative development. This sympathetic statement brings us closer to an understanding of forces which discourage or encourage growth.

The Little Boy

Once a little boy went to school.
He was quite a little boy.
And it was quite a big school.
But when the little boy
Found that he could go to his room
By walking right in from the door outside,
He was happy.
And the school did not seem
Quite so big any more.

One morning,
When the little boy had been in school awhile,
The teacher said:
"Today we are going to make a picture."
"Good!" thought the little boy,
He liked to make pictures.
He could make all kinds:
Lions and tigers,
Chickens and cows,
Trains and boats—
And he took out his box of crayons
And began to draw.

But the teacher said: "Wait!
It is not time to begin!"
And she waited until everyone looked ready.

"Now," said the teacher,
"We are going to make flowers."
"Good!" thought the little boy,
He liked to make flowers,
And he began to make beautiful ones
With his pink and orange and blue crayons.

But the teacher said, "Wait!
And I will show you how."

And she drew a flower on the blackboard.
It was red, with a green stem.
"There," said the teacher,
"Now you may begin."
The little boy looked at the teacher's flower.
Then he looked at his own flower.
He liked his flower better than the teacher's.
But he did not say this,
He just turned his paper over
And made a flower like the teacher's.
It was red, with a green stem.

On another day,
When the little boy had opened
The door from the outside all by himself,
The teacher said:
"Today we are going to make something with clay."
"Good!" thought the little boy,
He liked clay.

He could make all kinds of things with clay:
Snakes and snowmen,
Elephants and mice,

Cars and trucks—
And he began to pull and pinch
His ball of clay.

But the teacher said:
"Wait, it is not time to begin!"
And she waited until everyone looked ready.

"Now," said the teacher,
"We are going to make a dish."
"Good!" thought the little boy,
He liked to make dishes,
And he began to make some
That were all shapes and sizes.

But the teacher said, "Wait!
And I will show you how."

And she showed everyone how to make
One deep dish.
"There," said the teacher,
"Now you may begin."

The little boy looked at the teacher's dish.
Then he looked at his own.
He liked his dishes better than the teacher's
But he did not say this.
He just rolled his clay into a big ball again,
And made a dish like the teacher's.
It was a deep dish.

And pretty soon
The little boy learned to wait,
And to watch,
And to make things just like the teacher.
And pretty soon
He didn't make things of his own anymore.

Then it happened
That the little boy and his family
Moved to another house,
In another city,
And the little boy
Had to go to another school.

This school was even bigger
Than his other one,
And there was no door from the outside
Into his room.
He had to go up some big steps,

And walk down a long hall
To get to his room.

And the very first day
He was there,
The teacher said:
"Today we are going to make a picture."
"Good!" thought the little boy,
And he waited for the teacher
To tell him what to do.
But the teacher didn't say anything.
She just walked around the room.

When she came to the little boy
She said, "Don't you want to make a picture?"
"Yes," said the little boy.
"What are we going to make?"
"I don't know until you make it," said the teacher.
"How shall I make it?" asked the little boy.
"Why, any way you like," said the teacher.
"And any color?" asked the little boy.
"Any color," said the teacher.
"If everyone made the same picture,
And used the same colors,
How would I know who made what,
And which was which?"
"I don't know," said the little boy.
And he began to make pink and orange and blue flowers.

He liked his new school . . .
Even if it didn't have a door
Right in from the outside!

HELEN E. BUCKLEY[9]

STIMULATING BY QUESTIONING

Someone has called the ability to ask questions a verbal form of curiosity in action. It is undeniable that curiosity engenders the spirit of inquiry and should be nurtured through the school years of the child. Some evidence suggests that as the child moves

9. *School Arts* (October 1961). Used with permission. Helen Buckley Simkewicz is professor of English at State University of New York, Oswego, N.Y., and the author of several children's books published by Lothrop, Lee & Shephard Co.

through the grades his curiosity progressively diminishes, and that when he reaches high school this precious human quality is almost lost. The inquiring mind, highly prized as it is, seems manifest in all too few students. This is mainly attributable to inhibiting factors in the child's home and school environment.

Development of ideas and construction of projects should be encouraged so the child has the opportunity to formulate hypotheses and is prompted to speculate as a result of some bafflement or challenges—something he may be quizzical about but unsure of as to direction or focus. He may need the stimulation of questions by the teacher to push his thinking and stretch his imagination. Often it is the way the teacher frames a question (whether it has "lead-on" value or is one of factual inquiry) that will make a difference in whether there is closure or open-endedness. Good questions may help children interpret, translate, improvise, extrapolate, analyze, synthesize, discover, comprehend, observe, and identify.

Listed below are questions that have been gathered from teachers who have achieved some creative results through their use. How would you classify them?

What changes have been brought about?
What do you think?
Why do you think so?
Why?
Why do you say that?
How would you get the information?
Why do you think this is the information we need?
How can we find out?
How can you show what you think is true?
What makes you think it happened?
How can we find the answer?
How can you show us?
What do we need?
How does this help us?
What makes you think we have a right to move it?
How could you use it in an important way?
In what way will we disturb the place where it lives?
Can we care for it well in our classroom?
How soon can it be returned to its place?
What has happened?
In what way can you help?
What can you see?
What have we learned?
What might we do to find out more about this?
What changes should we make in our experiment?

When did it change?
Where did the change occur?
Why did it change?
Why is it inaccurate?
How do we do these things?
What are the safeguards to consider?
What agencies could we go to for help in gathering this information?
What people in the community could we call upon for information?
Where is it?
What is it?
What can it do?
What's to be done first?
How shall we begin?
What things did we do best?
How can we improve our way of work?
What did we do to be sure that our experiments showed us accurate results?
Where shall we look for an answer to that question?
Which are heavy?
Which are light?
What makes you say that?
What is it for?
How is it used?
What can we do to show others what we have learned?
How do we know this to be true?
How can we test it?
How can we be sure?
How can we show that what we say is true?
What did you do?
How is it different?
How do you know?
What changes do we see?
Why is this important?
How can we compare it?
Where do they go?
How do they change?
How can you tell?
What hobbies can you develop from this study?
How many can you see?
How did you check it?
What records did you make about what you saw?
What conclusions can you make from what you saw and tried?
What color is it?
How does it look like something else you know?
How does this compare with what we already know?
Why does this happen?

What does it do to stay alive?
How can we check this information?
How can you tell that the source is reliable?
How does it change?
What made it change?
Where do they come from?
Why should we try it?
How does it feel?
How does it look?
Why is it safe?
How can we make it safe?
How can we make it look better?
What can we do about this problem?
Which is the best for our use?
How does it smell?
How are they alike?

These questions may have been posed after an enriching experience prompted the children to submit their problems. They
help to develop interests that have been discovered or awakened
in the children; they tend to impel the children to a point where,
to overcome limited or inadequate data, they feel compelled to
explore and investigate further. The questions may also push the
children to the point where a counterintuitive or discrepant event
is discovered, the data appear disharmonious and conflicting. The
child thinks that they cannot all be true, and so further activities
are planned to get the data to satisfy their curiosity. Finding
answers may lead to construction projects, experimenting, seeking
out resources, observing, study trips, collecting and studying
samples, and a host of other activities.

MOTIVATION AND PROBLEM SOLVING

Science has always been one of the natural areas of interest for
children, and compared to most subjects in the curriculum little
stimulation has been required to motivate a class in science. However, the teacher's enthusiasm and skill in leading children to do
divergent thinking on some phase of the content being explored
will go far in sustaining and heightening their interest. Since
there are a wide range of abilities, interests, and ambitions in
every group of children, each child may be encouraged to develop
his own talents by sharing in the planning and being given a
choice of activity. All children will then learn different things.

Some will learn to think, observe, experiment, and demonstrate, and carry on a variety of investigative activities using quite different materials than others. Certain materials may be used by all, and certain common experiences may be shared by all, but the outcome may be as individual as the learner. There will, of course, be a core of common understanding of the principles involved in the subject at hand, but in this way a child's interest has been extended by his becoming totally immersed in a creative endeavor and moving as far as his abilities will take him.

Sometimes a highly motivated group may stimulate an individual to solve a group problem. A sixth grade class was confronted with the problem of learning to pilot an airplane, an outgrowth of a study on air transportation. They thought it best to start with a conventional airplane like a Piper Cub before exploring jets. The pupils said that they had learned all about the controls and now wanted the experience of using them. Bringing a link trainer into the classroom was out of the question of course. The class could have visited the airport, but even then they wouldn't get the experience of using controls in flight. Small

FIGURE 3-4. *A study of living things in the classroom always presents the problem of insuring survival. How does the teacher encourage the excellent care required? (SCIS Photo)*

commercial models of airplanes wouldn't have relieved the situation.

The problem was not solved that day but the next day a reserved though bright youngster exhibited some creative originality. He brought a small model of a plane that he had built. It was mounted on a vertical stick; thin threads ran from the movable parts of the plane to the base which was made from an old cigar box. The controls, all simulated and accurate, were on the top of the box. The child presented a lesson in flying by talking to the class and moving the controls. This was done so dramatically, clearly, and accurately that everyone felt that he had been a pilot that afternoon.

The incentive to build and create often comes after school hours as a result of some activity in the classroom. An illustration of this is a sixth grade class watching an experiment on buoyancy. The children were amused and awed to see a bottle rising and sinking like a submarine. The principle involved was simple. The water was expelled from the bottle by means of a tube which one blew into. When the tube was left open, water refilled the bottle and the weight of water and bottle made the bottle sink. A ratio of air and water controlled the depth of buoyancy of the bottle. A few days later there was a successor to our experiment. A boy brought in a metal diver that he had constructed of two tin cans with a cork-valve system that worked with dry ice. Instead of air, the dry ice in water yielded carbon dioxide, the pressure of which expelled the water. When the diver reached the surface, the cork-valve opened. Water rushed in and sank the diver. This process continued until all the dry ice was used up. The boy enjoyed his diver and so did his friends. As an outgrowth of this, he is working on a toy submarine made of discarded oil cans. He has run into some difficulty with the valve system, but is determined to work it out himself.

FOSTERING THE CREATIVE PROCESS

A teacher gives some objects to her pupils and they are asked to think of the most unique, unusual, and exciting ideas they can to either improve them or give them greater utility or purpose. The objects may be almost anything—a can opener, a wind-up toy, a bottle cap, a corkscrew, or some device around the home which challenges the child. The object should, however, be within the children's range of experience. For example, one class of youngsters with special ability in science who had learned many ways of using experiments to demonstrate principles were asked to think of new ways of explaining certain phenomena familiar to them. There are several ways of demonstrating that air has weight. Subjects were asked to review them quickly and to think of new experiments and demonstrate them to show the same thing—with some improvement if possible.

To test the resourcefulness of ten-year-olds, one enterprising teacher changed the numerals on the classroom clock. She found that the children soon learned to tell time just as easily—in fact, they did not wish the numerals changed back to the usual way.

Toys can illustrate a great many principles in the physical sciences and are often used by teachers. An interesting way of showing the application of principles that the children have already learned would be to have the children select a variety of toys from a basket and elicit from them as many principles as they can give from their selections.

If the teacher is to gain insight into the creative process, she may need to design new ways of getting children to reveal the process through the avoidance of stereotyped methods.

SUMMARY

Working creatively with children in science requires a high degree of understanding of children's development, cognitive styles, and a host of parental and community pressures that influence creative ability.

Creative learning can blossom only in a setting conducive to internal and external freedom. Since we know that children who are highly creative in one way are not always highly creative in other ways and learn differently, the greater the variety of instructional aids a teacher will use, the greater assurance will there be that more children will be reached. The challenges of learning creatively, which come from confrontation and problem solving, should be omnipresent.

Curiosity engenders the spirit of inquiry and should be nurtured through the school years. The inquiring mind needs an environment free of the inhibiting factors found in the home and school. The instructional environment should be designed for discovery and inquiry.

If a teacher realizes children have more than 100 talents and each child in her class is better than average in one of these she is more likely to teach for the development of talents. Discovery and inquiry teaching in the elementary school, because of their child-centeredness and freedom-to-explore orientation, make possible greater development of all talents than the teacher-centered approach. Carefully framed questions are needed to push a child's thinking and stretch his imagination. Enthusiasm and pedagogical skill are needed to lead children into paths of divergent thinking. Some valuable clues to creative thinking may come from observing the behavior of children engaged in problem solving designed to elicit imaginative responses.

QUESTIONS

1. Describe the requirements for working creatively with children.

2. Discuss Dr. Jean Piaget's viewpoint on creativity in the development of children.

3. To what extent have parents influenced the interest in science which many creative scientists acquired during their formative years?

4. List the ingredients needed to provide an ideal setting for creative learning in science.

5. Given unlimited resources, design a classroom that would reflect the spirit of science and scientific inquiry.

6. What is the role of discovery and problem solving in developing creativity?

7. How are discovery and inquiry related?

8. Devise several questions which elicit open-endedness, closure, "lead-on" value, and critical thinking.

9. How can insights into creative behavior be derived from observing children in specially designed activities?

10. Given a limited budget, how would you select equipment and facilities for a creative learning environment?

11. Why is freedom essential in fostering creativity?

12. What is the relationship of Teaching for Talent, the Implications of Projects Work, and Discovery Teaching?

13. After reading this chapter, summarize in one page your theory of instruction.

CHAPTER IV

Fostering a
Creative Science Program

> *We stand together, passengers on a little space ship, depen-*
> *dent on its vulnerable resources of air and soil, all com-*
> *mitted for our safety to its security and peace, preserved*
> *from annihilation only by the care, the work, and, I will*
> *say, the love we bestow on our fragile craft.*
>
> ADLAI STEVENSON

HOME AS THE SPARK CENTER FOR CREATIVITY

No one knows how much creative talent is lost because it is not encouraged in the home. Individuals grow through experience. If they have opportunities for creative experiences and are encouraged to be creative they are more likely to manifest this ability. The mind has been compared to a computer in that the input determines the output to a considerable extent. The environment of the child (the input) includes the home, community, and school. Each of these can play a major role in either stimulating or depressing creative talent. If a rich environment encourages creative activity, the input is of high quality, and it is reasonable to assume that the output will result in better-developed creative talent.

The extent and nature of the child's interests are largely determined by his home life; they are firmly rooted in his personality by the time he enters school. Parents can contribute to fostering the development of creative abilities in their progeny by giving recognition for creative achievements, showing an interest in their children's studies in science, and asking meaningful questions. Parents should realize that the behavior of creative children often does not follow the norm for their group. The creative individual, for example, may be much more interested in books than his peers, and parents can and should encourage such pursuits. Creative production comes from a prepared and enriched mind. The school obviously emphasizes learning from books, but if the home devalues reading it causes a serious conflict. Conflicts of this nature may arise particularly with the culturally deprived or in homes where the father is not overly concerned with academics and scorns the bookish interest of his son. The school should provide in its adult education programs, parent–teacher conferences, and at PTA meetings, suggestions to parents on how they can stimulate the creative abilities of their children.

Satisfaction of curiosity, so characteristic of the young, is the greatest possible motivation for science learning. A child wants to know what, how, and why. He tastes, smells, looks at, listens to, and handles many things in order to feel at home with the objects that surround him. The outdoors, too, is a constant source of stimulation and wonder. The child wants to know about the living things around him—trees, flowers, birds, dogs, cats, insects, turtles, snakes, rodents. A wide range of science experiences is available at home through the care of pets, gardening, and simple experiments involving food and household articles. Parents can encourage questions, frankly admit when they don't know the answers, and help the child to find the answers. At the same time, they should avoid giving him more information than he wants and be careful not to perpetuate superstitions or falsehoods, which could be worse than giving no answer at all.

Many important principles of science can be learned through play. A child is always eager to find out how his toys work. Some toys involve the use of gravity, magnetism, or friction. Others work by winding, pulling, or compressing. As a young child plays in water he discovers that some things float and others do not. Water causes a reduction in friction and the floor becomes slippery. As the child grows and learns, each bit of information leading to concept development becomes a building block for further knowledge. Often children's play involves making something to demonstrate ideas of their own, and this may contribute to their growing interest in science.

To get an idea of the child's real interests, observe his unguarded moments. What does he do or say or read? Is he a collector, a "fixer," a planner, a doubter? Is he curious—curious enough to tolerate failure to get answers? The school can supplement parents' observations with more concrete information about test scores, interest profiles, expressed occupational choices, and other records.

To encourage science interests effectively, the parent should know the child, know the school, and plan a variety of appropriate family activities. Parental support of the school program is a tremendous factor in shaping a positive attitude toward learning. The reverse—finding fault with the school—can provide a ready-made excuse for a pupil's apathetic performance. Guided by the knowledge of the individual child and his science activities at school, parents can devise practical ways of encouraging rapport between youth and science.

1. *Parents can surround the child with science-related books.*

   a. Reading families have children who can and will read.
   b. The right book is a gift long remembered.
   c. Subscribe to science magazines in the name of the student.
   d. Provide him with his own bookshelves and books.
   e. Explore libraries and bookshops with him.

The home library will be a source of enjoyment and help to students during their school years and later. If parents want some assistance in selecting books and magazines on science, they can consult the science teacher and librarian. Good lists are available in school and public libraries, and newspapers and magazines review books for all ages.

2. *Parents can plan a wide range of experiences.*

   a. In family discussion or "table talk" listen to questions and ask questions on science topics. Game-fashion, demand "the evidence, please" as a substitute for hearsay and irrational argument.
   b. Take the children to museums, nature centers and trails, zoos, laboratories, planetariums and observatories, aquariums, parks, wildlife sanctuaries, communication centers, water and power plants, construction projects, weather stations, airports, harbors, bakeries, the city dump.
   c. Include children, when appropriate, in activities such as science lectures, exhibits, conventions, nature walks, science club programs, summer institutes.
   d. Permit a space at home for a workbench, a darkroom, a chemistry lab, a growing plot.
   e. Support hobbies with your time and with money for

cameras, barometers, microscopes, models, science kits. Find time to work together on projects.

f. Encourage membership in 4-H clubs, science clubs, electronics clubs, hobby clubs, photography clubs, junior science societies, nature clubs, scouting.

g. Plan vacations—camps, jobs, courses, travel—to include seashore, mountains, desert, and other regions that will expand geographic and geological experiences.

Parents should learn to understand their boy or girl, encourage some action in the light of this knowledge, and praise all efforts. Only in an atmosphere of sympathetic understanding can parents foster a maturing interest in science. How would a parent you might know rate on the following checklist of possible ways of helping?

CHECKLIST FOR PARENTS

Family Activities   Yes No

1. Do you help your children to see the fun in discovering things of scientific interest in their own home, backyard, or neighborhood? — —
2. Do you take them to nearby places to see things they are studying about in science? — —
3. Do you help them find books or pictures that answer their questions and further their interest in science? — —
4. Do you select with your children worthwhile movies or radio and TV programs with science orientation? — —
5. Do you work with your childen on simple experiments? — —
6. Do you encourage them to make science collections? — —

Home Facilities

7. Do your children have their own science books and shelf space? — —
8. Do your children have a place to tinker, fix, build, and "try and see"? — —
9. Do you provide storage space for material collected for experiments and help the youngsters work out a plan to keep things in order? — —
10. Do you equip the playroom or study space with models, sky maps, charts of the solar system, aquariums, or other instructional aids for sciences? — —

11. Do you teach the children how to plant and care for a garden or tend potted plants?   — —
12. Do you allow them to have pets and teach them proper handling and care?   — —

Home-School Relations

13. Do you know enough about your school's science program to describe in a general way its strengths as well as its needs?   — —
14. Do you know what your boy or girl is doing now in the science class or lab?   — —
15. Do you consult the teacher, science supervisor, or school librarian about the choice of science magazines, books, or other science reading for your child?   — —
16. Do you consult with the teacher or science department head about the choice of gifts which support or stimulate interest in science subjects?   — —
17. Does your child bring home science books from the school or public library for further reading?   — —
18. Does your child talk to you about what would make a good science fair project?   — —

Interests and Attitudes

19. Can you name an area of science your boy or girl is especially interested in?   — —
20. Do you take time to help your children arrive at understandings and help them "find out" rather than give them the answers?   — —
21. Do you know how the work of a scientist differs from other jobs and what preparation is required for such work?   — —
22. Are you helping your children to observe carefully and make accurate statements?   — —
23. Do you, with your family, use books and other checks to judge the validity of statements?   — —
24. Do you, at opportune moments, encourage perseverance and point out the challenge of failure?   — —
25. While encouraging the seeking of facts, do you dispel the notion of absolute proof?   — —

Some parents, particularly from the upper-middle and upper classes, may consider science professions relatively low in status. People of these classes tend to have greater esteem for the business professions. They believe that scientists have poor income possibilities and are probably persons who couldn't succeed in the business or financial world. Other parents with life styles inimical to science and who hold science and technology responsible for the pollution of our cities and other social ills, direct their interests to the humanities and to urban and community problems. These views are often expressed by innuendo or in other ways to children. As a result, the child with creative scientific potential from these groups may be gradually directed away from his interest in science by the psychological and sociological pressures of the parents.

The home often inhibits curiosity, especially in young children. For example, "Don't play with fire" is an admonishment not to learn about fire. True, there are as in this case, safety reasons for not allowing children to investigate, but investigation can be done under supervision. "Don't bother me—can't you see I'm busy?" and "Don't do" this or that are admonishments against being curious. Unfortunately, such negative responses to curiosity on the part of the parents may become the pattern. After the child receives several instances of negative reinforcement or aversive behavior he soon learns it's safer not to be inquisitive or creative.

THE COMMUNITY: PROVIDER OF CENTERS FOR CREATIVE WORK AND SOCIAL RESPONSIBILITY

A good science program depends not only on the parents but on community leaders as well. Enlightened, action-minded parents will have the program they want. Parents can stimulate the science interests of children and broaden their science experiences by means of science-related books, trips, gifts, family talk, clubs, projects, lectures, films, and so forth. Parents should know what to expect of the school and what is going on there, and should respond to opportunities to work with the school, particularly in developing positive attitudes and shaping societal values. In recent years the need for closer linkage with the school has become imperative. The deterioration of the environment and problems in drug abuse require community and school action for solution. The political and social climate that provides impetus to change stems from the community.

One joint school-community effort might be science fairs, which serve as avenues for extending interest in the sciences in both the elementary and secondary schools. It is estimated that each year some 600,000 boys and girls in secondary schools, and lesser numbers in elementary schools, undertake experiments and science projects which they present in school exhibits and local or regional fairs. Many get recognition that enables them to participate in national science fairs. If you ever attended one of these fairs, no doubt you were amazed at the variety of interests illustrated there—demonstrations of how worms help the farmer, how animals build their homes, different kinds of noises and their cause, space science, conservation of natural resources, types of rocks found locally, motion of the earth, electrical circuits, advancement of communication, just to mention a few. One of the important educational values of these fairs, apart from the interest stimulated, is the development of skills a boy or girl utilizes in preparing exhibits. A project of his own choice also gives the student an outlet for his creative energy, since an exhibit should evolve from an original idea.

Another school-community action project is a clean-up drive to collect litter and trash defacing and polluting the environment. Parents and teachers and children can help in separating, at collection stations, litter into papers, cans, or bottles for transport to recycling centers. If centers are not available, organize or petition for them.

The federal government has become increasingly concerned with the education of the culturally deprived child. This concern comes from the realization of the influence of the home and the community in guiding the development of children. The Elementary and Secondary Education Act, Title I, provides multimillion dollar funding to meet the educational needs of children from low income, disadvantaged families. In fact, most of the U.S. Office of Education assistance programs are targeted towards the children of deprived minorities and marginal wage earners.

The action being taken by the government in supporting such activities as Project Head Start, Upward Bound, Talent Search, and Special Services, environmental and drug education programs, arises from an awareness of how influential the community can be in developing the potential of the child. It is clear that, unless a community strives to develop the intellectual and creative abilities of its young, these valuable assets never mature.

CREATIVE TEACHING OF ENVIRONMENTAL EDUCATION

One of the great challenges for the classroom teacher is the environmental crisis. It's almost impossible today to look at a newspaper, listen to the radio, view a TV program, or discuss problems of living without encountering some illustration of abhorrence over what man is doing to the world around us. If one is looking for the villain in our society, to whom should he point the finger— at the effluents of big industries, the sewage of towns, the farms pouring nitrogen fertilizers into streams, noxious emissions from auto exhausts, proliferation of junk yards, ugly strip mines, oil slicks from tankers, indiscriminate use of DDT, the litter in our cities, the crimes and attendant social disorganization? The finger is pointing at *us*—for all men are polluters, as in Pogo's prophetic remark, "We have met the enemy and he is us." The human implications resulting from mass contamination of the nation's air, water, and land have prompted a writer to announce that man is an endangered species. However, future survival is not the only issue. Survival is also an issue in our day-to-day living, the breath of life that we draw, our life expectancies, the blight of our inner cities, the traffic congestion, the despoiled countryside, the quality of life diminished. There is no doubt that alarm over the environmental condition is justified and a likely precursor to reform, but it also points up the urgency for the teacher to draw upon all of the resources available, assume the leadership required, and pursue an active program of creative teaching to cope with this grave problem of our time. The causes are complex and encompass population growth, technological advances, and the behaviors of people. Any way out of the present dilemma will require profound changes in political, social, and economic patterns as well as basic understanding of science and technology as they relate to ecological reality. (Could it be that the energy shortage will help teach us?)

Since any solution to the problem requires a new multidisciplinary approach to environmental education it may best be defined by the Environmental Education Act of 1970 (PL 91-516) in history-making legislation. The language of the Senate report explaining the act illustrates the national commitment for survival:

> Environmental education is an integrated process which deals with man's interrelationship with his natural and man-made surroundings, including the relation of population growth, pollution, resource allocation and depletion, conservation, technology, and urban and rural planning to the total human environment. Environmental education is a study of the factors influencing ecosystems, mental and physical growth, living and working conditions, decaying cities, and population pressures. Environmental education is intended to promote among citizens the awareness and understanding of the environment, our relationship to it, and

the concern and responsible action necessary to assure our survival and to improve the quality of life.

As stated in the Act, and in Chapter 12 of the report of the President's Council on Environmental Quality, environmental education (EE) is a process which will affect the entire continuum of American education. It is a design for reform because it will, through every aspect of formal and informal education, improve philosophies of life and help each citizen to acquire a new and more viable life style.

This objective was first defined by people in local communities and has been given the highest national priority by the President and by the Congress. Survival as a culture and even as a species may depend on environmental education.

The above description on environmental education is broad and all-encompassing. But integral to the definition is the role of ecology, an integrative science. The word, "ecology," was first proposed in the latter part of the 19th century by Ernst Haeckel, a German biologist to mean the study of the relation between living things and their environment (from the Greek "oikos"—home and "logos"—study). A study of the environment in all its broad implications requires information from the physical sciences, chemistry, physics, geology, astronomy and the like. An understanding of life means an understanding of biology and all related sciences. There is hardly an area in the field of science which does not touch upon the living world.

The ecologist conceives of the earth as a biosphere, which includes most of the earth's surface inhabited by plant and animal life and the lower atmosphere. He also views the biosphere in sections—parts or divisions—as ecosystems. An ecosystem means a self-sustaining community of living things that includes the

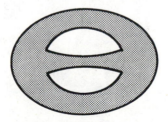

FIGURE 4-1. *This is a common symbol for ecology. Combining the letters E for environment and O from the Greek oikos ("home," "dwelling place"), it refers to the relationships between organisms and their environment.*

organic and inorganic environment. A pond is an ecosystem; so also is a lake or a stream, a woods or prairie, a lot or garden surrounding your house. A terrarium or aquarium in the classroom is an ecosystem in that it represents the functioning of living things and nonliving environment as a single unit. To understand ecology is to find out how ecosystems function—the interdependence of plants, animals, air, water, and soil, and the changes which time and man affect and the intricate balances of living communities. The study of ecology can provide the teacher with endless opportunity for children to test many of the principles of ecology both in and out of the classroom.

In teaching the science of ecology creatively, through a child's earliest levels, the teacher has begun the building of proper attitudes and environmental values that may be fortified through and beyond the formal years of education. Hopefully, the learner will come, in time, to react spontaneously and positively to his environment. But what of the program?

Some environmentalists would have the environmental education program support an expanded version of traditional conservation education. Others would build on the tradition of outdoor

FIGURE 4-2. *Environmental values are developed through a study of ecology. (SCIS Photo)*

education. Some scientists see it as a form of applied science education; social scientists would direct it toward the study of man-made environments.

Effective environmental education must combine all of these elements and serve as a vehicle for bringing about *innovation and reform in our educational systems*. Such reform must change not only what is taught but also how it is taught. Environmental education must emphasize the use of the environment in the education process itself and carry on throughout an individual's lifetime.

Environmental education then, deals with all forms and levels of life, their interrelationships, and our perceptions of them. This synergistic or cooperative action approach, the essence of environmental education, is concerned with what is meaningful and relevant to our times and our existence.

By pooling and redirecting available resources the aim is to create, in the President's words, "new knowledge, new perceptions, new attitudes . . . a basic reform in the way our society looks at problems and makes decisions." With this approach, environmental problems can be defined more clearly and, hopefully, resolved.

It is no great leap for the creative teacher to take one or several approaches in presenting environmental ecological concepts and processes. Some teachers have favored a multidisciplinary method in which all of the subject areas taught in science are based on specific environmental problems, other teachers have sought to integrate the basic environmental ecological principles into existing areas of study such as science, social studies, art, language arts, and health. Whatever the program, approach, or method, the objectives should be clear that the learner must evidence a positive change in behavior towards his environment.

The following pages from the Santee School District *Teacher's Guide*,[1] illustrates an approach that should lead to a change in both attitudes and action of pupils. The guide was written to focus attention on both the cognitive and affective aspects of environmental education.

Many of the activities both teachers and children will engage in to improve the environment should involve the out-of-doors and the community. The check list below can serve as a guide in surveying the categories and degree of pollution in your com-

---

1. *Environmental Education: A Teacher's Guide With Inquiry and Value Seeking Strategies,* Santee School District, Santee, Calif., Jackson Publications, 1972.

TABLE 4-1.   SUPPORTING CONCEPTS: LEVEL 1-1
(Suggested for Primary Grades)

A. In any environment, living things have similar needs.
B. Men live in different environments.
C. Men interact mentally and emotionally to the objects and events in their environment.

Performance Objectives	Teaching-learning Inquiries	Evaluation-terminal Performance
After investigating home and community environment, children will describe and illustrate deprivation of a healthy environment.	Through sociodrama, act out behaviors of polluters in and around school. —What are they doing? —What are they saying? (En)*	Children reveal their inner tensions and fears when their immediate environmental possessions are abused or destroyed.
	Look for evidences of children conserving their environment. —What are they doing? —What are they saying?	Children explore their feelings about an unhealthy environment.
	Illustrate or dramatize the actions. (En)	Children describe ways to handle their emotions and actions when angered, hurt or are fearful of an unhealthy environmental situation.
	Plan a large chart or bulletin board on pictures of what is happening and what should be happening as man seeks to secure his basic needs. —When children destroy their environment who are they hurting? —How are we affected when some one breaks a tree branch or pulls up flowers and bushes? —Why should we be careful with our toys? —What do we do?	

TABLE 4-1. SUPPORTING CONCEPTS: LEVEL I-1
(continued)

A. In any environment, living things have similar needs.
B. Men live in different environments.
C. Men interact mentally and emotionally to the objects and events in their environment.

Performance Objectives	Teaching-learning Inquiries	Evaluation-terminal Performance
Children will participate in activities which redeem the polluted environment at their school and home sites.	—What other things can we do? —Of what are we afraid? (En) Have children periodically collect scrap and refuse from schoolyard and home environment. Note kind and frequency of refuse. —Why should we clean up our environment? —Who pays for trash collection? —Where does the trash go? —How can we cut costs? —What does foul trash do to our health? (En-L) Introduce the concept of recycling of returnable bottles, aluminum cans and newspapers. If possible ask them to participate in local youth group projects. —Where does paper come from? (trees) —If we reuse newspapers, paper sacks and envelopes how are we helping save our trees?	Children begin to display evidence of caring for an aesthetic environment by clean-up activities which are self-motivated. Children begin self-correcting activities on litter control.

Courtesy, Santee School District, Santee, Calif.
* Abbreviations in center column: "En"—environment, "L"—land.

TABLE 4-1. SUPPORTING CONCEPTS: LEVEL I-1
(continued)

A. In any environment, living things have similar needs.
B. Men live in different environments.
C. Men interact mentally and emotionally to the objects and events in their environment.

Performance Objectives	Teaching-learning Inquiries	Evaluation-terminal Performance
	—If aluminum cans can not rust away we have to reuse them. How can we help collect them? —What other kinds of things that we see thrown around in our environment could we reuse or collect and recycle? (En)	
	Illustrate contrasting scenes with before and after land trash pollutants. (see bulletin board ideas) (En-L)	
	Create dioramas of a healthy city, healthy rural, healthy desert, or healthy forest environment to live in. (L-En)	
Men live and survive in different environments.	Use local audio-visual listings to select and to view films on various homes, habitats or modes of shelter throughout the world.	Children focus their attention on other modes of living than their immediate environment.
Children identify different environments.	—What kinds of shelters are there? —What do we need a house for? —Where do we get houses? (En)	Children examine reasons for different kinds of structures and how it is adapted to its environment.
After reviewing illustrations of man-made shelters, children will select and illustrate a type or types of homes	Have children compare and contrast homes other people choose to live in.	Children weigh advantages and disadvantages of various

TABLE 4-1. SUPPORTING CONCEPTS: LEVEL 1-1 (continued)

A. In any environment, living things have smiliar needs.
B. Men live in different environments.
C. Men interact mentally and emotionally to the objects and events in their environment.

Performance Objectives	Teaching-learning Inquiries	Evaluation-terminal Performance
which would appeal to them to live in and to give reasons for their choice.	Illustrate pictures of homes with extreme temperatures such as igloos and jungle huts. View films on mountain forest homes and desert homes and note structure and size differences. Read to the children the poem "If I could Build a House," from Ranger Rick, January 1971. See appendix about the possibilities of living in different environments of a child's choice. —Children select and illustrate their choice of home sites and state reasons for their choices. —Children may role-play "buying" home sites and ask questions about environmental conditions in the community which will determine their purchase. (En) Children begin to compare various modes of living. Children draw pastoral scenes of country living. Note pleasing atmospheres and reasons for desiring to live there. Note clouds, clear skies, running water, green meadows, etc. —Where do we play? Grow food? Build houses? —Why do we like or dislike country homes? (En-L.)	living quarters and select a home-style consistent with their values.

TABLE 4-2. ENVIRONMENTAL CHECKLIST: RATE YOUR
COMMUNITY

*This form may be used to survey the degree of pollution in your com-
munity. After rating the community in the various categories of pollution, you can use the third column to indicate whether government,
private business, or individuals are responsible for the problem. In the
fourth column you can suggest possible remedies.*

Possible Source of Pollution	Rate Problem in Your Area*	Who or What is Responsible?	How can Problem be Alleviated?
Sewage Disposal	_____	_____	_____
Industrial Pollution of Streams	_____	_____	_____
Air Pollution by Factories, Incinerators, etc.	_____	_____	_____
Motor Vehicle Exhausts	_____	_____	_____
Auto Junkyards	_____	_____	_____
Dumping in Vacant Lots	_____	_____	_____
Garbage Disposal	_____	_____	_____
Agricultural Pollution	_____	_____	_____
Construction/Mining Projects	_____	_____	_____
Traffic Noise	_____	_____	_____
Aviation Noise	_____	_____	_____
Other Forms of Pollution	_____	_____	_____

* Serious, getting worse, minor problem, or no problem.
Special permission granted by *Issues Today* Teacher's Edition, published by Xerox Education Publications, © Xerox Corp., 1970.

munity and by providing both learning and suggestions for
positive action for teacher and children.

A variety of charts and posters and the usual instructional aids
with an ecological theme may be used to help the pupil understand relationships and to focus attention on pollution factors
and ways to take immediate and practical action on the problems.

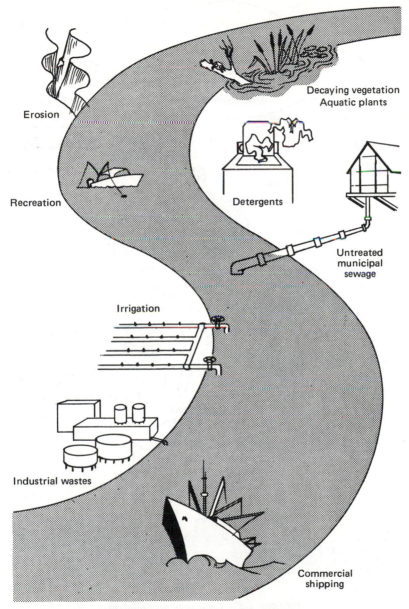

Erosion

Recreation

Irrigation

Industrial wastes

Decaying vegetation
Aquatic plants

Detergents

Untreated
municipal
sewage

Commercial
shipping

FIGURE 4-3.   *Causes of water pollution.*

Adapted from a chart in *Clean Air and Water,* published by E. I.
du Pont de Nemours & Co. Used with permission.

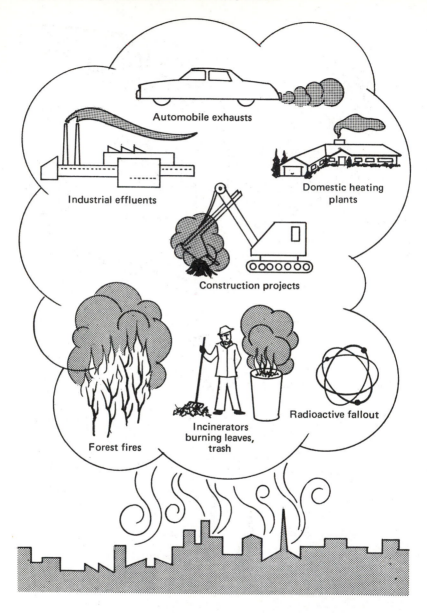

FIGURE 4-4. *Causes of air pollution.*

Adapted from a chart in *Clean Air and Water,* published by E. I. du Pont de Nemours & Co. Used with permission.

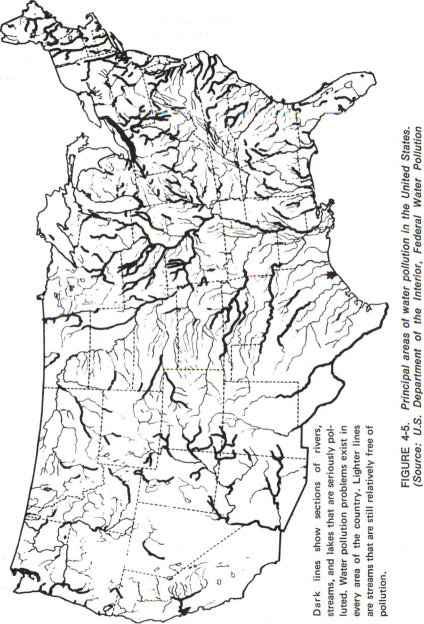

Dark lines show sections of rivers, streams, and lakes that are seriously polluted. Water pollution problems exist in every area of the country. Lighter lines are streams that are still relatively free of pollution.

FIGURE 4-5. *Principal areas of water pollution in the United States. (Source: U.S. Department of the Interior, Federal Water Pollution Control Administration.)*

87

SELECTED SOURCES OF ENVIRONMENTAL–CONSERVATION EDUCATION MATERIALS

American Forest Institute
1835 K Street, N.W.
Washington, D.C. 20006

American Forestry Association
919 17th Street, N.W.
Washington, D.C. 20006

Bureau of Outdoor Recreation
Division of Information
U.S. Department of the Interior
Washington, D.C. 20240

Bureau of Sport Fisheries and Wildlife
Office of Conservation Education
U.S. Department of the Interior
Washington, D.C. 20240

The Conservation Foundation
1250 Connecticut Avenue, N.W.
Washington, D.C. 20036

Consumer Protection and Environmental Health Service
Office of Public Affairs
U.S. Department of Health, Education and Welfare
Washington, D.C. 20204

Federal Water Pollution Control Administration
Office of Information
U.S. Department of the Interior
Washington, D.C. 20242

Forest Service
Information Division
U.S. Department of Agriculture
Washington, D.C. 20250

National Air Pollution Control Administration
Office of Education and Information
U.S. Department of Health, Education and Welfare
801 North Randolph Street
Arlington, Va. 22203

National Park Service
Division of Information
U.S. Department of the Interior
Washington, D.C. 20240

National Wildlife Federation
1412 16th Street, N.W.
Washington, D.C. 20036

Resources for the Future, Inc.
1755 Massachusetts Avenue, N.W.
Washington, D.C. 20036

Soil Conservation Service
Information Division
U.S. Department of Agriculture
Washington, D.C. 20250

Soil Conservation Society of America
7515 N.E. Ankeny Road
Ankeny, Iowa 50021

U.S. Geological Survey
Information Office
U.S. Department of the Interior
Washington, D.C. 20242

Educational information might also be obtained from local branches of the Sierra Club, Audubon Society, Friends of the Earth, Society for the Protection of New Hampshire Forests, Save the Redwoods, and many others.

Further assistance can often be obtained from your state fish and game department, forestry department, parks division, or county agent. Consideration should also be given the various city offices that might be helpful—health department, parks and recreation division, city engineer, or board of zoning, for instance.

WILDERNESS AREAS

Most communities are accessible to ecological areas offering choice opportunities to study natural science and to see how the factors of the environment interplay and influence living organisms. The study of animal and plant communities can be fascinating if children are actively involved in determining how life changes in the community and if attempts are made to correlate these alterations with the changes in the weather and seasons.

Exploring an empty lot can be an exciting ecological expedition offering possibilities for creative involvement. For example, the children might be encouraged to discover the variety of plant and animal life and the interrelationship of living things. They could

89

suggest how they would determine the population of the plant and animal community, the distribution of insects in the grass or in the top layers of the soil, how life is dispersed in the lot, and what factors they think influence the distribution of the various types of life they find and the harmful effects of pollutants on the balance of nature.

If earthworms are found, a study might be made to determine how deep earthworms go in the soil and why, the characteristics of earthworms, and importance to soil. Other possibilities for experiments to be done at home, at the science museum, or in the classroom will undoubtedly arise from the investigation of a lot or wilderness area. The study of the interrelatedness of life with the physical and biological factors affecting it offers many opportunities for leisure pursuits involving investigation, inventiveness, and creative enterprise. It is of little importance who fosters this interest—the parents, the local, state, or federal government, community organizations, or the school, but it is important that the child have a chance to learn about his environment and see its leisure-time possibilities.

Ecological studies can also lead to better understanding of conservation principles and provide opportunities for children to see how these principles might be applied to prevent environmental disaster. Many forward-looking communities have been instrumental in establishing wilderness areas, forest preserves, and parks to serve as outdoor laboratories for this purpose. Teachers particularly have done much to convince communities to investigate the desirability of establishing such areas. They accomplished this objective by involving children actively in ecological studies and then publicizing what the children were doing to clean up the environment. As a result, the communities were alerted to the educational value of field study. Once members of a community see this value, they are more inclined to provide funds to acquire and maintain preserves for future generations. High school science teachers, college science professors, professional scientists, agricultural advisers, conservationists, state fish and game personnel, and other related service groups are keenly aware of the value of maintaining natural ecological areas and teaching environmental education and can be called on for assistance. They may become, as a result, valuable teaching allies offering extensive aid in field work. The scientific and intellectual stimulation of the teacher and pupils, as a result of their involvement in this type of activity, is more likely to be enhanced and such alliances provide greater opportunities for creative involvement.

DRUG EDUCATION IN THE ELEMENTARY GRADES

Drug abuse has become a problem of national concern which is impacting on the schools of the nation. An alarming trend is the misuse of drugs by younger and younger age groups. Reports show that elementary school children have experimented with marijuana and other drugs and, therefore, teaching about potentially dangerous drugs must begin at the early levels and continued throughout their school experience. In the formative years of a child's life, particularly between 8–12, his personality and nervous system are more vulnerable than in later life and, consequently, the results of drug abuse can be irreparable. It is not within the scope of this book to discuss the social milieu which has brought about our "drug culture" nor discourse on the complexities of the problem except to emphasize the responsibility of the teacher mainly in education, prevention, and referral when identified.

Look at the child's world and the influence of the media on his daily living—the commercials that blare out pills for headaches, sleep, tensions, stomach disorders, and the like. Even the cartoons will frequently depict a character taking some potion and being transformed into a superman and committing magical feats. In the child's immediate family, the use of alcohol and tobacco may be common and pervasive so that program in drug education requires great creative skill in reaching the young child in the context of his home, school, and neighborhood setting. Drug education, not unlike environmental education, must go beyond the cognitive level—it must include attitudes, values, and behavior.

In the second report of the National Commission on Marihuana and Drug Abuse,[2] the Commission has attempted to define Drug Education by stating that in one sense, it is simply drug information transmitted in a school classroom and that, unfortunately, too many programs make no more of it than that. Teachers who have received no special training in the task simply read, repeat, or pan out materials from other sources, show films, or bring in guest speakers from outside organizations or agencies. Worse yet the untrained teacher may feel obliged to add his or her own input to the class, contributing misinformation or personal prejudices in the form of facts.

At its best drug education can be much more than this. First it

2. *Drug Use in America: Problem in Perspective, Second Report of the National Commission on Marihuana and Drug Abuse* (Washington, D.C.: U.S. Government Printing Office, March 1973).

is a systematic presentation of information to a particular group of recipients; it is designed specifically for those recipients and attuned to their own level of sophistication, their knowledge, and their views. Second, proper drug education employs a teacher trained not only to use materials at hand but also to relate to the recipients at a personal level and to use that relationship itself as an educational device. As one expert grandly put it, "drug education is a concept placing emphasis upon utilizing the total influence available to affect the individual's social physical and mental well being with respect to drugs" (McCune 1973).

The Commission strongly indicates that in spite of many and varied efforts made thus far in drug education, the incidence of drug use for self-defined purposes has continued to rise and raises the troubling possibility that something basic is wrong with our pedagogy. It is possible to speculate that the avalanche of drug education in recent years has been counterproductive, and that it may have stimulated rebellion, or simply raised interest in the forbidden. In the main, two approaches have been tried: 1) that information about potential harm will have a beneficial impact on behavior, and 2) deemphasize the problem and avoid whetting young appetites. Though our society has tried both approaches, we still have no way of knowing which method works best.

To quote from the report, "In recognition of ignorance about the impact of drug education, the commission recommends that policy makers should also seriously consider declaring a moratorium on all drug education programs in the schools, at least until programs already in operation have been evaluated and a coherent approach with realistic objectives has been developed. At the very least, state legislatures should repeal all statutes which now require drug education courses to be included in the public school curriculum."

In the Commission's view, programs oriented solely towards drugs are unlikely to serve us well. Education should integrate information about drugs and drug use into broader mental hygiene or problem-solving courses. In this way, the overall objective of encouraging responsible decision making can be emphasized, without placing the teacher in the position of defending drug policy.

A Commission-sponsored survey reveals an increasing trend toward integrating drug-related instruction into the total school curriculum, wherever appropriate (Boldt et al., 1973). If elementary education succeeds in teaching children the basic lesson —that education can offer them something they want as well as need—the task for secondary schools will be much easier.

In keeping with the Commission's report, consider the educational implications for the elementary school child. Before developing a program in drug education, the teacher must have access to accurate scientific information and a clear understanding of the facts before attempting instruction. The most natural area to begin drug education is in the life or health sciences. Every good program in science provides a program for teaching principles of health on every level. When dealing with good health practice, concepts and attitudes concerning drugs are developed through investigatory activities in which the learner makes discoveries and relates them to his own physical and mental well-being.

On the subject of nutrition, the child learns that food is important to health but certain nonfood substances may be injurious. In primary levels, the child learns not to put things in his mouth for it could be harmful and also the danger of accepting favors from strangers. In every classroom, you will find that children who have a knowledge of drugs will cover the whole spectrum from total innocence to frightening sophistication. Children from neighborhoods where drug problems are common are, naturally, well informed. Regardless of their background, free expression and inquiry will reveal much to the teacher who can begin to deal with the problem with factual data. If the answers are not known, then teacher and child together can probe the questions and thereby establish a mutual bonding experience in the process. The learner should gain some perspective and appreciation for the guardians of health of the community and the important health services which doctors, dentists, nurses, and pharmacists provide. The child can discover the validity in properly administered prescription drugs, learn they are to protect or restore health and at the same time come to realize that there is no magic or cure-all properties in any single medicine but deal with the question of the role medicine plays in maintaining good health and disease prevention and distinguish between facts and fantasy. There are many directions teachers can take in providing avenues for exploration. Children are curious about their body and what effects it. Instruction can begin with many topics and questions on drugs that are science related, for example:

1. Edible plants are important as food.
2. One should learn to know poisonous and nonpoisonous plants.
3. Drugs are derived from plants.
4. Drug products affect health.
5. Household products have good uses but can be abused.

6. Medicine cabinets contain a variety of drugs that are carefully labeled.
7. What is the importance of labeling?
8. Medicine used for purposes other than intended ones may be injurious.
9. Anything that touches or enters the body has an effect on it.

There are more resources now available that provide information on drug education than ever before, such as books, pamphlets, magazines, newspaper articles, films, filmstrips, and charts easily obtained from book publishers, health associations, pharmaceutical manufacturers' association, mental health associations, and local and state health centers. Resource people may also be sought for information such as pharmacists, doctors, scientists, botanists, customs officers, police officers, county health officers, district drug advisors, narcotic agents, probation officers, and the school nurse. Perhaps, the best deterrent to drug abuse is a child who begins to understand the value of good health as a factor in effective living and is highly motivated in a learning environment to develop his potential through constructive channels.

The Commission notes that an effective drug education policy, once developed, should not be limited either to school or to youth. If we are ready to accomplish the task of encouraging responsible decision making, we must broaden the scope of our concern beyond youth. Community-wide adult education programs are no less important than teenage programs. The family can only perform its vital role effectively in dealing with youthful drug use if parents appreciate the complexity of drug-taking behavior, the perceived needs it allegedly fills, and the importance of their own behavior in shaping that of their children.

SCIENTISTS AND ENGINEERS HELP

The scientists living in the community can help convey an understanding of what scientists do, how they work, and how they wage constant war on misconceptions and false beliefs. When a busy scientist takes part in school or community activities, the students associated with him will learn how he thinks. They may be struck by his open-mindedness and the noticeable respect he has for the point of view of others. Or they may perceive that he always looks for cause and effect relationships and is willing to change his mind when evidence is offered to disprove his views. They may learn that a man working in theoretical or basic science seeks knowledge for its own sake and may not particularly care what practical use is made of scientific discoveries. The importance of pure research can hardly be overemphasized, since new knowledge must be acquired before any use can be made of it. A man working in applied science or technology put to practical use the results of basic or pure science, and this may result in the design of a product such as a refrigerator, vacuum cleaner, automobile, or rocket.

Some schools use professional scientists as consultants when there is a particular problem or research project in which the child needs guidance. In many parts of the country scientists and engineers have established, with the support of scientific industries, special councils to act as liaison groups with the schools. Some of these are the Southern California Industry Education Council, the Frontiers of Science in Oklahoma, the Washington Joint Board of Science Education in Washington, D.C., and the Mid-Hudson Science Advisory Council of New York. There are many more. You can probably find out if there is one in your area by contacting a high school science teacher or a scientific society such as the American Chemical Society or the American Engineering Society. If the school needs a special piece of equipment, wants a speaker or a scientific demonstration, needs judges for the science fairs, information on pollution control or drug abuse or in other ways requires assistance, the council endeavors to come to their aid. The activities of these organizations have been mainly directed toward the secondary school, but they are also available on the elementary level.

Many scientific and technological industries have extensive programs to motivate children's interest in science. They provide free publications, films, filmstrips, and kits, give special tours of research facilities, and sponsor special addresses given by learned scientists. The talks they give are usually informational in nature. The teacher should, prior to such a tour or talk, suggest to the scientist that he outlines possibilities for creative activities in his field for children to do relative to their level of understanding. The teacher should work closely with him and suggest ways for best adapting his talents to meet the needs of children.

THE LOCAL LIBRARY

The availability and quality of the public library can contribute immeasurably to science interest, particularly during vacation periods. The library can be used to reinforce and supplement the work of the school. There is no reason why children should remain mentally dormant during vacation periods, especially in the summer, and the library can in many ways provide educational experiences of wide variety for children during these periods.

Many libraries throughout the nation are presently offering special educational programs for children. Others need to be encouraged and should receive financial support to implement similar programs. Obviously, the standard of the library science collection is important, but this needs to be supplemented by an active educational science program sponsored by the library. A science program should include discussion groups, films, talks, and demonstrations by scientists, science educators, and resource people from related professions. Personnel from scientific and technical professions can also make a contribution if the program is carefully planned with teachers. Local and regional science teachers associations can be called upon to sponsor and assist in developing and implementing the program. The library staff should encourage discussion leaders to include creative elements in their science presentations. Some consideration should be given to rewarding children for creative activity at the end of a vacation period; for example, there might be a display of what the children did during the vacation, and awards can be made then. Recognition for all participants is desirable, with different rewards for quality of work based on the child's potential level of achieving.

THE SCIENCE MUSEUM

Many of the large metropolitan communities have built and maintain science museums. These museums, as a rule, do not serve as just archives of knowledge but have active educational programs consisting of several types of tours and discussion groups. They also sponsor student projects and research work. A visit to a science museum can be a visit to a palace of wonder for elementary school children. To most of them it is as exciting and filled with mystery as the story of *The Wizard of Oz*. Visits to the museum, provided they are followed by discussions, help to motivate and suggest activities for creative investigation. A guide from the museum should be enlisted to direct the tours, and parents should be encouraged to come along, particularly if they have an interest in or are trained in the sciences.[3] It is desirable to keep the groups small

3. For further suggestions on the use of a museum for teaching science consult John R. Saunders, "How to Visit a Museum," *Science and Children* (December 1958), pp. 5–7.

so that questions can be handled and viewing facilitated. If museums are large—with more displays than can be seen within a reasonable time period—several trips should be planned and areas covered in sequence.

THE SCHOOL: MAGNIFIER OF CREATIVE TALENT

The school has a major responsibility to provide opportunities for creative growth for children and to educate parents and the community as to their roles in encouraging creative development. To date it is in the arts that the school probably has been most successful in fulfilling this obligation. A concerted effort is needed now to insure that this is broadened to include the sciences. How can the school be effective in fostering creative science activity? There is no easy answer to this question, but certainly an important ingredient in developing interest in any area of study is that it be made provocative, challenging, and pleasurable. Not only is this being done by teachers during the academic year but in very creative enrichment programs in the summer as well.

HOW TO MAKE CREATIVE LEARNING OF SCIENCE EXCITING

How does one make learning science exciting, engaging, and pleasurable? Dr. David Hawkins, past director of the Elementary Science Study project, after several years' experience in the program, has said:

> If education were defined, for the moment, to include everything that children have learned since birth, everything that has come to them from living in the natural and the human world, then by any sensible measure what has come before age five or six would outweigh all the rest. When we narrow the scope of education to what goes on in schools, we throw out the method of that early and spectacular progress at our peril. We know that five-year-olds are very unequal in their mastery of this or that. We also know that their histories are responsible for most of this inequality, utterly masking the congenital differences except in special cases. This is the immediate fact confronting us as educators in a society committed, morally and now by sheer economic necessity, to universal education.

To continue the cultivation of earlier ways of learning, therefore, to find in school the good beginnings, the liberating involvements that will make the kindergarten seem a garden to the child and not a dry frightening desert, this is a need that requires much emphasis on the style of work I have called "Messing About." Nor does the garden in this sense end with a child's first school year, or his tenth, as though one could then put away childish things. As time goes on, through a good mixture of this with other phases of work, "Messing About" evolves with the child and thus changes its quality. It becomes a way of working that is no longer childish, though it remains always childlike, the kind of self-disciplined probing and exploring that is the essence of creativity.[4]

Dr. Hawkins believes it is important for science instruction (initially at least) to follow the way a child learns naturally in the preschool years. He emphasizes the need for children to have

FIGURE 4-6. *How would you use these children's "messing about" as a springboard for other science lessons? (Photo by Lee Young-blood)*

4. Reprinted with permission from *Science and Children,* vol. 2, no. 5 (February 1965). Copyright 1965 by the National Science Teachers Association, 1201 Sixteenth Street, N.W., Washington, D.C. 20036.

time to "mess about" with the science materials and ask questions about them. He has found that when this is done the attention span of the children increases immeasurably. He further believes there must be guidance and some discussions led by the teacher, but that they should be a minor part of the instruction. Dr. Hawkins is pleading for greater involvement of children in experimenting and discovering on their own. In this plea, he is in complete agreement with the consensus of the science educators in this country.

The National Society for the Study of Education 46th Yearbook on Science Education expressed a similar viewpoint as far back as 1947. An excerpt outlining this view is included below:

The child of elementary-school age is characterized by searching, questioning proclivities. He explores freely his physical environment and, as he matures, he explores the realm of ideas. Mitchell writes:

"The evidence is overwhelming that the essay in discovery is a native drive of children from kindergarten through high school. If children of these ages do not show this drive, I think we can hold adults responsible—not the children themselves. . . . Curiosity about how things work is one of the strongest drives of young children."

The spontaneous drive and curiosity of children in exploring their environment are not dissimilar to the drive and curiosity of scientists. The persistent inquisitiveness of children in exploring their world, in discovering facts, and in finding how things work can be readily utilized through science education.

It has often been noted that maturing children seem to lose some of their zest for inquiry. Environmental factors undoubtedly play the major role in this loss. One factor is the lack of a scientific outlook among many teachers and parents. The absence of open-minded inquiry and the reluctance to suspend final judgment create a fertile field for the habit of accepting ready-made ideas whether they be explanations, superstitions, prejudices, or taboos. Another factor is the school's tendency to assume an authoritarian view of knowledge with emphasis upon the assimilation of predigested information. Needless to say, there is a place for giving information to children, but making this the entire instructional program has the effect of discouraging children from investigation. Prescott notes that:

"There is no real possibility that it [loss of questioning spirit] appears because schools check the normal maturing of concepts, which come as experience accumulate. Indeed, affective factors may play a large role due to the unpleasant feelings aroused by so many interests and by the frustration of so much natural inquisitiveness during the early years of school."[5]

Another advantage of allowing children to make alternative choices involving activities, hypotheses, and collecting what they think are relevant data, is that it helps to motivate them and to prevent boredom.

GUIDING CREATIVE DEVELOPMENT

Creativity cannot be taught, since it is a process that takes place in the actions of an individual. The teacher and the school, however, can provide an environment likely to enhance and reinforce creative development. This requires that the teacher provide situations that demand imagination, invention, originality, and problem solving. Research involving the creative processes is now receiving greater attention from psychologists, and it is possible to make several suggestions likely to contribute to the creative development of pupils as well as teachers. These suggestions not only include psychological and sociological aspects, but the physical environment as well. The discussion of the influence of the physical environment is covered in some detail in Chapter V.

1. *Recognize that nonconformity may be an asset.* Allow for considerable flexibility and freedom when children want to investigate or experiment. If, for example, an experiment involves planting two seeds in a carton with some soil in it and a child asks what would happen if twenty seeds were planted, encourage him to find out, particularly if it relates to the investigation at hand. If a child working with pulleys wonders how they work under water in systems of different combination, encourage him to test them. Many of the current materials produced by local and state syllabuses, national curriculum projects, and publishers of elementary science books contain science activities that are relatively structured. In using these materials teachers should try to stimulate children to look for other possibilities for experimentation arising from these studies. If the children want to deviate from the outlined procedure in the program, or perform original experiments in their investigations, they should be en-

5. *N.S.S.E. Forty-Sixth Yearbook* (Chicago: University of Chicago Press, 1947), pp, 63–64.

couraged to do so. These structured materials should be supplemented by experiences which give children opportunities to make hypotheses, collect data, test their findings, make inferences, and discuss theories.

2. *Reinforce creative endeavor by positive recognition.* When a child makes a creative suggestion, give him approbation through some act or word of praise—"That's really a good idea!" "That sounds like it would be thrilling to do—let's try to find out!" In some way show the child how pleased you are that he is thinking in a creative way. This, however, does not imply that you are indiscriminate in your judgment of praise. When a child has a problem, particularly a child in the upper elementary grades, allow him to "mess about," to devise experiments and explore, and to perform tests to get answers. Constantly try to eliminate a negative response to an idea or a suggestion made by a pupil, even though you may think it worthless. He may have a very good idea that he can't explain. Often, because of the difficulty children have in communicating, teachers mistake what the child is trying to say. A teacher may react negatively as a result and say, "No, that won't work," or "I don't think that's a very good idea," or "That's wrong." This type of response hinders inquisitiveness. Even though the child's idea appears to be foolish, the teacher should still commend him for his contribution. Instead of completely rejecting a child's statement and inhibiting him as a result, it would be better to guide him to other approaches or suggest some ideas to consider before he renders a final judgment and the class decide what they think is best. In this way the teacher saves the pupil embarrassment, is not telling the child to stop thinking because his thinking is poor, but is suggesting there are other ways of looking at the problem. Don't be the teacher who destroys a child's willingess to take a chance, a chance that might enable him to use his mind to produce a unique and creative idea. Strive to develop support by positively demonstrating your belief in the worth of each individual and develop similar respect when the children interact with each other in class discussions.

The effect that teachers have had in stifling response is probably no more keenly evident than in college classes. Generally, when a professor asks the members of the class a question for the first time there is silence. Few if any students are going to "take a chance" on being wrong. Why are college students hesitant about making suggestions or answering questions? Elementary teaching probably has contributed at least to some degree in shaping this type of behavior.

3. *In making evaluation in science give particular recognition for a child's ability to suggest hypotheses, design experiments, collect data, make inference, generalize, and draw conclusions.* In other words, attempt to recognize his ability as a problem-solver.

4. *Attempt to provide opportunities for children to learn that there are several ways of looking at a problem and possibly several methods of finding an answer to it.* This is particularly important with children in primary grades. The research of Jean Piaget has revealed that children in the primary age group are egocentric.[6] They tend to think there is only one way of looking at something—the way they see it. However, if they are given opportunities to interact with other children who view a problem in a different manner, they are presented with alternate views. This may lead them to seek verification in testing their opinions.

5. *For the child who is outstanding in creative ability and two or three grades above his grade level, attempt to provide activities with other talented children so they can have opportunity to interact and become acquainted.* This procedure can help to kindle creative potential by preventing a child from becoming bored. The teacher should try to see that the child doesn't become a creative isolate and should prevent peer group sanctions that might be used against him because of his success. Some school administrators have been particularly concerned about this problem and have provided interest groups which are voluntary and held after school. The Palo Alto, California, School District has been particularly successful in programs of this type. The University Elementary School at the University of Hawaii has tried interest groups in the third grade, one of which was in science. The Detroit Public Schools provided "special ability" classes for children with special aptitudes and strong interests in certain subject fields. Science was selected by enough children to establish over twenty-five centers. It was exceedingly popular and successful. Classes were held after school and Saturdays. The participants shared their experiences with children in their regular classes benefiting even larger numbers of children. Groups of this type should be organized around investigation and researches involving solving problems related to the interests and abilities of the children and providing opportunities for them to be creative.

6. *Attempt to keep the curiosity of the child alive.* This can be done by providing materials and activities that will stimulate

6. Jean Piaget, *The Child's Conception of the World* (Paterson, N.J.: Littlefield, Adams and Co., 1963), p. 33.

curiosity. When, on the school grounds, on a field trip, or in the classroom, you observe a child in activity, engage him in discussion—ask him what he is doing and what he is thinking about. Stimulate him with queries and problems. Show how pleased you are that he is responding, and encourage him to pursue his interests. Remember, one of the best ways to keep the spirit of curiosity alive in children is to be an example of a curious human yourself.

7. *Encourage inquiry.* Curious children can find answers to their questions by inquiring. When questions arise, ask the children how they think they could be answered.

One important aspect of inquiring is the opportunity to discover. The instructor who gives children the answer robs them of the opportunity to find out for themselves. The process of discovering is an important part of behaving like a scientist, and children should be given every opportunity to experience the thrill of discovery, particularly in scientific activities. If a teacher gives the solution to a problem she stops the possibility of inquiry and seriously limits potential for learning science as a process. Furthermore, when children are actively involved in solving problems they are more likely to discover more problems and questions than answers about the phenomena they are investigating. Such is often the case in any real scientific endeavor. Dr. Jonas Salk once remarked, "If scientists asked the right questions, all the viruses that torment men could be conquered." A researcher often sees additional engrossing scientific questions in the process of solving his problem. If this were not so, there would probably be few scientific specialists devoting their entire lives to a minute area of scientific knowledge.

8. *Team work should not be overemphasized.* Creative scientists usually have a high degree of independence of action and autonomy. Sometimes group action is important and desirable, but if a child prefers to work on some activity alone he should be allowed to do so.

9. *Children should be allowed to take their time on project work.* It is in unhurried activity that curiosity is likely to be stimulated and creativity incubated. To rush through a project to achieve the objective of the lesson may result in a loss of far more desirable objectives.

10. *Give children as many opportunities as possible to participate and do experiments.* There still are a great many elementary school teachers who seldom have their children involved in any but passive activities, such as reading an elementary

science text, reading about experiments, reading about activities. These teachers may cover science material but they don't teach science. What they teach is descriptive science—the story about science. There can be little demonstrable creative endeavor without involvement in living science. Elementary science books should be used to stimulate ideas for inquiring and as a source of information. They should never become the whole design or *raison d'être* of the science program. As one youngster said after observing the results of his experiment, "Let's see if the textbook agrees with what we found out." The major purpose should never be to cover the science book for a grade level, but rather to give children opportunities to investigate in diverse ways so that they learn answers to their questions through inquiry and experimentation. An important avenue to finding answers to scientific questions is through experimentation, and designing and carrying out experimental work which offers many opportunities for creative responses.

11. *Give children choices.* In teaching science creatively we must give children some choice in the selection of activities for inquiry. These choices may arise naturally out of materials chil-

FIGURE 4-7. *Hands-on experience represents the most important single factor in planning inductive teaching experiences. (Photo from Los Angeles Unified Schools—A Model Educational Program in Ecology, ESEA Title III)*

dren bring into class, reading they do in the elementary science books, or class discussions. An astute teacher is sensitive to her children's particular interest in and fascination with a topic. When they react this way, she should question them to see if they would like to investigate further. In engaging in a science activity, possibilities for further experimentation often arise. The children, if they choose, should be encouraged to follow these paths of inquiry.

12. *All children do not have to perform the same activity.* Let the children take initiative and responsibility for developing lessons and doing demonstrations and other experiments to supplement the class work. All children do not learn equally well under the same method of instruction. Dr. Torrance has emphasized the importance of using several teaching approaches. He says, "The evidence seems rather clear that whenever we change our ways of teaching in significant ways, a different group of children become the star learners or high achievers." He goes on to say, "Alert teachers probably knew when they changed their method—slow learners or even nonlearners became outstanding achievers and some of their former star learners became slow learners."[7] All children need not perform the same experiment at the same time. In fact there is probably more learning when there is diverse activity within a rather broad framework of some unit on science; when performing different types of research the children can share their findings with each other in discussions. There is some less obvious learning going on here because of the inquisitive nature of children; they try to find out what their peers are doing and learn from each other as a result. This is analogous to what goes on in a science laboratory or in a meeting of scientific specialists who read their papers to each other. They share their knowledge and the field progresses.

13. *Reinforce an attitude of perseverance and meeting adversity, if it comes, as a challenge.* It is better to try and fail than not to try at all. Much of the history of scientific endeavor has been, in a sense, failure. But to a scientist failure has many meanings. He may, for example, have the hypothesis that a certain chemical will cure or arrest cancer, but in trying the chemical finds that it won't work. Many laymen would say he has failed. But, on the contrary, he has succeeded in advancing knowledge because now investigators at least know that this chemical won't

7. E. Paul Torrance and Robert D. Strom, *Mental Health and Achievement—Increasing Potential and Reducing School Dropout* (New York: John Wiley & Sons, Inc., 1965), p. 252.

work. Edison, trying to develop a metal filament for his incandescent lamp, failed 500 times. When asked about these failures, he replied that he had learned of 500 things that didn't work. Dr. Paul Ehrlich developed 605 chemicals and tested them before he created his famous "606," which was effective in controlling syphilis. It could be said he failed 605 times before he found the answer; but each of these so-called failures gave him direction for continuing his studies because he considered, as scientists do today, that a negative answer to a hypothesis is a valuable answer.

Children often set out to accomplish a task and feel they have failed if they don't reach their goal. An instructor can give them a more sophisticated understanding of what they are accomplishing. For example, a fifth-grade boy was trying to maintain a saltwater aquarium in class but was continually faced with problems. The water became foul and many of the organisms in the aquarium died. He consulted some books and asked the local pet shop owner what was wrong. He tried several times but, although the problem took longer and longer to arise, each time the aquarium became cloudy again. He was discouraged until his teacher showed him how he was becoming, in a sense, successful. She said, "Why are you discouraged? Haven't you been able to keep the aquarium going better longer? Haven't you learned a lot about maintaining life in it? If you try three or even six times more, don't you think you will be able to maintain life in the aquarium even better? Do you think a scientist usually gets the answer to the questions he asks by performing just one experiment? Part of the fun of science is the challenge of failure and learning from it." She encouraged him to try again and he did. The year progressed with several more trials, none of which was completely successful; but the teacher felt success, and the boy, too, for that matter. It was also interesting to see the participation of other members of the class as they asked questions, gave suggestions, and acted like junior consultants to their classmate. This one boy's aquarium project spilled over into the class and involved them all. The failures of the aquarium became a motivational force for learning about the nature of the scientific process.

14. *Be creative yourself in the methods you use.* Vary the method of instruction frequently; emphasize experimentation, demonstrations, and inquiring methods of teaching. Constantly inquire into your ability to motivate inquiry. When something "clicks" in the method or approach you use, keep a record of it and throw out what doesn't work. Be experimental in your approach, collecting data and evaluating your teaching. Above all,

attempt to encourage creativity by being creative yourself. Unfortunately, there are those teachers who become tradition-tied. They seldom alter their instruction, use lesson plans with little change over the years, and get into a rut. Teaching is an art as well as a science. Motivating children and designing an educational environment can be as challenging and as much fun as when an artist selects his pigments and develops a design for a canvas. Teachers who lose sight of this creative aspect of teaching become less and less inspiring. They grow bored, and their boredom reflects not only in their personalities but (worst of all) in the children they teach.

15. *Show examples of creative work to your children.* Displaying creative work is not only a form of positive reinforcement but a stimulus for children to become creative. Don't restrict the creative work to just the children in your classes. Bring in examples of work from other classes as well. It can be helpful at times to have a child come in from another classroom and explain his creation. A particularly effective approach is to have children from the upper grades illustrate some of their science projects to a grade below theirs and discuss some of the problems they had developing it.

16. *Have high school students interested in science relate their interest to younger children.* Some school systems have future teacher associations for high school students, who are sometimes given opportunities to work for a short period of time with the elementary grade teachers. These students interested in science should be encouraged to work with children in the elementary schools on some science activity. Children usually enjoy discussing their ideas with high school students. These visiting "acting science teachers" can be especially motivational because they are closer to the elementary children in age and usually have intense interest in their subject. The elementary grade instructor who wishes to sponsor a high school student "science teacher" will usually receive cooperation from the high school science teachers and administration. You should know what area of science you would want the student to work in and the best ways you can make use of him. The San Mateo High School District, San Mateo, California, in cooperation with the elementary schools in its district, has encouraged and supported this type of activity. Many other school systems throughout the nation have similar programs. They have found that fostering such a program helps elementary school teachers utilize an important community resource, creates greater science interest in the children, and moti-

vates the high school student to learn with greater understanding the material he is going to present as well as giving him opportunities to think seriously about teaching as a profession.

17. *Foster work in the creative arts to stimulate science interest, and suggest ideas for creative work.* Children like to draw and paint and sculpt. Encourage them to do science drawings, such as life in prehistoric times, ecological communities, variations of life, or how machines work. Some of these could be used as bulletin board displays, dioramas, cycloramas, and murals. A room where there is science activity should be as stimulating as possible; the pupils' art work on any level can contribute to this objective. The writing and presenting of a play depicting the work of some scientist, a famous discovery or invention, or writing a science fiction story can provide opportunities for creative expression.

18. *Stimulate the children's imagination by asking what they think the city, car, boat, and house of tomorrow will look like and why.*

19. *Participate in science nights.* Some school systems have science nights when the parents are invited to come to school and walk through the science activity centers, watch children engage in science study, see science and audio-visual equipment in use in the school, observe science project work, and see a film or hear a special speaker on some scientific subject of interest. Often school districts have instituted this type of program in preference to participating in science fairs, because the staff believe it involves more students and the community receives a more realistic view of what the school is trying to do. Success in this enterprise is to have as many children as possible involved in some investigation and demonstrate it through experimentation or exhibit or by dramatizing in some unique fashion data they have collected. The displays may range from simple collections with little apparent creative value to inventions or experiments that state a problem, suggest an hypothesis, show a record of the data made from observations, and list conclusions.

20. *Rely as much as possible on first-hand experience.* The actual thing is always better than the substitute. The more children can feel, hear, touch, smell, taste, and involve their senses with the phenomena they are studying, the greater the possibilities for learning and creative activity.

21. *Make science kits.* With the children, prepare and use kits containing materials for carrying out a scientific investigation. A simple kit might contain just marbles and a list of some questions

FIGURE 4-8. *How would you use this child's experience to kindle his creativity? (Photo by Lee Youngblood)*

such as, "What can you find out about all the ways marbles will move? How can you make a marble move without touching it? What does the speed or the angle at which a marble hits another have to do with its motion? What does the weight (mass) have to do with it?" Materials for science kits can be stored in cigar boxes, coffee cans, or shoe boxes and labeled. When a child has opportunity or is motivated, he can obtain a kit and take it to his desk, science work area, or home. This can all be done without disturbing or interrupting other class activities.

22. *Periodically display a science surprise box.* The box may contain some scientific equipment or other material related to science. On the outside write statements that will stimulate the children to curiosity. For example, the box might have on it the following: "It is hard. It swings. It swings at a different rate when short than when long. What is it? How is it made?" The teacher should allow the children to ask questions and make guesses from time to time about the contents of the box. She should give only yes or no answers to pupils' questions so that inquiry will continue. After the children have discovered the contents of the box, the teacher can conveniently lead them into a study of phenomena related to the pendulum. For example: How does its length affect its rate? If two pendulums are hanging from the same support string, will anything happen to the other one when one starts to swing? How high will a pendulum go when you let go of it? What will happen when it hits another pendulum? She may give some pendulums to the children and allow them to inquire into what else they can find out about them.

Another surprise box might contain something living. The riddle posed on the outside of the box might read: "I am at room temperature. My temperature changes when the room's temperature changes. I move sometimes. My skin is rough. I am a friend of the gardener. I should be out in the garden now. If you listen closely, you might get a hint as to what I am. What am I?" This, of course, would be a toad. When the children guess what it is, the teacher can take the toad out and use it as a basis for study. Some of the following questions might be asked: "How does it move? Are its legs designed well for the kind of movement it has? Why? How does it protect itself? What superstitions have you heard about toads?" Many more questions might be suggested. The children should have time to expand their interest with toads to discover, gain insights, and pose questions.

23. *Prepare or have the children make a science discovery chart.* A discovery chart usually consists of some drawing, photograph, or objects placed on the bulletin board. Discovery charts often consist of photographs of some scientific phenomenon which lead from the picture to small pieces of paper. Each child is given the opportunity to place his name and what he thinks the picture represents on one of the pieces of paper and next to the picture. The display is left up for a week and the child may

change what he writes on the paper as many times as he chooses. At the end of the week, the teacher leads an inquiring discussion of what the picture represents.

If diagrams are used, they might include orbital paths of satellites, part of the solar system, galaxies, strata in rock, a contour map, a vegetation map, migration routes, or magnetic lines of forces. Real objects such as a pendulum, rocks, fossils, and a magnet may also be used in a similar way.

24. *Prepare a collection of discovery lessons, inquiring discussions, pictorial riddles, inquiring experiments, demonstration ideas for possible inventions, and counterintuitive activities.* Ideas on how to prepare these materials and examples of each are given in Chapter VIII.

25. *Occasionally, in the upper grades, hold brainstorming sessions.* Brainstorming is a group technique used by academicians, government men, businessmen, engineers and others, where ideas are suggested in rapid succession on a particular subject. Criticism of the ideas is not allowed and quantity is encouraged. Individuals within the group try to improve and build on ideas suggested. There is some argument among psychologists as to whether this technique nurtures more unique, high-quality suggestions than thinking on an individual basis. Brainstorming, however, does achieve the objective of setting a mood for creativity. Dr. Ernest Hilgard believes it is probably a good method for teaching creativity but that after an individual has gained the learning value from the process he should be allowed to do creative work alone if he so chooses.[8]

Scientific problems by their nature lend themselves well to brainstorming techniques. A science instructor, for example, might ask a class: "What can be done to get plants to grow rapidly?" He should then encourage all answers, allow no criticism, and use other suggestions as a stimulus for additional ideas. At the end of the brainstorming session, the ideas should be recorded for later use as a resource for possible experiments. The actual testing of the ideas experimentally should be fostered.

When creative endeavor seems to stagnate, a teacher can use brainstorming to move the class from its plateau. The technique requires considerable adaptation by most teachers because they are not used to playing the role of nonevaluator of ideas. In addition, once having used it successfully, the teacher should guard

8. Ernest R. Hilgard, "Creativity and Problem Solving," in *Creativity and Its Cultivation*, Harold H. Anderson, ed. (New York: Harper and Brothers, 1959), p. 171.

against the natural tendency to employ the technique more than warranted. The success or failure of brainstorming depends to a considerable extent upon the nature of the problem the teacher gives the children; it must be one that can capture their interest and offer a wealth of possible responses. Success in this teaching technique is more likely to occur if the teacher looks at the procedure as an enjoyable activity and brings to it her full zest for inquiry and creative endeavor. Role-playing that enacts a scene and dramatizes a scientific event is especially effective with children in the early grades and lends itself well to the study of the history of science and special events involving personalities in science.

SUMMARY

An individual's behavior is shaped largely by the type of "input" stimulation received. If the home, community, and school provide rich opportunities for creative involvement, children's creative potential will be more easily realized because of the chances this potential has to manifest itself. Unfortunately, much needs to be done to educate the parents, community leaders, and school personnel. Parents often harbor attitudes, particularly about science, which are antithetical to the development of creative ability in their children. They may, by their negative reactions to inquisitive questions, suppress the curious nature of the child. Some parents, for a variety of reasons, may harbor notions that are inimical to science. Teachers and parent-teachers organizations can help modify these views by offering educational programs for parents, emphasizing the importance of encouraging creative ability of children through science study. Many communities and interested groups within them have supported science fairs and congresses, library programs, museums, planetariums and observatories, have provided tours of scientific industries, and have sponsored science discussions to help motivate children to study science. Educational parks, public parks, wilderness areas, ecological plots, and conservation camps have been established in various parts of our country to be used as learning laboratories. They provide opportunities for children to design and solve problems requiring creative responses about their environment and how to preserve it. The environmental crisis makes it incumbent on every teacher to draw upon the most effective resources to creatively teach environmental education. When started at the child's earliest level, positive attitudes and environmental values can be developed that will make the child more responsive to the pollution problems of our times. Environmental education must become integral to the educational process if the quality of life is to be improved.

Drug abuse is a national problem which has had its impact on the school child. Drug education, not unlike environmental education, must deal with attitudes, values, and behavior. Programs in science can provide factual information about plant life from which many drugs are derived and develop principles of health and safety to which the child can quite naturally relate.

Teachers can contribute to the creative development of their pupils in science as follows: by not overemphasizing conformity or team work; by giving positive recognition for creative endeavor; by providing opportunities for them to see there may be several ways of looking at a problem; by arranging for children with creative ability to meet with gifted children; by stimulating the child's natural curiosity; by encouraging first-hand experience and experimentation; by allowing children to choose areas and problems for study; by providing for individual differences so that all children don't have to engage in the same science experiences or at the same time; by showing examples of creative work done by other pupils; by using outside students to stimulate interest; by fostering work in the arts; by having science nights; by using brainstorming sessions; by preparing science kits, discovery charts and lessons, and surprise boxes; by inquiring types of experiments, demonstrations, and counterintuitive activities. Approaches of this kind are the thrust required to reach a child's latent creativity. But it must not stop there. Having reached the child, continuity of experience is required for further growth and development. Re-stimulation through a variety of activities will insure a more constant level of performance throughout childhood and into adulthood.

QUESTIONS

1. How can the home encourage children to be creative?

2. How many parents retard the creative abilities of children?

3. It has suddenly come to your attention that the local community is not really doing much to encourage creative development. What would you do to change this situation?

4. How would you enlist local scientists, industrial technical personnel, and other human resources to help develop the creative

abilities of children, particularly in providing environmental education experiences? What would be your criteria for selection?

5. The community in which you live provides few activities for children during the summer. What would you do to change and improve the situation?

6. How would you use a science museum to foster creativity?

7. What would you do to encourage children's creative activity on an ecological field trip?

8. How are children similar to scientists when they explore and make discoveries?

9. Why isn't it possible to teach a person to be creative?

10. How might structuring of an instructional program hinder or encourage creativity?

11. Why should positive reinforcement be used in teaching children?

12. Children tend to center their attention on one approach in solving a problem. What would you do to try to get them to broaden their views?

13. How would you provide for individual creative differences in science?

14. How would you stimulate curiosity among children?

15. How can learning to inquire contribute to creative science objectives?

16. How would you use team work so as to encourage and not diminish creative work?

17. Why should teaching approaches be varied?

18. How can failure contribute to creative activity?

19. If, in doing an experiment, part of the equipment fails to function properly, and you don't get the results you expected, what would you do to turn the situation into an exciting learning activity?

20. Why should you endeavor to be creative in your methods of teaching?

21. What is basic to a program for environmental and drug abuse education for young children?

22. Describe several activities which would build awareness in children of the problems of pollution.

23. How would you develop positive values in combating drug abuse in the later elementary years?

24. Discuss how to organize a bottle reclamation project and how to establish redemption centers.

25. How would you conduct an anti-litter beautification and recycling contest?

26. What individuals would you invite to your class to stimulate creative activity?

27. How would you use a science night as an opportunity for creative involvement by your pupils?

28. Describe how you would prepare a science kit to be used by a child so as to provide creative experiences for him.

29. List two examples of something you would use as a teaching device in a science surprise box.

30. Describe how you would use brainstorming or role-playing in the grade you teach.

CHAPTER V

Significant Factors
for Creative Teaching

The most creative aspect of the science education of chil-
dren is the fact that it is the process in which human re-
sources are developed creatively—the process through
which the girls and boys of today can become scientifically
oriented toward their own optimal fulfillment.

LAURA ZIRBES

THE CREATIVE TEACHER

The teachers are most directly responsible for the quality of
modern science instruction. Regardless of the type of program
followed in the elementary classroom, the teacher is the key to
success. Modern facilities, equipment, books, and courses of
study matter little if teachers are unprepared, indifferent, or overworked.

Reference has already been made (see Chapter 4) to the many
ways in which a teacher can implement creative enterprise in the
classroom. But, even more important than these techniques for
setting the environment, the teacher must feel secure in what she
is attempting to do and at ease with science content. First, she
should not hesitate to learn with her children. Teaching is supposed to be an intellectually stimulating profession on all levels of
instruction. What better way is there to grow than to become involved in new learning experiences to which you do not know
the answers? No one can know all the science in any one subject

area today let alone in all the areas of science. If your children raise questions or pose problems that you are relatively un-informed about, don't be afraid to say: "Let's see what we can find out about it together." Children enjoy having their teacher, at times, learn with them. After all, some of their fondest ex-periences have come from active involvement in learning together with their parents. Even if a problem arises with which the children and you are having difficulty, you should seek help from a consultant or supervisor in the central office, county, or state office. Colleges or universities often provide science services to teachers. You can probably get help from the many resources available in or near a community, and high school and university science teachers can often provide information in their field of teaching. Science academies and science clubs are useful sources for aid.

There is no substitute for a good background in the sciences. Most elementary school teachers have not had extensive training in the sciences because they had to prepare to teach in many fields. This can be alleviated in part by outlining and following a program of self-enrichment and renewal in the sciences.

Activities for Self-improvement

1. *Self-enrichment reading program.* One way to improve your background is to read. Too often a teacher is too short of time and training to engage in technical reading. However, reading lists, bibliographies, and guides to selected listings are available from many sources such as: publications of the Office of Education, U.S. Government Printing Office, Washington, D.C.; *Science Books,* a quarterly review, American Association for the Advancement of Science, Washington, D.C., and many commercial listings by publishers. Colleges and universities—science education depart-ments—also produce lists for teachers. In these lists, teachers can find publications written in an interesting manner and contain-ing substance. Today there has been an explosion of science books offering wide selections. There are literally hundreds of paperback books covering a wide scope of scientific areas; often these require little background in the sciences for comprehension.

Elementary school teachers can also improve their backgrounds and keep up-to-date in science by reading periodicals devoted to science education. Three that are particularly useful are *Science and Children, Science Teacher,* and *Science Newsletter. Science and Children* is the publication of the National Science Teachers Association written specifically for elementary school teachers. It is published monthly during the school year. *Science Teacher* is also published by NSTA but is more general, having articles more weighted for secondary and college teachers.

Many ideas for experiments and student activities with creative possibilities appear in almost every one of these issues. *Science Newsletter* is a simply written weekly publication of a few pages describing the latest scientific developments. This publication gives the teacher the advantages of finding out quickly some of the current developments in science. As a result, he is better informed and prepared to cope with children's questions. Other helpful publications are *Nature and Science, Current Science* (student and teachers' edition), and *Science World*. The sources of all the above publications are listed in the Appendix. There are, of course, many more science journals—all of a technical nature. These usually require more time to read and often a greater sophistication of scientific background than the publications just mentioned. From these, teachers can select and maintain several files of science materials including articles and pictures for reference and class use.

2. *Continued and supported programs for advanced training.* Continued education for a teacher, particularly in the sciences, is mandatory. Teachers should return as often as possible to colleges or universities to obtain further background and techniques for improving science instruction. In addition to extension courses and special programs for improvement in science during the academic year, most colleges now offer science institutes, workshops, and special courses during summer sessions, and many of these are specifically designed for the elementary school teacher.

Improvement programs supported by the National Science Foundation (N.S.F.) will be more sharply focused on specific major problems of science education and educational institutions. N.S.F. provides in-service, summer, and academic year institutes for secondary school (grades 7-12) teachers, supervisors of science, mathematics, and social science. Indirectly, they may also support workshops to train elementary teachers to use the modern science curriculum. To keep current on developments, one may write to the National Science Foundation.[1]

1. Instructions and lists of the colleges and universities offering summer institutes supported by the Foundation can be obtained from the National Science Foundation, Washington, D.C. 20550.

FIGURE 5-1. *A workshop for teachers in action. (Photo by Fish-leder)*

3. *Special workshops.* Many colleges and school districts give special workshops during the year or summer vacation to help teachers learn how to use the new curriculum materials being produced by several nationally supported programs. (More will be said about the modern curricular materials in a later chapter.) Because of your awareness of the problems of teaching the creative child, as a result of reading books on creativity, you are probably better qualified to speak about the problem than most of the teachers in the workshops. A teacher should ask workshop directors how materials can be modified to develop creative ability. Asking questions about creativity insures its becoming a topic of discussion which might have been overlooked.

4. *Revisions of school curriculum.* Often school districts have committees working on the revision of the science curriculum. This activity not only affords you opportunity to contribute but is a special way to get a wider perspective of the science program, makes you influential in insuring that the curriculum stresses more activities requiring creative endeavor, and affords you opportunities to be creative yourself in designing a curriculum.

5. *Team teaching.* Team teaching can contribute to creative teaching. In deciding to teach science as a team with another

teacher you have the advantage of being able to interact with this instructor in designing programs requiring creative responses. The old adage that two heads are better than one can be especially true in teaching science—particularly if each of you has a particular competency which contributes to the team effort. If organized properly, and with sharing of work loads, more time may be allowed for preparation. In addition team teaching gives you the advantage of having someone evaluate your instruction while you teach. After a class session you can interact with the other instructor to consider whether the class should be less structured, more inquiring, or more confined to productive work. When you evaluate each other, you are given opportunities to compare how each of you might structure the class in a more creative fashion. If these evaluations are seriously considered and your instruction is modified as a result, your ability to teach and provide a more creative environment will be likely to improve.

If team teaching does not meet your requirements, team plan, share instructional materials, and evaluate each other's work. Share the planning work load! If you write a discovery exercise, make a list of divergent questions, or construct a science kit, share them with another teacher and ask him to review your work with a focus on creativity. Tell him you will reciprocate with the materials and lessons he plans. This is the essence of teaming and if you interact to build the self-concepts of your team members you are bound to enjoy teaching more and further develop your creative teaching potential.

6. *Video-taping for teacher self-analysis.* Some schools are presently using portable video tape recorders to assist in the improvement of instruction. These machines are used to tape the class proceedings. The instructor may tape a science demonstration or an activity where children are experimenting. At the conclusion of the lesson the recorder is turned off. When the teacher is alone and has time, she may replay the video tape and observe her teaching practices. By using this approach, she can better evaluate her teaching to determine how successful she is in encouraging or inhibiting creative activity. By repeating the process of taping several class sessions and analyzing her instruction, she can gain added insights into how to become a more creative teacher. The teacher might also enlist other teachers or the science supervisors to watch the playing of the tapes and suggest how the science instruction could provide for more creative involvement by children.

THE PHYSICAL ENVIRONMENT

The Self-contained Classroom

A stimulating, well-equipped physical environment is as necessary for science teaching as it is for art or music. In the elementary school, science teaching either takes place in a self-contained classroom or there is some form of departmentalized system where science rooms and special activity rooms are used. The use of a self-contained classroom often presents a major problem in the storage of scientific apparatus and materials. Also, some science experiments require considerable time to complete, particularly in the study of the life sciences. As a matter of fact, many of the elementary science study units in current use may require several weeks and a considerable amount of space. For this reason, it is particularly difficult to involve all the children at once in these activities on an individual or team basis in a small crowded classroom. If they are to be successful in teaching science in a creative fashion in a self-contained classroom, teachers must have space,

FIGURE 5-2. *Individual or small group viewing stations, utilizing inexpensive filmstrip viewers, may considerably expand opportunities for using nonprint media within a realistic school setting. (Photo from Los Angeles Unified Schools—A Model Educational Program in Ecology, ESEA Title III)*

104801 121

equipment, and materials of instruction. Several flat tables on which experiments can be performed should be available. In self-contained classrooms the science activities, because of the limitations of space, are often done on an individual basis or by small groups. The information and results the children collect are then reported to the class for discussion.

The Special Science Room vs. the Self-contained Classroom

Scientific apparatus companies now provide furniture especially designed for use in elementary school classrooms. This furniture includes permanently installed laboratory desks fitted with the utilities needed to perform most experiments on an elementary level. Because of the possibilities for better inquiring activities, a well-stocked laboratory is to be especially encouraged in the grades above the primary level. The maintenance and teaching in this facility are usually done by an elementary school teacher particularly interested in science. Some schools have hired special teachers to teach science, but though there have been specialists in elementary school in music and physical education for years, only recently has the use of science specialists gained acceptance. Among other arguments, it is said by those who do not favor such specialists that when science opportunities arise during regular class instruction they must be held in abeyance until the children go to the special science class and meet with the specialist. This need not be the case. Children could still perform some experiments on an individual basis in the regular classroom. The science teacher could also be informed of their interest and encourage the children to investigate related problems in the laboratory. It has also been said that, because a science specialist is likely to have a better science background, he is more able to devise inquiring activities, ask insightful questions, and provide creative experiences for children. Some schools with large enrollments have selected children on an interest-in-science basis and have placed them all in one class with a teacher who likes science and knows how to teach creatively. Reading, spelling, and most activity center around scientific investigations. Although the children's range of ability and background is as varied as in other classes, discipline problems are considerably lower and the achievement is higher. However, such a plan depends on having a teacher particularly interested in science. The pioneer spirit and zestful interest of the teacher play a large part in the success of such a plan. There is no evidence that children receiving this type of instruction are in any way less prepared in the three R's than students in other classes.

Although the type of organization necessary affects the facilities and equipment needs, a given curricular organization—whether the self-contained classroom or the departmentalized program— does not in itself assure that better learning will take place. The significant factors in a good science-learning activity are the teacher and the quality and kind of activities the pupils engage in each day. All manner of science activity requires enough room for the pupils to manipulate materials, explore, demonstrate, experiment, and carry out both individual and group investigations. Given the space for activities, a setting can be worked out for creative learning.

Special Laboratory Equipment

1. *Science furniture.* Several science furniture manufacturers produce a number of different vivaria. A vivarium may include an aquarium, animal cage, and terrarium. Some specially designed vivaria are small self-contained greenhouses containing controls for temperature, humidity, and light. If vivaria are maintained and used for experimental study, they can be valuable tools in presenting problems for inquiry and creativity.

2. *Science kits.* Science kits and so-called packaged science are of particular concern to program builders because of their potential misuse. The busy administrator who lacks the time to select and order separate items from the various catalogues looks upon the kit as a solution to his program and equipment problems. The teacher who is inexperienced in building a science curriculum also welcomes the ready-made program. Although the cost of some kits is higher than the cost of the collected items of equipment, they do contain useful materials. Some supervisors of science, however, have emphasized that an overdependence on science kits may have a limiting effect on an instructional program. Like all equipment, these kits can be used effectively or ineffectively. Some persons are concerned with the stereotyped use of equipment leading to the so-called cookbook method which would stifle creativity. To a large extent the kit may determine the program.

The several commercial kits familiar to most teachers and available in elementary schools range widely in price depending on the amount and quality of the contents. They contain a variety of physical science items such as magnets, spring-balances, thermometers, and magnifiers. They are usually marketed in specially built boxes with handles, which make them convenient to carry.

Most of the new curriculum projects and new programs of sequentially developed textbooks have specially prepared kits. Much of the cost of these goes for the packaging. A science supervisor, particularly in a large school district, can economize by purchasing the material individually from scientific supply house or local department or discount stores. Kits generally cost too much for what is in them, but they do provide convenience and availability of materials. It should be remembered, however, that kits usually have expendable items in them that will need replenishing. Some plan should be worked out to provide for this eventuality with a minimum of effort by teacher and supervisor.

Some schools or school systems make their own kits; they construct the box and obtain the materials for it from many sources. One type of school-built kit is designed to provide materials for the study of concepts in a specific unit or area of elementary science such as earth science, the night sky, light, heat, sound, magnets, and weather. In some school systems these kits are called "shoebox kits"; in others they are called "science-concept boxes."

Some kits emphasize the assembly of a particular kind of equipment such as a toy motor, telegraph set, question-and-answer boards, or optical system. The skills developed in putting the component parts together would justify the activity, providing its purpose is clear at the outset.

3. *Mobile laboratories*. There are presently on the market several types of mobile laboratories—demonstration desks on wheels, with water, portable gas burners, and, usually, electric plugs. They may be stocked with several types of scientific apparatus. Mobile laboratories have the advantage of being transportable from one room to another with little effort. There are also mobile laboratories consisting of stacks of large plastic trays on wheels, each of which provides most of the materials needed for a class to perform scientific investigation. In some of these laboratories the materials, workbooks, and teachers' guides come completely stocked with the trays. Because the science activities outlined are fairly directive, they may hinder creative responses by children, but a teacher could adapt them to suit her purposes.

Both types of mobile laboratories mentioned above are relatively expensive but now, because much of their cost can be borne by federal funds under certain programs, they are becoming more common in the elementary schools.

4. *Homemade equipment*. Because of the opportunities for invention and creation (and to belie the notion that science can only be learned in a gleaming laboratory), children and teacher should explore the possibilities in improvising equipment.

Materials found in the home may be adapted for use in science. Parents with home workshops are often more than willing to participate in class and school projects. By helping, the parents have opportunities to work with their children and to become more involved in the school program. Such an involvement can lead to a better understanding of how they can contribute to the creative efforts of their children. For example, peanut butter jars can become beakers for mixing things, and large (one gallon) commercial-size mayonnaise and pickle jars can be used for many purposes (such as terraria). Clean baby food jars have a multitude of uses such as test tubes, storage jars, and collecting containers. Small boards, parts of shingles for instance, can become inclined planes, levers, or material to demonstrate how sound vibrates. The latter can be shown by holding one end firmly and hitting the other

FIGURE 5-3. *Shoe boxes may be used for the storage of individual equipment and can be filed on shallow shelves when not in use. (SCIS Photo)*

to make it vibrate and produce a sound. A board can also be used to show the power of a moving body as a hand moving at great speed hits it sideways and breaks it. Tin cans or paper drinking cups can serve as speakers for a string telephone. Bottles inverted over water can illustrate that there is something in the bottle that keeps the water out. A piece of peg board with hooks and clips on it nailed to a two-by-four can serve, among other purposes, to hold test tubes. Cartons can be turned into trays to store kits or made into storage cabinets. Note the creative ways of illustrating principles of science in the use of homemade equipment. Endeavor to increase your supply of such equipment so that you have ample materials available to carry out investigations children suggest.

5. *Inexpensive materials.* The local grocery, drug, discount, and department stores offer a wealth of scientific materials—usually at far less cost than that asked by a scientific supply house. For example, many large department stores sell beakers, test tubes, burners and other materials at a price far below that of the usual science purchasing service. They also have kitchen units that can turn a classroom into a science laboratory at a fraction of what regular scientific furniture costs. Almost every local hardware store has portable burners sold at a relatively low cost. Other useful teaching aids may be obtained from materials to be discarded by repair shops, garages, radio-television shops, and hospital laboratories.

Get accustomed to being inventive and creative yourself in using equipment and materials from your environment. If you need a chemical for some special purpose, consult a nearby chemistry teacher or your local druggist; utilize your local resources as much as possible. You will be amazed at how easily you can enrich your science program at low cost. Also, your example may stimulate children to look for new uses for old things, thereby giving them more opportunities to be creative. A word of caution here: As valuable as improvised equipment may be to the creative process, careful appraisal should be made to see that the learning to be derived from the experience justifies the time and effort expended in the "making."

SUMMARY

Creative opportunities for children in science can be increased by the actions of a teacher in a rich school environment. A good teacher can overcome, although with difficulty, poor facilities, but excellent facilities cannot make up for an incompetent teacher. Elementary school teachers should outline a program for self-enrichment in the sciences—including subscribing to and reading publications in elementary school science—in order to keep up-to-date and improve their backgrounds. Teachers should also become aware of and participate in programs supported by the National Science Foundation and the United States Office of Education. These programs offer stipends and subsidies, and support and encourage teachers to return to universities and colleges in order to receive increased training.

Science is taught in the elementary schools either in self-contained classes or special science rooms. The self-contained class is generally the type of class used in the elementary grades, but there seems to be a swing back to the use of special science rooms in the upper grades. The special science rooms, particularly in a departmentalized system, are usually staffed by a science specialist and may provide some advantages in facilities and equipment over the self-contained room. Some schools have grouped together children with an interest in science under an instructor having a special interest in the subject. In these classes, science and math instruction is central to other areas in the curriculum. The general achievement of the children in these classes has ranked favorably with that of students in other types of groupings with the addition that children in the science interest classes complete more scientific projects and participate to a greater extent in science fairs.

There is a wealth of special laboratory apparatus provided by scientific companies for the elementary school. These include rather elaborate vivaria, science kits, and mobile laboratories. Teachers can find substitutes for many commercially prepared pieces of apparatus at less cost by improvising equipment, or they can obtain useful materials from local sources. An instructor should constantly look for materials that are often discarded and could be used creatively in a science class. Instructors who become accustomed to being creative and inventive in discovering uses for laboratory equipment and materials serve as a creative example to the children they teach. Although improvised material may lend itself to invention and creativity, careful note should be made that the learning derived from the experience justifies the time and effort expended in the making.

QUESTIONS

1. If you were going to design an elementary science laboratory so that it would provide for more creative work by the children, what would you do?

2. What are the advantages of a special science room or science laboratory in the upper elementary grades over a self-contained classroom? What are its disadvantages?

3. What will you do in order to improve your creative teaching competence over the next five years?

4. List some ways inexpensive or free materials from the local community might be used in science teaching instead of more expensive equipment.

5. How would you use team teaching to improve your creative teaching?

6. If you were paired with another teacher in a team teaching situation, and she wasn't very creative, how would you help her improve this ability without hurting her feelings?

7. If you were assigned a practice teacher, what would you do the first week to orient him to creative teaching in science?

8. You have just been assigned to an old elementary school. You walk into the class and there is no equipment other than desks. What would you do to make the room a rich environment for creative science activities, given a very limited budget?

9. If you were presented with the problem of convincing a school board of the necessity of increasing the budget for science supplies and equipment, what approach would you make and why?

10. In what ways would you use tin cans, quart and gallon jars, paper clips, and small rubber balls for science instruction?

CHAPTER VI

National Studies Programs—
The Concern for Creativity
in Curriculum Reform

I shall operate on the assumption that discovery, whether by a schoolboy going it on his own or by a scientist cultivating the growing edge of his field, is in its essence a matter of rearranging or transforming evidence in such a way that one is enabled to go beyond the evidence so reassembled to additional new insights. It may well be that an additional fact or shred of evidence makes this larger transformation of evidence possible. But it is often not even dependent on new information.

JEROME S. BRUNER

THE NATIONAL REVOLUTION IN SCIENCE CURRICULUM REFORM

Prior to the launching of the Russian satellite Sputnik in 1957, the community of professional scientists in this country were concerned about the kind of science taught in a majority of American secondary schools. They felt that many of the science texts contained out-of-date material and failed to give a suitable picture of modern scientific research and philosophy.

A group of physicists in the Boston area, many of whom taught at Massachusetts Institute of Technology and Harvard University, were the first to take steps to explore the possibilities for improving science teaching. They met with other scientists, teachers, and educators interested in improving the level of physics instruction in the secondary schools. Under their direction conferences were held to plan a course of action. An outgrowth of these conferences was the establishment of the Physical Science Study Committee in 1956. The committee obtained funds from several sources, including the federal government, to support their investigation, the devising of new texts, laboratory manuals, films, and supplemental reading sources, and the publication of reports describing the committee's purpose and progress. The first objective of the PSSC, as it came to be known, was to produce a physics text and a laboratory manual to accompany it, and to design inexpensive apparatus for the course. Science teachers, educators, and professors worked during the summer to produce these materials. They were then tested in a small number of high schools throughout the nation and feedback was sent to the project's center in Cambridge, Massachusetts. The materials were then revised and retested on a larger group of students the following year. This was followed by another revision and testing. The third and final revision of the initial part of the project was completed in 1960 and the materials were released commercially in the fall of that year for use by any school district.

The founding of the Physical Science Study Committee and its approach to the revision of instructional materials began a revolution in science curriculum modification for American education. It was revolutionary for two reasons: It was the first time a large group of individuals outside the public schools—professional scientists in this case—worked with teachers and educators to improve science instruction; and the materials were produced by committees and were tried and revised for three years before they were released for wide distribution. The inclusiveness of the number and types of materials included in the program and the method of support for its work was new and different. The PSSC produced not only texts, a laboratory manual and inexpensive equipment, but supplemental monographs and films as well. These were meant to be integrated with the course. The committee set a precedent by obtaining, for the first time in American history, tremendous financial support from the federal government for curriculum revision. The federal government supported the activities of the PSSC by giving it several million dollars to carry out its work. No group before the PSSC ever received as much money to produce materials for school use. The PSSC is still in operation today and is working on other projects to improve secondary school physics teaching.

Since the PSSC was founded, many other groups have been constituted to improve science teaching: HPP (Harvard Project

Physics), BSCS (Biological Science Curriculum Study), CHEM Study (Chemical Education Material Study), CBA (Chemical Bond Approach), and ESCP (Earth Science Curriculum Project). High school, junior high school, and all grade levels of science teaching in the elementary school have been included. The methods of operation, production and testing of materials, and financial support of all these follow somewhat the pattern established by the PSSC. Some commercial firms have followed similar procedures, except that they provide the financial support.

After PSSC became established, several elementary science curriculum projects came into being most of which had as their objective a process-oriented system of instruction. Dr. E. Paul Torrance has stated that he thinks the new elementary science curriculum revisions require more imagination, intuition, decision making, formation of hypotheses, testing of different patterns of thinking, and communication than do many of the traditional curricula, and because of this they provide better chances for creative thinking.[1] Other critics have pointed out that many of the curriculum projects fail to achieve their stated objective and are not designed specifically to develop creativity. It is unwise, generally, to accept the idea that because new materials produced by one of the curriculum projects are used, creativity will automatically be taught. The materials in themselves do not insure creativity. The properly motivated teacher is the key to the success of the new programs in science at the elementary level. The attitude, methods, and adaptation of the materials for the creative enterprise can have a far greater influence on the children than the activities do by themselves. Although the elementary school curriculum projects have incorporated modern subject matter and are based on a philosophy of inquiry, teachers could teach them in a traditional manner. Dr. Calvin W. Taylor has stressed that the emergence of new instructional materials by no means lessens the need to teach for creative involvement.[2]

Devising a curriculum or a science course of study can be a creative enterprise. Many local school districts, and in some cases regional groups involving several districts, have had committees working on the revision of science curricula. Some school districts have employed teachers during summer vacation to revise and improve the elementary school science curriculum with the help

1. E. Paul Torrance and Robert D. Strom, *Mental Health and Achievement—Increasing Potential and Reducing School Dropout* (New York: John Wiley & Sons, Inc., 1965), p. 259.
2. Calvin W. Taylor, "Creativity and Science Education," *News and Views of NABT* (December 1963), p. 7.

of a science supervisor and college consultants. The number of groups active in science revision on the elementary level are too numerous to be included in this book. (A complete list of these, including international projects, may be obtained from *Eighth Report of the Information Clearinghouse on New Science and Mathematics Curricula,* College Park, Md.: Science Teaching Center, University of Maryland, 1972. The report was edited under the direction of J. David Lockard, the project a joint undertaking of the Commission on Science Education of the American Association for the Advancement of Science and the university. Only a few prominent ones taken from this source are discussed here. The analyses of the creative aspects of the programs are the authors' own.

ELEMENTARY SCIENCE STUDY (ESS)

PROJECT DIRECTOR:
Christopher Hale, 55 Chapel Street, Newton, Mass. 02160 (617) 969-7100 X519.

PROJECT HEADQUARTERS:
1. Contact: Eleanor Jenner, Project Administrator, 55 Chapel Street, Newton, Mass. 02160, (617) 696-7100 X517.
2. Special facilities or activities available for visitor viewing: Display area containing teacher's guides and some materials. Group visits should be made by appointment only.

PRINCIPAL PROFESSIONAL STAFF:
Emily Romney, Staff Developer.

PROJECT SUPPORT:
1. Funding agencies: National Science Foundation.
2. Associated agencies: Education Development Center, Inc. (formerly Educational Services, Inc.).

PROJECT HISTORY:
1. Principal originator: Education Development Center, Inc. (formerly Educational Services, Inc.).
2. Date and place of initiation: 1960; Cambridge, Mass.
3. Evolution and development of the project: Development of materials for teaching science from kindergarten through eighth grade started on a small scale in 1960. The work of the project has since involved more than a hundred educators in the conception

and design of its units of study. At every stage of development, ideas and materials were taken into actual classrooms, where children helped shape the form and content of each unit before it was released to schools everywhere.

PROJECT OBJECTIVES:
1. Overall project purpose: It is our intention to enrich every child's understanding, rather than to create scientific prodigies or direct all children toward scientific careers.
2. Specific objectives: Rather than beginning with a discussion of basic concepts of science, ESS puts physical materials into children's hands from the start and helps each child investigate through these materials the nature of the world around him. We have tried to incorporate both the spirit and the substance of science into our program in such a way that the child's own rich world of exploration becomes more disciplined, more manageable, and more satisfying. Careful attention is given to all materials used so that all equipment looks like materials which are normally accessible to children in their own environment and not imposingly "scientific." A mix of university scientists and master teachers work together in the laboratories and in classrooms to test and revise their ideas before the materials are released to schools.

FIGURE 6-1. *How is the instructor of these children applying the principle of utilizing basic experiences as suggested by Piaget? (Photo by Lee Youngblood)*

UNIQUE CHARACTERISTICS OF THE PROJECT:
ESS materials have been used successfully in middle-class
suburban and low socioeconomic areas, large cities and small
towns, and a great variety of different situations.

Children are scientists by disposition. They ask questions and
use their senses as well as their reasoning powers to explore their
physical environments; they derive great satisfaction from finding
out what makes things tick; they like solving problems; they are
challenged by new materials or by new ways of using familiar
materials. It is this natural curiosity of children and their freedom
from preconceptions of difficulty that ESS tires to cultivate and
direct into deeper channels.

SPECIFIC SUBJECTS, GRADE, AGE AND ABILITY LEVELS:
Science K–9, all students.

MAIN METHODS OF INSTRUCTION USED
IN THE PROJECT:
Independent study, laboratory investigations, discussion sessions,
and films and film loops.

PRESENT COMMERCIAL AFFILIATIONS:
Webster Division, McGraw-Hill Book Company, Manchester Road,
Manchester, Mo. 63011.

DESCRIPTION OF MATERIALS ALREADY PRODUCED:
1. *ANIMAL ACTIVITY* (Grades 4–6). This unit involves children
in a direct study of the activity of small animals. It introduces
several techniques for observing and measuring animal behavior
under different conditions. The children use a small exercise
wheel coupled to a counter. When a small mammal—such as a
mouse, gerbil, or similar rodent—runs on the wheel, the counter
keeps track of the number of complete revolutions of the wheel.
The number of revolutions in a given span of time is a measure of
the animal's activity. This apparatus encourages children to design
experiments, keep records, and analyze their data. Equipment:
animal activity wheel; Printed matter: Teacher's Guide, student
booklets—*Experiments on Animal Activity* and *The Curious
Gerbils*.
2. *ANIMALS IN THE CLASSROOM* (Grades K–4). This book was
written with two purposes in mind. The primary objective is to
present teachers with an illustration of the way in which an
interdisciplinary curriculum can be built around a central theme
—in this case, animals. The book contains a teacher's account of a
year in which the desert animals in her primary classroom became the focus for language, mathematics, social studies, and
science activities. The book is also a resource book to encourage
and to help teachers keep animals of all kinds in their classrooms.
It describes in some detail methods for keeping gerbils and two
kinds of lizards; a checklist of things to consider, whatever

animals you have; descriptions of a variety of simple, inexpensive cages; and a short bibliography of books on animal care.

3. *ATTRIBUTE GAMES AND PROBLEMS* (Grades K–9). This unit provides an opportunity for children to deal with problems of classification and the relationship between classes. The kinds of problems worked on here lend themselves to applications in many curriculum areas—science, social studies, mathematics, or whatever classification and dealing with relations between classes are called for. The same colorful materials (A Blocks, Color Cubes, People Pieces, colored loops, stickers, and label cards) are used, though in different ways, from kindergarten through ninth grade and beyond. Equipment: three kinds of blocks, loops; printed matter: Teacher's Guide, problem cards (in English and Spanish), geometric stickers.

4. *BALLOONS AND GASES* (Grades 5–8). This unit gives children an opportunity to prepare and collect gases and to discover some of their properties. Preliminary work is done with acids and bases and a colored indicator, bromothymol blue. Students generate a number of common gases and conduct tests which enable them to distinguish the bases from one another. The Teacher's Guide contains recipes for making "mystery gases" which students can generate and attempt to identify on the basis of their previous experience. The chemical reactions by which the gases are produced offer interesting avenues for further study. Equipment: crystals, powders, glass tubing, medicine droppers, balloons; printed matter: Teacher's Guide.

5. *BATTERIES AND BULBS* (Grades 4–6). This unit is an introduction to the study of electricity and magnetism. In the course of this study, each child carries out experiments with simple and safe equipment—flashlight batteries, small bulbs, various kinds of wire, magnets, and a compass—and draws conclusions based on his observations. Equipment: flashlight batteries, small bulbs, various kinds of wire, compresses, magnets; printed matter: Teacher's Guide, student prediction and project sheets.

6. *BATTERIES AND BULBS II* (Grades 5 and beyond). This resource book contains illustrated suggestions for almost fifty different battery-operated gadgets and projects. All the gadgets are relatively simple and can be constructed with simple tools from common scrap materials. The descriptions are intended to be used as a source of ideas rather than as models to be copied. The book also suggests where to buy hard-to-find items, such as earphones and diodes. Included is an extensive bibliography of background books and a list of free booklets available from electrical suppliers.

7. *BEHAVIOR OF MEALWORMS* (Grades 4–8). *Behavior of Mealworms* stimulates children to ask questions about the observable behavior of an unfamiliar animal and then directs them to ways of finding the answers for themselves. As children

observe and experiment, they learn some things about the process of scientific inquiry. Equipment: mealworms, food, containers; printed matter: Teacher's Guide, two student booklets—*How Barn Owls Hunt* and *How a Moth Escapes from Its Cocoon*, set of pictures; film (for teachers) one 16mm black and white, sound film: *How to Make a Mealworm Back Up.*

8. *BONES* (Grades 4–6). This unit engages the students in becoming familiar with a variety of bones, noticing similarities and differences, and making skeletons. Equipment: disarticulated skeletons, assorted bones; printed matter: Teacher's Guide, two student booklets—*Bones Picture Book,* and *How to Make a Chicken Skeleton;* film: five 8mm loops, black and white: *X-ray Motion Pictures Head and Neck, X-ray Motion Pictures Shoulder, X-ray Motion Pictures Knee and Elbows, X-ray Motion Pictures Hand, X-ray Motion Pictures Foot.*

9. *BRINE SHRIMP* (Grades K–4). Brine shrimp are small, salt–lake crustaceans, easily hatched and cared for in any classroom and fascinating to study. Children can easily watch their own animals hatch, grow, and eventually have young of their own. Each child, working alone or with a classmate, can raise and maintain his own brine shrimp because the animals are small and easy to maintain. Equipment: brine shrimp eggs, salt water, magnifiers, containers; printed matter: Teacher's Guide; film: one 16mm, color, silent—*Brine Shrimp;* two 8mm loops, color—*Brine Shrimp I, Brine Shrimp II.*

10. *BUDDING TWIGS* (Grades 4–6). In this unit, planned for late winter and early spring, children examine in the classroom the structure of twigs and the development of buds forced into bloom out of season. Through observation and dissection, children become aware of the varieties and complexities of plant construction. Later they observe the development of buds outdoors. They are encouraged to collect twigs and to try to predict what the buds will become. As the study progresses, they design experiments to answer their own questions. The guide contains teaching suggestions, some possible avenues of exploration, information about collecting twigs, and a list of materials needed for the activities. Equipment: twigs, containers; printed matter: Teacher's Guide.

11. *BUTTERFLIES* (Grades K–5). Children can witness the complex and fascinating life cycle of an insect by raising butterflies in their classroom. While the children watch and care for their own animals, they ask many questions about them. In time they find answers to some of their questions and begin to develop a sense for the way in which an animal lives, grows, and reproduces. Equipment: butterfly eggs, cocoons; printed matter: Teacher's Guide; film: one 16mm, silent, color—*The Life Cycle of a Butterfly;* six 8mm loops, color—*Black Swallowtail Butterfly: Egg Laying, Hatching, and Larvae; Black Swallowtail Butterfly: Larval Molt; Black Swallowtail Butterfly: Preparing to Pupate (1); Black*

Swallowtail Butterfly: Preparing to Pupate (2); *Black Swallowtail: Pupal Molt; Black Swallowtail Butterfly:Emergence.*

12. *CHANGES* (Grades 1–4). This unit gives children an opportunity to see, distinguish, and understand something about the changes in organic and inorganic substances that are caused by the growth of living organisms, such as bacteria, as well as those brought about by non-living processes, such as rusting and melting. In the course of this unit, the children make direct observations of the continual change that characterizes the universe. Equipment: plastic boxes, baby food jars, foods, liquids, metals, crystals, powders, seeds; printed matter: Teacher's Guide.

13. *CLAY BOATS* (Grades 2–6). Children investigate the possibility of making a lump of clay float in a container of water. The children make shapes out of the clay and, when they have made a shape that floats, they experiment to see how much "cargo" their "boats" will hold. At the conclusion of the activities, most students will begin to accept the fact that objects which sink can be made to float. They will also be aware that some shapes are better than others for boats. Equipment: clay (oil base), containers— uniform weights for loading materials; printed matter: Teacher's Guide.

14. *COLOR SOLUTIONS* (Grades 3–8). This unit utilizes food coloring, water, salt, and transparent containers to introduce children to ideas associated with density and the layering of liquids. In time, the children develop a scheme for ordering the liquids they are exploring according to "weight for the same amount." Equipment: plastic trays and cylinders, salt solutions, eye droppers, and food coloring; printed matter: Teacher's Guide.

15. *CRAYFISH* (Grades 6–8). Crayfish are interesting and manageable animals to keep in a classroom. Children enjoy handling crayfish and investigating their behavior. They may be collected in most parts of the country at all times of the year or purchased inexpensively enough to give each pair of children an animal to work with. Equipment: crayfish containers; printed matter: Teacher's Guide.

16. *DAYTIME ASTRONOMY* (Grades 5–8). *Daytime Astronomy* is built around children's observations of the shadows the sun casts on the earth at different times of the day and throughout the year. Children become familiar with the apparent motion of the sun by recording changes in the length and direction of the sun's shadows. The resulting "shadow-clocks" are used for telling time, for finding directions, and for developing theories about the movement and relative position of the earth and sun. Working with globes indoors and outdoors, children can investigate conditions that occur all over the real world. An earth–moon scale model allows them to simulate the role which sunlight plays in phases and eclipses. Equipment: metal globes, pasteboard globes, magnets, protractors; printed matter: Teacher's Guide.

17. *DROPS, STREAMS, AND CONTAINERS* (Grades 3–4). This unit is a guide to play and investigation with liquids. Children examine flow, drop formation, and other properties of water, soapy water, oil, and other available liquids, using a variety of containers, surfaces, drops, and tubes. Equipment: bottles with holes, caps with holes, eye droppers, medicine caps, tubing, paper towels and wax paper; printed matter: Teacher's Guide, problem cards.

18. *EARTHWORMS* (Grades 4–6). Children examine the habits and preferences of these small, easy-to-care-for animals. Students devise ways to find out what kind of soil, how much moisture, and how much light earthworms prefer. Field trips are a central part of the unit. By searching for the animals outside, children can test their ideas about where earthworms can be found. They are sometimes surprised at the places they find worms and are stimulated to experiment further in the classroom. Printed material: Teacher's Guide.

19. *EGGS AND TADPOLES* (Grades K–6). This unit encourages children's natural interest in living things through the exploration of frog eggs and tadpoles. Whether the eggs are collected from a pond or purchased from a supplier, they are exciting to watch as they change in a few days from nondescript blobs to living, swimming animals. Many questions can be answered from the children's own observations. Often, they go back to watch a second batch of eggs develop and hatch. Equipment: fertilized frog eggs, aquaria, pond water; printed matter: Teacher's Guide; film: two 16mm, color silent—*Frog Development: Fertilization to Hatching; Frog Development: Hatching through Metamorphosis;* eight 8mm loops, color—*Frog Egg I: First Cell Division to Early Neural Fold; Frog Egg II: Development of the Body Regions; Frog Egg III: Continued Development to Hatching; Frogs: Pairing and Egg Laying; Artificial Fertilization of Frog Eggs; Frogs: Pituitary Preparation; Tadpoles I; Tadpoles II.*

20. *GASES AND "AIRS"* (Grades 5–8). This unit is composed of closely linked laboratory experiments investigating the nature of air and the changes it undergoes when interacting with common. objects in our environment. Early experiments demonstrate that air is "real" even though it can't be seen, and that its presence can be proven. Students undertake investigations with the gasses of the atmosphere ("air") and the "things" of the universe (rock, iron, water, seeds, a candle). As the unit progresses, students begin to analyze "airs" for oxygen content and gain experience with an essential tool of experimental science—the control. Equipment: tubes, candles, steel wool, seeds; printed matter: Teacher's Guide, worksheets; film: one 16mm, black and white, sound—*Gases and "Airs" in the Classroom* (for teachers); four 8mm loops, color—*Candle Burning Techniques; Candle Burning I; Candle Burning II; The Mouse and the Candle.*

21. *GEO BLOCKS* (Grades K–6). The *Geo Blocks* are a set of unfinished hardwood blocks small enough to be used on school desks. They come in a wide range of shapes and sizes that make possible a great variety of structures and designs, both simple and complex. The blocks are related to one another in volume, and all but three can be made up from the smaller blocks in the set. When a child runs out of large blocks, he can match them with combinations of smaller ones, thus gaining a sense of volume equivalents. Equipment: 330 blocks; printed matter: Teacher's Guide and picture cards.

22. *GROWING SEEDS* (Grades K–3). This unit gives children an opportunity to become acquainted with science as early as the first grade—an opportunity to discover ways to find answers to their own questions about the world. At first they gather and bring in small objects they think might be seeds. They ask questions and devise ways to find their own answers. Children soon discover that they can distinguish a seed from things it resembles by planting it and watching to see if it will grow. Equipment: seeds, soil, containers; printed matter: Teacher's guide; film: two 8mm film loops, color—*Bean Sprouts; Plant Growth-Graphing.*

23. *HEATING AND COOLING* (Grades 5–7). This unit deals primarily with heat and heat conduction through a variety of materials: metal sheets, wires, rods, and screens. Small candles are the source of heat. With equal-size rods of different metals, glass rods, and rods of different diameter, children compare the effect of size and substance on heat conduction. Equipment: expansion frame, various rods (aluminum, brass, copper), assorted wire, screens, cardboard tray; printed material: Teacher's Guide, problem cards.

24. *ICE CUBES* (Grades 3–5). Almost all children are familiar with freezing water and with ice. This unit asks questions to which children can find answers through direct experimentation. The students experiment with ice cubes to determine which factors influence the rate at which ice melts. They try insulating ice cubes with a variety of materials. They race different shapes of ice to see the effect on the melting rate of larger or smaller amounts of surface area. Equipment: thermometers, ice, containers; printed matter: Teacher's Guide.

25. *KITCHEN PHYSICS* (Grades 5–8). The student examines liquids—how they form drops and puddles; how they fall and break up; how fast they flow through various sizes of openings; how they heap up, are absorbed, evaporate, mix, and dissolve. He assembles and uses simple equipment, such as a balance, which he then modifies for use as a tensiometer.

26. *LIFE OF BEANS AND PEAS* (Grades K–4). Children plant beans and peas, tend them, and observe them throughout one life cycle and on into a second generation grown from class-produced seeds.

27. *LIGHT AND SHADOWS* (Grades K–3). In exploring the world of light and shadows, both outdoors and indoors, children find new meanings in a number of ordinary objects and phenomena. When children are exploring shadows, they are experimenting with spatial relationships in simple ways. This unit has been taught in Grades K–3 and could be extended to the middle grades as well. The scheduling is quite flexible and will often depend on the weather (for outdoor activities) or a child's inspiration. Printed matter: Teacher's Guide.

28. *MAPPING* (Grades 5–7). Youngsters learn to describe their environment in terms of symbols. In mapping, children must devise ways to describe locations in words or pictures, to represent three dimensions in two, and to show the relative position and size of objects in a space.

29. *MATCH AND MEASURE* (Grades K–3). This is a resource book for the primary grades, illustrating many ways in which children can work with measurement as a practical tool in the context of other classroom projects. The purpose of the book is to encourage teachers to use an informal approach in teaching measurement to young children. Through such an approach, teachers can help children use more formal measuring techniques with understanding. The activities in the book deal with measuring lengths, areas, and volumes; the approach is applicable to other kinds of measurement as well. Equipment: measuring wheels, calipers; printed matter: Teacher's Guide.

30. *MICROGARDENING* (Grades 4–7). This unit introduces children to the molds—a group of microscopic living things very different from the trees, shrubs, wild flowers, and other plants with which they are familiar. Children working with microgardening become familiar with principles and procedures that have contributed to man's knowledge and understanding over the past 200 years. The five areas of study covered in the unit are: What are molds like? What influences the growth of molds? Where do molds come from? What influences the rate of mold growth? What can molds do? Equipment: containers, nutrient media; printed matter: Teacher's Guide; booklet—*Illustrated Handbook of Some Common Molds;* film: seven 8mm film loops— *Alternaria, Rhizopus, Fusarium, Penicillium, Trichoderma, Growth Rings, Rotting Pear, Mushroom Growth,* and *Reaction.*

31. *MIRROR CARDS* (Grades 1–7). The basic problem posed by *Mirror Cards* is one of matching, by means of a mirror, a pattern on one card with a pattern shown on another card. The children find the colors and shapes on the cards pleasing and fun to work with. They enjoy the challenge presented and require little supervision from the teacher. Equipment: cards (twenty-one different sets), four mirrors; printed matter: Teacher's Guide.

32. *MOBILES* (Grades 2–3). The unit describes very simple ways in which children can experiment with balance by

making constructions that are provocative and delightful to look at. It may be presented as an activity that is an end in itself, or it may be incorporated into more systematic explorations involving balancing and weighing, such as the ESS unit, *Primary Balancing*. Equipment: reeds, twine, hangers, clips; printed matter: Teacher's Guide.

33. *MOSQUITOES* (Grades 3–9). Most people know little about mosquitoes except that they bite, yet these insects are fascinating to study, easy to raise, and readily available. *Mosquitoes* is a resource book for information and experiments to help anyone who is interested find out more about mosquitoes. Teachers can use the book as a guide for class activities. Children will find it a helpful resource for individual or small-group projects. The book contains information on raising mosquitoes, some ideas for experiments to try, and descriptions of experiments scientists have performed on mosquitoes. There also is a list of materials for raising mosquitoes and information on sources of mosquito eggs. Printed matter: resource book.

34. *MUSICAL INSTRUMENT RECIPE BOOK* (Graded K–adult). Making musical instruments combines craftsmanship with an exploration of the physical properties of devices that produce sound. There is great satisfaction to be derived from building an instrument which is pleasing and which works. This resource book contains illustrated instructions for making over twenty stringed, wind, and percussion instruments from inexpensive, readily available materials. It can be used as a construction manual and as a source of ideas for building original instruments. Printed matter: resource book.

35. *MYSTERY POWDERS* (Grades 3–4). The activities in *Mystery Powders* deal with the properties of ordinary white powders (starch, baking soda, plaster of Paris, granulated sugar, and salt) and the use of indicators in identifying them and detecting their presence in mixtures. The powders are safe for children to handle and taste and are inexpensively obtained from drug, grocery, and hardware stores. From beginning activities in which they use their senses to become familiar with the powders, students progress to more sophisticated analysis, utilizing indicators and other laboratory techniques. Equipment: sugar, salt, baking soda, starch, plaster of Paris, vinegar, iodine, heat source, containers; printed matter: Teacher's Guide.

36. *OPTICS* (Grades 4–6 and beyond). Students observe and analyze many of the interesting properties of light by direct experiment. They look at light itself and its interaction with transparent objects and with things that act as mirrors. While they investigate the various optical phenomena and raise questions about what they see, children also are exploring why the world looks the way it does to us; that is, what the properties of light have to do with our visual experience. Equipment: light

sources, mirrors, containers, or color filters; printed matter: Teacher's Guides.

37. *PATTERN BLOCKS* (Grades K–6). This set of 250 flat blocks includes six shapes and colors. Except for the two-inch sides of the trapezoid, all the sides are an inch long. This allows children to build closed as well as open designs and to acquire a feeling for the size and shape relationships among the blocks. Pattern blocks lend themselves to work in counting and arithmetic, combinations and equivalents, linear and area measurement, congruency and similarity, symmetry, angle measurement, series, sequences, and modular form. Equipment: 250 blocks, mirrors; printed matter: Teacher's Guide.

38. *PEAS AND PARTICLES* (Grades 4–8). Children deal informally with estimation and large numbers in ways that may be new to them. They answer questions—How many? How big? How far away?—not with worksheet or arithmetic-test precision, but as we tend to answer questions ordinarily, with estimates and "educated" guesses. Children are ingenious when it comes to thinking of methods of counting and estimating large numbers. How important is rounding off? When is an exact answer needed? These are some of the questions that children discuss in their work with *Peas and Particles*. Equipment: rice, peas, beans, balls, containers; printed matter: Teacher's Guide, picture packet.

39. *PENDULUMS* (Grades 4–6). Children have the chance to observe, investigate, and reflect upon the many physical phenomena associated with swinging objects. A variety of bobs, differing in weight, size, and shape, lead the children to ask questions about a pendulum's behavior and to find their answers from the pendulum itself. The students make and test their predictions in a readily controllable situation. Equipment: frame, string, bobs; printed matter: Teacher's Guide; film: five 8mm loops, color—*Sand Pendulum I: Drawing Circles; Lines and Ellipses; Sand Pendulum II: Drawing on a Turntable; Sand Pendulum III: Drawing Lines on a Traveling Table; Sand Pendulum IV: Slowing Down; Sand Pendulum V: Pouring Sand into Soda Straws*.

40. *POND WATER* (Grades 4–7). Pond Water introduces children to an exciting array of living creatures, invites them to make their own collections on field trips, distinguish their finds through observation and description, and go on to study the tiny animals they have collected. They can begin to understand the complicated interactions of pond life. And most important, they will learn to use their eyes and their minds to find out about the world in which they live. Equipment: pond water, containers, microscopes; printed matter: Teacher's Guide, study cards.

41. *PRIMARY BALANCING* (Grades K–4). Children explore balancing and weighing at first hand. They develop a general understanding of weight and balancing from weighing, compar-

ing, sorting, counting, and balancing a large assortment of items on equal-arm balances, on flat wooden beams, and in suspended pans. Preliminary experiences with balancing are followed by more specific investigations into the physical laws of balance and the idea of weight and its measurement. Equipment: walking boards—four foot balance boards, pan balances, things to weigh; printed matter: Teacher's Guide.

42. *PRINTING* (Grades 1–6). *Printing* makes available a simple printing press for classrooms and a resource book for the teacher. When a printing press is an everyday part of the classroom furniture, children will use it as a tool to carry out work in many areas. One child may print a poem, or a group of children may decide to put out a newspaper. Equipment: printing press, type, printing ink, type rack, ink rollers; printed matter: Teacher's Guide.

43. *ROCKS AND CHARTS* (Grades 3–6). *Rocks and Charts* encourages children to look closely at the characteristics of rocks (and other things), to establish their own ways of comparing objects, to agree upon useful standards, and to find greater possibilities in their own collections. Equipment: rocks, balances, streak plates, hand lenses; printed matter: Teacher's Guide.

44. *SAND* (Grades 2–3). The unit uses graded, colored sand which, appealing aesthetically, invites a wide variety of explorations of a scientific nature. Sand can be thought of as analogous to water, and poured, measured, and dripped. Sand can also be sorted, piled, looked at through a hand lens, rolled down various surfaces, strained, crushed, and weighed. Children make sand clocks, sandpaper, sand sculpture, and sand pendulums. Equipment: graded colored sand, sieves, sand table; printed matter: Teacher's Guide.

45. *SENIOR BALANCING* (Grades 4–8). Children hang washers on strips of pegboard suspended from a nail. They learn how to identify problems involving balance and to make use of various strategies to solve the problems. An intuitive understanding of moments of force and center of mass underlie the study. Equipment: pegboard, nails, washers, and others; printed matter: Teacher's Guide, cards.

46. *SINK OR FLOAT* (Grades 2–7). This unit offers children experiences with displacement of volumes of liquid and with buoyancy. The activities are intended to help provide a base upon which a more formal conception of the density of materials can be built. Equipment: containers, Plasticine, materials of different densities, salt; printed matter: Teacher's Guide.

47. *SMALL THINGS* (Grades 4–6). *Small Things* is an introduction to the microscopic world, the instruments needed to make it accessible, and the appearance and structure of minute living and nonliving things. Equipment: microscopes, balances, eye dropper, hand lens, tweezers; printed matter: Teacher's Guide.

48. *SPINNING TABLES* (Grades 1–3). A spinning table is a simple piece of equipment with which a child can explore the paradoxical behavior of things that move in circles. The table, a free moving, circular disc, can be turned by hand or with a hand crank. A smooth chalkboard insert for the table makes it possible to draw circles, spirals, and other shapes on the table. A pegboard insert for attaching objects to the table allow children to watch how objects behave as the table spins. Equipment: hand-driven turntables, marbles, tubes, blocks; printed matter: Teacher's Guide.

49. *STARTING FROM SEEDS* (Grades 3–7). In this unit, children are given seeds, and vermiculite and containers in which to grow them. Numerous questions arise immediately—"Which way should we plant the seeds?" "How deep?" "Will they grow in the dark?" Equipment: various types of seeds, containers, vermiculite, slides; printed matter: Teacher's Guide.

50. *STREAM TABLES*. In the classroom children study such events as the behavior of streams, erosion and soil conservation problems, and the action of waves on beaches. Equipment: plastic sheeting, Tri-Wall cardboard, pump, plastic tubing, tape, connectors; printed materials: Teacher's Guide, problem cards.

51. *STRUCTURES* (Grades 2–6). As the children build with materials (newspaper, clay, sticks, Scotch tape, and others) they begin to see the relationship between material, function, and form. By slowly working with a set of various materials, a wide range of experience is provided. Equipment: clay, straws, string, Plasticine, paper, tape, and pins; printed matter: Teacher's Guide.

52. *TANGRAMS* (Grades K–8). The tangram is a fascinating geometric puzzle consisting of seven pieces dissected from a square. This adaptation includes a set of problem cards that begin with smaller groups of the seven-piece set in order to help the children develop skill in dealing with basic geometric relationships before they confront more complex problems. Equipment: tangram pieces (seven pieces); printed matter: Teacher's Guide, tangram cards (120 patterns of varying difficulty divided into three sets).

53. *TRACKS* (Grades 4–6). Children learn to use their eyes and their minds to unravel the events that shaped the tracks they find in pictures and in their everyday environment. A track can indicate many things: the identity of an animal, the direction in which it was going, whether it was moving quickly or slowly, how long ago the animal lived, its mood, and, in some cases, even its sex, the food it ate, and the environment it needs in order to survive. Printed matter: Teacher's Guide, picture book for students, track card sets—mystery cards (ten cards), small track cards (fifty-two cards), animal photographs (fourteen); one 8mm loop, black and white—*The Horse: Walk, Trot, and Gallop, in Slow Motion.*

54. *WATER FLOW* (Grades 5–6). This unit takes advantage of the natural appeal of water play to enable children to improve their insight into water flow in closed systems. Students construct their own water systems in vertical support frames, using plastic tubing, tubing containers, and water bottles. The unexpected behavior of the water, a desire to make the water flow a different path, a question about their designs, or a new piece of apparatus prompts children to make changes. Equipment: support frame, vinyl tubing, connectors, rigid plastic tubes; printed matter: Teacher's Guide, student cards.

55. *WHERE IS THE MOON?* (Grades 3–7). This is an informal introduction to observational astronomy. During a three-month period, children are given approximately fifty notes called "Reminders." Each note describes an event that the children can see in the sky. Their observations of the sky—specifically of the moon in relation to Venus, Jupiter, and the sun, and its shape and position in relation to familiar landmarks—are the basis of the study. Children observe, make predictions about what they will see, keep records and notes of their observations, and begin to look for patterns from month to month. Printed matter: Teacher's Guide, student booklet—*Where Was the Moon; Reminders* (series of approximately fifty notes on the sky and moon).

56. *WHISTLES AND STRINGS* (Grades 4–5). Working with materials that produce sounds of definite pitch—such as stiff and flexible plastic tubing, straws, and different kinds of string—children explore the relationship between objects and the sounds they make. By altering and combining these and other materials, they investigate the physical conditions necessary to produce sounds, and to change the pitch, volume, and tone quality of sounds. They construct sound-making contraptions for experiments and make simple musical instruments. Some children compose music for their instruments and play music together. Equipment: plastic tubing, straws, various types of string, scrap wood; printed matter: Teacher's Guide.

MATERIALS AVAILABLE FREE:
Brochure describing ESS (*Introduction to ESS*—limited to twenty copies), reprints of several articles, Newsletter which is published irregularly and sent to the mailing list. Upon request, interested institutions, scientists, or educators are added to this mailing list.

MATERIALS PURCHASABLE:
Price list and catalog available from Webster Division, McGraw-Hill Book Company, Manchester Road, Manchester, Mo. 63011.

ADDITIONAL MATERIALS BEING DEVELOPED:
A summary report of the history of the Elementary Science Study, and a materials resource book.

LANGUAGE IN WHICH MATERIALS:
1. Were originally written: English.
2. Have been translated: Some in French and Spanish.

COUNTRIES IN WHICH MATERIALS ARE USED:
Canada, Korea, Japan, England, and Israel.

PROJECT IMPLEMENTATION:
It is estimated that 3,000,000 students have used some of the materials.
Name and location of selected schools where this program is in use: Fairfax County Schools, Fairfax, Va.; Gates-Chili Central School District, Rochester, N.Y.; San Diego, Calif.; Dixie School District, San Rafael, Calif.; Greece Central, Rochester, N.Y.; Wellesley, Mass.; Stoughton, Mass.; Lincoln, Mass.; Cardozo Model School District, Washington, D.C.; Abington, Pa.; Orange, N.J.; Belmont, Mass.; Portland, Oregon; Minneapolis, Minn.; Lompoc, Calif.

TEACHER PREPARATION:
1. Consultant services available for teachers using the materials: Regional consultant list is contained in *A Working Guide to the Elementary Study* (available from ESS at $3.00 per copy); the Webster Division of McGraw-Hill Book Company also has a science consultant service.
2. Activities conducted for pre-service and in-service teacher training: ESS is no longer able to conduct in-house workshops. ESS workshops available in various regions will be listed in our next Newsletter. They will not be run by ESS, but by the people in the region in which they are held.
3. Available pre-service and/or in-service teaching materials for science educators to use in preparing teachers: no specific materials. Some suggestions are made in *A Working Guide to the Elementary Science Study*. The following films are available for rental and/or sale from the EDC film library: *Another Way to Learn, Balancing, Bones, Choosing to Learn, Classrooms in Transition, Gases and "Airs" in the Classroom, a Small Things Classroom, Kitchen Physics, Pond Water, Things Classroom, Kitchen Physics, Pond Water.*

PROJECT EVALUATION:
The effectiveness of the materials has not been evaluated.

PROJECT PUBLICITY:
1. Hawkins, David, "Messing About in Science," *Science and Children* (February 1965).
2. Hein, George E., "Children's Science is Another Culture," *Technology Review* (December 1968).
3. Hawkins, David, "The Informed Vision: An Essay on Science Education," *Daedalus.*

4. Zacharias, Jerrold R., "What's Ahead in Elementary Science," *Instructor* (January 1967).

5. Rice, Michael, "Water Flow," *Science and Children* (December 1969).

6. Rogers and Voelker, "Programs for Improving Science Instruction in the Elementary School, Part I, ESS," *Science and Children* (January–February 1970). May be obtained from ERIC Information Analysis Center for Science Education, Columbus, Ohio.

BRIEF SUMMARY OF PROJECT ACTIVITIES SINCE 1970 REPORT:
Time has been spent doing research for the above mentioned books to be published soon, publishing *A Working Guide to The Elementary Science Study* and *The ESS Reader*, responding to verbal and written requests concerning ESS materials, and overseeing the filming of two new classroom films: *Pond Water* (two parts), and *Kitchen Physics;* and overseeing commercial publications.

PLANS FOR THE FUTURE:
ESS funding ended in September 1972. While the project work is complete, information and a display area are still available at EDC.

Creative Aspects

The objectives of the Elementary Science Study are to give children opportunities to observe and isolate factors involved in their observations. In *Kitchen Physics*, for example, the children are confronted with situations that cause them to think about properties of liquids—their "heaviness" (density), "thickness" (viscosity), "stickiness" (cohesion or adhesion), and others. In the process of trying to answer some of their questions, the children learn to formulate hypotheses, devise tests, assemble equipment, collect data, and draw conclusions. They are encouraged to examine and experiment from many viewpoints.

Dr. Nichols of the Elementary Science Study points out how this might be done in *Kitchen Physics*. He says:

> They begin to devise ways of testing their own conjectures. They assemble a simple equal-arm balance that can measure the "heaviness" of various liquids. By modifying their balances slightly, they can measure the "grabbiness." How many washers do you have to add to one arm of balance beam to make the opposite arm lift a plastic plate off the surface of the various liquids? They begin to explore the

skinlike [sic] effect that may be observed on the surface of liquids. They use the balance to check how much water a paper towel can absorb and to measure its variation with time, indicating the effect of evaporation. They use blotter strips to examine the rise of various liquids in blotters of various widths and on the capillary block. These phenomena are so interrelated that children performing experiments to seek the answers to one series of questions almost inevitably notice a new collection of effects that lead to a new set of experiments. It is when they try to relate the results of several experiments that they gain insight into scientific principles.[3]

Dr. Nichols says further that not all children will do the same experiments. Some will want to follow original ideas arising from their investigations.

Most of the Elementary Science Study units have been tested in a wide variety of classrooms with teachers of varied backgrounds, and rewritten. The testing program of the Elementary Science Study has shown that capable teachers, regardless of their backgrounds, make the most capable elementary science teachers of the units. This is believed to be so because the instructors are more likely to encourage enthusiasm and eagerness of investigation on the part of their pupils and demonstrate these qualities themselves in their own personalities. Under the guidance of a creatively oriented teacher, these materials could be adapted to contribute to creativity.

SCIENCE—A PROCESS APPROACH (AN ELEMENTARY SCHOOL SCIENCE CURRICULUM PROGRAM DEVELOPED BY THE COMMISSION ON SCIENCE EDUCATION OF THE AMERICAN ASSOCIATION FOR THE ADVANCEMENT OF SCIENCE)

PROJECT DIRECTOR:
John R. Mayor, Director; Arthur H. Livermore, Deputy Director; 1515 Massachusetts Avenue, N.W., Washington, D.C. 20005. (202) 467-4462.

PROJECT HEADQUARTERS:
1. Contact: Project Director.
2. Special facilities or activities available for visitor viewing: The printed materials and kits of materials of *Science—A Process Approach*.

3. Benjamin Nichols, "Elementary Science Study Two Years Later," *ESI Quarterly Report*, Summer–Fall (Watertown, Mass. ESI 1965), pp. 8–9.

PRINCIPAL PROFESSIONAL STAFF:
John R. Mayor, Director; Arthur H. Livermore, Deputy Director;
Richard G. Netzel, Acting Deputy Director of Education;
C. Charles Peterson, Staff Associate; Hermenegilda Margate,
Research Assistant.

PROJECT SUPPORT:
1. Funding agencies: National Science Foundation.
2. Associated agencies: American Association for the Advancement of Science and Xerox Corporation.

PROJECT HISTORY:
1. Principal originator: Commission on Science Education of the
American Association for the Advancement of Science.
2. Date and place of initiation: 1962; Washington, D.C.
3. Evolution and development of the project: *Science—A Process Approach* was developed over a six-year period by more than 100 scientists and teachers working in five summer writing sessions. Fourteen school systems across the country cooperated in the tryout each year with more than 300 teachers reporting regularly on the exercises as they were taught. Each exercise of the program was tried out, evaluated, and modified as a result of the tryout during three or more school years.

PROJECT OBJECTIVES:
1. Overall project purpose: *Science—A Process Approach* is designed to present instruction which is intellectually stimulating and scientifically authentic. It is based on a belief that the scientific approach to gaining knowledge of man's world has a fundamental importance in the general education of every child. Instructional materials of *Science—A Process Approach* are prepared for the teacher, while kits of materials are available for use by the children. Topics covered sample widely from the various fields of science, including some exercises in mathematics and the social sciences. The exercises are ordered in a sequence of instruction to provide a developmental progression of increasing competence in the processes of science. Each exercise is designed to achieve clearly stated objectives. Methods for evaluating pupil achievement and progress are an integral part of the program. A guide for in-service instruction is also provided. This description was taken from the brochure, *Science—A Process Approach: Purposes, Accomplishments, Expectations*. Copies of the brochure are available upon request.
2. Specific objectives: *Science—A Process Approach* is organized in seven parts, each of which has twenty or more exercises. In each exercise there are carefully stated performance objectives. A sequence chart in each exercise indicates the prerequisite skills for the exercise and the skills to be taught later that will depend on

FIGURE 6-2. *How would you design field experiences to have children learn about their environment? (Photo by Lee Youngblood)*

the exercise. Each exercise also includes a competency measure to test the achievement of the objectives.

UNIQUE CHARACTERISTICS OF THE PROJECT:
Science—A Process Approach was prepared for all elementary school children in kindergarten through grade 6. Special characteristics of the program include:
1. The identification of the acquisition of skills in the processes of science as the primary objective of the program.
2. The careful statement of objectives and competency measures to test the achievement of the objectives for each exercise, as described under G-2.
3. The sequential arrangement of the program, determined by a hierarchy of skills in the processes of science.
4. The selection of content from the natural and behavioral sciences and mathematics.
5. Teacher texts and associated kits of teaching materials for the children.

SPECIFIC SUBJECTS, GRADE, AGE AND ABILITY LEVELS:
Science for kindergarten through grade 6. Some schools are using the materials also in grades 7 and 8.

MAIN METHODS OF INSTRUCTION USED IN THE PROJECT:
Independent study, laboratory investigations, discussion sessions
and field experiences.

PRESENT COMMERCIAL AFFILIATIONS:
Xerox Education Sciences. Sales offices: 555 Gotham Parkway,
Carlstadt, NJ. 07072. Editorial offices: 191 Spring Street,
Lexington, Mass. 02173.

DESCRIPTION OF MATERIALS ALREADY PRODUCED:
1. *Science—A Process Approach*, Parts A–G (grades K–6).
2. Kits of teaching aids for *Science—A Process Approach*, Parts
   A–G.
3. Process Hierarchy Chart for *Science—A Process Approach*,
   Parts A–D.
4. Process Hierarchy Chart for *Science—A Process Approach*,
   Parts E–G.
5. *Commentary for Teachers*.
6. *Guide for In-service Instruction*.
7. Kits of teaching aids for *Guide for In-service Instruction*.
8. *Science Process Instrument* (A–D experimental edition).
9. *The Psychological Bases of Science—A Process Approach*,
   2nd edition, 1967.
10. *Science—A Process Approach: Purposes, Accomplishments,
    and Expectations*.
11. *How To Plan for Science—A Process Approach*.
12. *Supplementary Science Reading for Children*.
13. *Developments in Elementary School Science: A Report of
    Seven Regional Conferences for School Administrators*.
14. *Newsletter*, AAAS Commission on Science Education.

MATERIALS AVAILABLE FREE:
Items 9 through 14 available from Commission on Science Edu-
cation, AAAS, 1515 Massachusetts Avenue, N.W., Washington,
D.C. 20005.

MATERIALS PURCHASABLE:
Items 1 through 7 available from Xerox Education Sciences, 555
Gotham Parkway, Carlstadt, N.J. 07072. Price list available from
same address. Item 8 available from Commission on Science Edu-
cation, AAAS, 1515 Massachusetts Avenue, N.W., Washington,
D.C. 20005. ($5.50).

ADDITIONAL MATERIALS BEING DEVELOPED:
Not answered.

LANGUAGE IN WHICH MATERIALS:
1. Were originally written: English.
2. Have been or will be translated: Spanish for use in the schools
of Puerto Rico. German for use in an experimental program in
Gottingen.

COUNTRIES IN WHICH MATERIALS ARE USED:
United States and Canada.

PROJECT IMPLEMENTATION:
1. Total number of teachers using any of the materials: 70,000.
2. Total number of students using any of the materials: 2,000,000.
3. Total number of schools using any of the materials: Not possible to make a reasonable estimate.
4. The totals stated in 1 and 2 are estimated.
5. Name and location of selected schools where the program is in use: Des Moines Public Schools, Harold Rathert, Supervisor of Science; District of Columbia Public Schools, Mary Harbeck, Assistant Director, Science Department; Flint (Michigan) Community Schools, Hugo Pinti, Coordinator of Science Education; Lakewood (Ohio) Public Schools, Dora Dean, Coordinator, Elementary Science; New Albany–Floyd County (Indiana) Consolidated School Corporation, Glen Linnert, Science Coordinator; Philadelphia Public Schools, Margaret W. Efraemson, Head Start Follow Through Program; Shamokin (Pennsylvania) Area School District, Lyman Weaver, Principal, Washington School; Springfield (New Jersey), Roseanne Gillis, Science Supervisor; Tampa, (Florida), Guy T. Cacciatore, Supervisor of Elementary Science, Hillsborough County Public Schools; Tucson (Arizona) Public Schools, David T. Smith, Coordinator of Science.

TEACHER PREPARATION:
1. Consultant services available for teachers using the materials: Xerox Education Sciences, publisher and distributor of the program, provides consultants to schools purchasing Xerox materials. The Commission on Science Education has prepared a list of consultants, including persons who have worked in the development of the program or with in-service programs, that can be sent upon request.
2. Activities conducted for pre-service and in-service teacher training. During the past four or five summers, on their own initiative, at least thirty colleges and universities have offered pre-service and in-service teacher training in *Science—A Process Approach*. The Commission on Science Education itself does not conduct pre-service or in-service teacher training classes. It assists Xerox Education Sciences in its pre-service and in-service teacher training and colleges and universities upon request.
3. Available pre-service and/or in-service teaching materials for science educators to use in preparing teachers: Teacher training materials of *Science—A Process Approach* consist of *Commentary for Teachers*, planned as a self-instructional text for teachers of all levels of the program, and *Guide for In-service Instruction* which, as the name describes, is planned for use in in-service classes. Both of these teacher aids are developed in a form comparable to that of the exercises of *Science—A Process Approach*. The

Guide for In-service Instruction consists of twenty-one modules covering the processes of science and teaching strategies. *Commentary for Teachers* sells for $7.00 per copy and *Guide for In-service Instruction* sells for approximately the same price.

PROJECT EVALUATION:

1. Has the effectiveness of your materials been evaluated:
Yes, internally.

2. Published research studies:

(a) The principal in-house research with *Science—A Process Approach* was reported in *An Evaluation Model and Its Application*, 2d Ed., 1967. This report is now out of print but is available in libraries and science teaching centers.

(b) Ayers, Jerry B. and George E. Mason, "Differential Effects of *Science—A Process Aproach* Upon Change in Metropolitan Readiness Test Scores Among Kindergarten Children," *The Reading Teacher,* vol. 22, no. 5 (February 1969), pp. 435–39.

(c) Carter, Heather L., "A Study of the Ability of Primary School Children to Generalize Behavioral Competencies Acquired in Science to Other Content Settings," Ph.D. thesis, University of Maryland, 1969. Available from Xerox Microfilms.

(d) Day, David E. and Louise Y. George, "Effecting Change in Inner City Schools: Some Reflections," *Journal of Negro Education,* 39 (1970), pp. 4–13.

(e) Kolb, John R., "Effects of Relating Mathematics to Science Instruction on the Acquisition of Quantitative Science Behaviors," *Journal of Research in Science Teaching,* 5 (1968), pp. 174–182.

(f) Walbesser, H. H., and Heather L. Carter, "Acquisition of Elementary Science Behavior by Children of Disadvantaged Families," *Education Leadership,* vol. 25, no. 8 (May 1968), pp. 741–48.

(g) Walbesser, H. H. and Heather L. Carter, "The Effect on Test Results of Changes in Task and Responses Format Required by Altering the Test Administration from an Individual to a Group Form," *Journal of Research in Science Teaching,* no. 7 (1970), pp. 1–8.

3. Brief abstraction of in-house or unpublished research: In the tryout of *Science—A Process Approach* over a five-year period scores of children in kindergarten through grade 6 on competency measures on the exercises of the program were reported and analyzed. From these data one can conclude for the children in these studies that inner city children did as well as children from privileged classes, but that they did not complete as many exercises in any one year as children from privileged situations. Data also showed that children who had been in the program for one or two years scored consistently higher on competency

measures than those in the program for the first year. (For example, in a class of children working with Part C exercises, some children may have worked with Part A or Part B or both and some may not have had experience with either.) Data on teachers in the tryout did not show a relationship between success of children and number of college science courses in the teacher's preparation program.

4. Evaluative data available to interested individuals: Not answered.

PROJECT PUBLICITY:
1. Dennis, J. T., and C. C. Peterson, "Coping With Change, Science—A Process Approach" Science Activities (to be published).
2. Gagné, Robert M., "Elementary Science: A New Scheme of Instruction," *Science*, 151 (1966), pp. 49–53.
3. Gagné, Robert M., "Why the 'Process' Approach for a Modern Curriculum," *The EPIE Forum* (April–May, 1968), New York: The EPI Institute.
4. Kurtz, Edwin B., Jr., "Biology in Science—A Process Approach," *American Biology Teacher*, 29 (March 1967), pp. 192–196.
5. Livermore, Arthur H., "The Process Approach of the AAAS Commission on Science Education," *Journal of Research in Science Teaching*, 2 (1964), pp. 271–82.
6. Livermore, Arthur H., "Curriculum Research in Science," *Journal of Experimental Education*, 37 (1) (1968), pp. 49–55.
7. Livermore, Arthur H. and John R. Mayor, "Curriculum Change in Other Sciences," *Geotimes*, 13(3) (March 1968), pp. 21–25.
8. Mayor, John R., "Science and Mathematics: 1970s—A Decade of Change," *The Arithmetic Teacher*, 17 (April 1970), pp. 293–97.
9. Mayor, John R. and Arthur H. Livermore, "A Process Approach to Elementary School Science," *School Science and Mathematics* (May 1969), pp. 411–16
10. Rathert, Harold, "Science—A Process Approach in Des Moines Elementary Schools," *IAS Bulletin* (April 1970), pp. 24–26.

BRIEF SUMMARY OF PROJECT ACTIVITIES SINCE 1970 REPORT:
Part F of *Science—A Process Approach* and *Commentary for Teachers* were published by Xerox Education Sciences in 1970, Part G in 1971, and *Guide for In-service Instruction* in 1972. An experimental edition of *Science Process Instrument* was published by the Commission on Science Education in 1970. This instrument, a test to be administered to children individually, has not been fully validated and should be used for experimental rather than for diagnostic purposes. Xerox Education Sciences also produced the kits for Parts F and G and for *Guide for In-service Instruction*.

PLANS FOR THE FUTURE:
Work has been started on revision of *Science—A Process Approach* looking forward to the time in which the program goes into the public domain beginning in September, 1974.

Creative Aspects

A search of the literature published by the Commission does not indicate that this project is fundamentally concerned with the development of creative ability. In fact, many of the lessons produced thus far seem fairly structured. If a teacher were to follow them explicitly, there would be little chance for children to explore and test their own ideas. Each lesson has its stated objectives and teachers are directed to teach toward them. There has been an extensive evaluation of this curriculum, which involves testing children to see if they attained the behavioral objectives outlined by the Commission. The emphasis on achieving these objectives is outlined in a statement made in the Commission Newsletter as follows:

> Several writers took the opportunity to try to teach their new materials to the children and, with the help of experienced teachers, learned much about how to ask questions so that the children would eventually be induced to give the desired answer. Writers were admonished not to write "lead the children to . . ." unless they could tell the teacher how to do it.[4]

This quotation suggests the teacher is supposed to lead the students to make discoveries and attain the described objectives. Teachers already do this in many traditional lessons, but leading children should not be the primary emphasis in teaching, nor should it interfere with opportunities for creative expression. Leading creates a tendency for the teacher to race the children toward the behaviorial objectives of the lessons at the expense of stifling creative expression. *Science—A Process Approach* can be used by instructors in a creative manner provided they encourage creative enterprise. On the other hand, following the lessons as prescribed and teaching only for the defined objectives will contribute much less toward the manifestation of creativity.

4. "What Is Science—A Process Approach," *Commission on Science Education Newsletter,* vol. 2, no. 1 (October 1965), American Association for the Advancement of Science, Washington, D.C.

SCIENCE CURRICULUM IMPROVEMENT STUDY (SCIS)

PROJECT DIRECTOR:
Robert Karplus, Professor of Physics, Associate Director of The Lawrence Hall of Science, University of California, Berkeley.

PROJECT HEADQUARTERS:
1. Contact: Herbert D. Thier, Assistant Director, Science Curriculum Improvement Study, Lawrence Hall of Science, University of California, Berkeley, Calif. 94720. (415) 642-4541.
2. Special facilities or activities available for visitor viewing: Participants in the SCIS Implementation Program (see item R) meet with SCIS staff members and visit classrooms in the Berkeley schools.

PRINCIPAL PROFESSIONAL STAFF:
Robert Karplus, Director; Herbert D. Thier, Assistant Director; Chester A. Lawson, Director of Life Sciences; Diane Bramwell, Administrative Assistant and Senior Editor; James Eakin, Schools Coordinator; Jack Fishleder, Implementation Program Leader; Robert Knott, Biologist; Laurence Malone, Biologist; Marshall Montgomery, Coordinator, Equipment Development; George Moynihan, Project Coordinator; Rita W. Peterson, Evaluation Specialist; John Quick, Film Director; Suzanne Stewart, Newsletter Editor and Editorial Assistant; Anthony Calica, Art Director.

PROJECT SUPPORT
1. Funding agency: National Science Foundation.
2. Associated agencies: University of California, Berkeley.

PROJECT HISTORY:
1. Principal originator: Robert Karplus.
2. Date and place of initiation: 1962; University of California, Berkeley.
3. Evolution and development of the project: Since 1962, the project has maintained a full-time staff of physicists, biologists, psychologists, and teachers. The staff has developed ideas for units, tried out these ideas during exploratory teaching in Berkeley Trial Center Schools, produced preliminary edition units that were taught by regular classroom teachers, and revised them for final edition.
The procedures for developing and perfecting the SCIS Teacher Education Program are similar to those used in developing the elementary science program. Procedures and materials are proposed, subjected to criticism, and tried out in exploratory teaching. The materials and procedures will then undergo more extensive testing in districts using SCIS units.

The philosophical view of SCIS toward evaluation has always been best described in the introductory material to a unit. There, the idea is presented of on-going and continual teacher evaluation of the children. As the teacher stops traditional teaching and directs his attention toward observing and listening to the children, he will find the clues he needs to determine how much and how well they understand. When such evaluations need translation into tangible records, the teacher will find alternate forms of evaluation useful. SCIS has recently created a design for evaluation and evaluation supplements for *Interaction and Systems* and *Life Cycles* which have been published in trial edition. Documented evaluation, as provided in the new evaluation supplements, helps the teacher communicate his findings objectively to parents and administrators. Through documented evaluation, the teacher can systematically gather each student's reaction to a specific activity developed for the purpose of assessing a major objective of the unit. It also provides the teacher with criteria for identifying attainment of objectives, so he will not have to rely exclusively on his intuition to decide if a child has achieved a goal.

SCIS's long-term goal—scientific literacy—combines an understanding of both content and process-oriented concepts with a positive and inquiring attitude toward science. A single test score would belie the multifaceted nature of the program. Thus, the evaluation supplements identify three phases of a pupil's growth and assess them separately: attitudes in science, perception of the classroom environment, and concept–process objectives. Because of enormous differences among children, teachers, and community needs, a national standard seems completely irrelevant to science teaching. The program could guarantee certain minimum accomplishments only by completely violating the open-ended and exploratory nature of the SCIS program, depriving the teacher of the freedom to develop each child's capabilities and interests at his own level. The teacher is encouraged instead to identify the progress of each child throughout the year. With the evaluation, the teacher diagnoses the areas in which the child has weaknesses, provides further help according to his needs, and repeats the appraisal after he has had an opportunity to make progress. Objectives are evaluated several times because individual children may achieve desired levels of accomplishment at different stages during the teaching program.

PROJECT OBJECTIVES:

SCIS usually capsulizes its purposes as the development of scientific literacy. But it is important to delineate exactly what is meant by that term, and how the state hopes to achieve this goal. An important meaning of scientific literacy is sufficient knowledge and understanding of the fundamental concepts of both the biological and physical sciences for effective participation in twentieth century life. A second implication of scientific literacy is the development of a free and inquisitive attitude and the use of rational procedures for decision making. In the SCIS program, children learn science in an atmosphere of intellectual freedom, where their own ideas are respected, where they learn to test their ideas by experiment, and where they learn to accept or reject ideas, not on the basis of some authority, but on the basis of their own observations. Ideally, some of these experiences will carry over to other areas of life and allow children to make decisions on a more rational basis after weighing the factors or evidence involved more objectively. Each unit of the SCIS program presents activities which lead to the understanding of important scientific and process-oriented concepts. The sum of these concepts may be considered a sound base from which the scientifically literate person may seek answers to his questions.

UNIQUE CHARACTERISTICS OF THE PROJECT:
The SCIS program is designed for elementary school children in grades K through 6. The program has been successful with disadvantaged inner-city children in many of the country's urban centers, as well as with disadvanaged rural children in a compensatory education, language development project. In addition, Adapting Science Materials for the Blind is adapting SCIS materials for use with visually impaired children (see page 163).

SPECIFIC SUBJECTS, GRADE, AND AGE LEVELS:
Sequential physical and life science curriculum suggested for grades K–6.

METHODS OF INSTRUCTION USED IN THE PROJECT:
SCIS uses a materials-centered approach in which the elementary classroom actually becomes a laboratory. In their first explorations of a new concept, the children are allowed to manipulate or observe selected materials, sometimes freely in any way they wish and sometimes under the guidance of the teacher. As a result of these preliminary explorations, the children have a new experience—direct physical contact with natural phenomena. As the next step, the teacher introduces the scientific concept that describes or explains what the children have observed. This is called the invention lesson. Following the invention lesson, other experiences are provided that present further examples of the concept. These are called discovery lessons. Through this procedure, the child is expected to recognize that the new concept has applications to situations other than the initial example. In other words, the discovery experiences reinforce, refine, and enlarge upon the concept.

PRESENT COMMERCIAL AFFILIATIONS:
Rand McNally & Company, P.O. Box 7600, Chicago, Ill. 60680.

MATERIALS PRODUCED:
1. The first year. The first-year units are *Material Objects* and *Organisms*. These units have certain common objectives to sharpen children's powers of observation, discrimination, and accurate description.

> (a) *Material Objects*. Common objects and special materials provided in the kit are described by their properties: color, shape, texture, hardness, and weight. Children study these as they observe, manipulate, compare, and even change the form or appearance of objects. All the activities stimulate language development because each child acquires experiences about which he is eager to talk. At the same time, these concepts basic to the science program are introduced and used repeatedly: object, property, material, serial ordering, change, evidence.

> (b) *Organisms*. Children become familiar with some of the requirements of life as they set out seeds and watch the growth of plants. This experience is extended when the class builds aquaria with water plants, fish, and snails. Three natural events occurring in the aquaria are observed and discussed: birth of guppies and appearance of snail eggs; growth of guppies and snails; and death of organisms. When they explore the school yard, nearby park, or nature area, children discover plants and animals living outside the classroom. They are led to the concept of habitat as they compare these land organisms with those living in the aquaria.

2. The second year. The second-year SCIS units are *Interaction and Systems* and *Life Cycles*. In both the theme is change, observed either as evidence of interaction or by the development of an animal or plant. Both units require children to add the mental process of interpreting evidence to the observational skills they developed in the first year.

> (a) *Interaction and Systems*. The central concept of the entire SCIS program, interaction, is introduced in this unit. The children's work with objects and organisms in the first year has given them the background necessary for understanding the interaction relationship. Concepts are developed in the unit, as are the children's skills in: 1) manipulating experimental equipment, 2) reporting observations, and 3) recording observations during experiments. The student manual plays a key role in developing the children's recording skill and assists in introducing them to these major concepts: system, interaction, evidence of interaction, interaction-at-a-distance.

> (b) *Life Cycles*. The investigation of ecosystems begun in

Organisms is continued in *Life Cycles*. The unit, however, focuses on individual organisms, which alone show the characteristics of the phenomenon we call "life." For the time being, the interrelationships and interdependencies within the ecosystem are given secondary importance. Seeds are planted and their germination observed. Plants are cared for until they reach maturity, produce flowers, and form a new generation of seeds. Fruit flies, frogs, and mealworms are observed as they develop through the stages of their life cycles. As one gener-

FIGURE 6-3. *How could you involve children creatively in learning about their ecosystems? (Photo by Lee Youngblood)*

ation of organisms produces another, children are led to consider biotic potential and the effects of reproduction and death on a population. Each experience with living organisms helps increase the children's awareness of the differences between living and nonliving objects.

3. The third year. The children observe and experiment with phenomena of increasing complexity as they build on the first two years of the SCIS program and move toward an understanding of energy, matter, and ecosystems.

(a) *Subsystems and Variables.* The subsystems concept is introduced to give the children a grouping of objects intermediate between a single object and an entire system. Subsystems may be the grains of sand in a mixture of sand, salt, and baking soda, the salt in a salt solution, or the arm and rivets in a whirlybird system. This concept helps the children as they investigate these and other systems.

(b) *Populations.* The children's attention is directed toward populations of organisms rather than to individual plants and animals. They observe the growth, eventual leveling off, and decline of isolated populations. They relate increase in population numbers to reproduction, and population decline to death. The children's experiences with aquaria and terraria continue the study of ecology begun in *Organisms* and *Life Cycles.* They serve as background for the introduction of these important biological concepts: population, food chain, food web, and community.

4. The fourth year. The investigations of the fourth year make use of the measurement skills and scientific background developed in the first three years.

(a) *Relative Position and Motion.* Faced with the problems of describing the position and motion of objects in their environment, children become aware that they use reference objects to do so. The *Relative Position and Motion* unit introduces into the SCIS program activities dealing specifically with spatial relationships. It also enhances the children's abilities to think critically, interpret evidence, and work independently, which are broad process objectives of the entire SCIS program.

(b) *Environments.* The children design and build terraria at the beginning of the unit to contain several different plants and animals. Because the environmental requirements of the organisms vary, the growth and survival of the organisms differ widely among the containers. These differences can be correlated with variations in environmental factors, such as temperature, amount of water, and intensity of light. The term environment is introduced as the combination of all the environmental factors affecting an organism.

5. The fifth year. The conceptual development of the SCIS program continues with the introduction of energy transfer. In

the physical science unit, *Energy Sources*, energy transfer takes place between interacting physical systems; in the life science unit, *Communities*, the energy that is transferred from plant, to plant eater, to animal eater in the food chain is considered. In these units the interactions of objects and of organisms are investigated from a more comprehensive point of view, in which their dynamic interdependence is taken into account.

(a) *Energy Sources*. The children continue their study of matter and energy and also extend their skill in conducting scientific investigations. Their attention is focused on the energy transfers that accompany the interaction of material in solid, liquid, and gaseous forms. The children experiment with warm and cold water, stopper poppers, rolling spheres colliding with movable targets, melting ice, dissolving sodium thiosulfate, and dissolving magnesium sulfate. Although the principle of conservation of energy is not stated, the children's qualitative descriptions of energy transfer from a source to a receiver prepare them for later quantitative investigations of energy exchange.

(b) *Communities*. The children investigate the food relations within a community of plants and animals. They first experiment with germinating plants and discover that food stored in cotyledons supports the early development of the seedling. After the cotyledons are consumed, the children discover that green plants support their growth through photosynthesis. They observe the feeding behavior of animals in terraria containing various plants and animals, and identify the food chains. The children infer from their experiments and observations that photosynthesis in green plants not only supplies food for the plants but indirectly also for the animals in the community.

6. The sixth year. The last year of the SCIS program represents both a climax and a new beginning. The study of ecosystems in the life science sequence integrates all the preceding units in both physical and life sciences as the children investigate the exchange of matter and energy between organisms and their environment. The physical science unit, *Models: Electric and Magnetic Interactions*, introduces the concept of the scientific model, and thereby opens a new level of data interpretation and hypothesis making.

(a) *Ecosystems*. Children investigate evidence of the water cycle, oxygen–carbon dioxide cycle, and food–mineral cycle and discover the importance of these cycles in the maintenance of life. When the children understand the concept of a community interacting with its environment, the term ecosystem acquires its full meaning. Experiments in which aspects of the cycles are altered leads to the definition of pollution: a sequence of changes in which the normal functioning of the ecological cycles is disrupted.

(b) *Models: Electric and Magnetic Interactions*. Activities are directed toward increasing the children's understanding of electrical and magnetic phenomena both at the level of concrete experiences and at the level of abstract thought. The principal device to accomplish the latter is the concept of the scientific model, which is introduced early in the unit and applied in all later parts.

MATERIALS AVAILABLE FREE:
The SCIS Newsletter is published quarterly. When other free materials are available from the project, they are announced in the current issue of the Newsletter.

MATERIALS PURCHASABLE:
1. SCIS units. A SCIS equipment kit is developed for each unit in the program. These include materials to teach a class of thirty-two children, a teacher's guide, and student manuals. For life science units, order forms are also included to obtain organisms when they are needed. Write to Rand McNally & Company, Customer Service Department, P.O. Box 7600, Chicago, Ill. 60680, for information on the availability and price of kits. See section L for a list of the units.
2. Individual guides and manuals. SCIS teacher's guides and student manuals may be purchased individually from SCIS. The purchase prices of these materials are listed in each issue of the SCIS Newsletter.
3. Films. As of February 1972, twelve films are available showing SCIS in the classroom. The films may be rented from the Extension Media Center, 2223 Fulton Street, Berkeley, Calif. 94720. They may be purchased from SCIS. A booklet describing each of the films is available from SCIS.

ADDITIONAL MATERIALS BEING DEVELOPED:
1. SCIS sourcebooks. A sourcebook is being developed which will contain original papers on the theoretical, historical, and psychological foundations of the SCIS program. A number of original papers providing background information in areas of science and education closely related to the SCIS program are being prepared. A trial edition of the primary level *SCIS Elementary Science Sourcebook* has been published and used since the spring of 1968. An upper-grade trial sourcebook is now being prepared. It is planned that a single SCIS sourcebook will be produced as a result of combining and modifying both of these trial editions.
2. Special Education. The Lawrence Hall of Science, in conjunction with the Alameda County Schools and the California School for the Blind, has received a Title III grant to develop a curriculum program in science based on SCIS for visually impaired children. The project, under the direction of Herbert D. Thier, SCIS Assistant Director, is titled Adapting Science Materials

for the Blind. *Material Objects, Organisms, Interaction and Systems, Life Cycles, Subsystems and Variables, Communities,* and *Energy Sources* have been adapted to the needs of the visually impaired, and trial teaching of other SCIS units is underway. Materials are developed to be used in three types of organized educational programs: special classes, such as California School for the Blind; resource rooms in public schools where there are clusters of several visually impaired children; and classes where a single blind child is taught with sighted children. It is expected that the program will eventually affect science teaching of visually impaired children throughout the country. Experience with these adaptations during the next few years should be valuable for any future efforts of adapting the SCIS program to other areas of special education.

LANGUAGE IN WHICH MATERIALS:
1. Were originally written: English.
2. Have been or will be translated: The Institut de Recherches Psychologiques, Inc., Montreal, Quebec, Canada, has translated SCIS materials into French. Experimental translations are being designed in Israel, Japan, Denmark, Sweden, Taiwan, Chile, and other countries.

COUNTRIES IN WHICH MATERIALS ARE USED:
United States.

PROJECT IMPLEMENTATION:
The materials produced by SCIS are being used by schools in practically every part of the country. Some school districts are in the initial pilot phase, using the materials with a selected segment of the district's schools in order to observe and evaluate the effectiveness of this approach to science education. Many others are following through on a planned implementation program. The materials are being effectively used in urban, suburban, and rural districts throughout the United States. If additional information with regard to specific districts using this material is wanted contact Paul Lindquist, Rand McNally & Company, P.O. Box 7600, Chicago, Ill. 60680. It is estimated that the number of children using SCIS, based on kit sales of preliminary and final editions, is approximately 800,000.

TEACHER PREPARATION:
1. Consultant services available for teachers using the materials: SCIS Awareness Conferences. Rand McNally & Company is maintaining consultant services for all districts interested in the SCIS program. Arrangements can be made for such conferences through local Rand McNally representatives. In addition, those districts implementing the SCIS program can make arrangements with Rand McNally for on-going consultant services for teacher education.

2. Activities conducted for pre-service and in-service teacher training:

(a) Implementation Program. SCIS began an Implementation Program in the fall of 1967. During the school year, university science educators, school district supervisors, and other key people in education visit the project from one to two weeks and become familiar with the philosophy, methods, and materials of the Science Curriculum Improvement Study. After completion of his study–visit, the science educator will be able to act as consultant to various communities as they plan and set up new science programs and develop teacher education programs. During any one week, from two to four educators are involved in this program. As of February 1972, about 420 science educators had participated in this individualized leadership program. The Study maintains the services of the Implementation Program leader, as well as other staff consultants, to assist districts in their problems in helping teachers implement the SCIS program.

(b) CCSS Workshops. The National Science Foundation through its Cooperative College–School Science (CCSS) program, assists school systems in the training of teachers in a new science program like SCIS with the school district making a commitment of supplying the actual materials to be used by the children. In 1972, there were twenty-seven such SCIS–CCSS workshops funded by NSF. These projects are located in Tempe, Ariz.; Fullerton, Calif.; Rohnert Park, Calif.; Irvine, Calif.; Colorado Springs, Colo.; Washington, D.C.; Honolulu, Hawaii; Terre Haute, Ind.; Gambling, La.; Baltimore, Md.; Westfield, Mass.; Detroit, Mich.; Lorman, Miss.; Hattiesburg, Miss.; Havre, Mont.; Hempstead, L.I., N.Y.; Jericho, N.Y.; Greenville, N.C.; Oxford, Ohio; Clarion, Pa.; Philadelphia, Pa.; Cedar City, Utah; Blacksburg, Va.; Tacoma, Wash.; Pullman, Wash.; Madison, Wis.; Stevens Point, Wis.

(c) Resource Personnel Workshops. Summer Resource Personnel Workshops in SCIS have been sponsored by the National Science Foundation since 1967. During the summer of 1972, leadership people in science education were trained in SCIS at University of Colorado, Denver, Colo.; Western Kentucky University, Bowling Green, Ky.; Michigan State University, East Lansing, Mich.; and Temple University, Philadelphia, Pa. A conference that will include SCIS along with other curricula will be held at Southern Utah State College, Cedar City, Utah. Science and science education professors, science supervisors, and administrators who receive this special training will become active teacher–education specialists and implementers of the SCIS program.

(d) Conferences for Administrators. NSF has also funded ten Conferences on Science Course Materials for Administrators and Others Interested in School Curricula for 1972. These were held at University of California, Berkeley; University of Colorado, Boulder, Colo.; University of Southern Florida, Tampa, Fla.; Purdue University, Lafayette, Ind.; University of Iowa, Iowa City, Iowa; University of Southern Mississippi, Hattiesburg, Miss.; Eastern Montana College, Billings, Mont.; Portland State University, Portland, Oreg.; Memphis State University, Memphis, Tenn.; University of Virginia, Charlottesville, Va.

3. Available pre-service and/or in-service teaching materials for science educators to use in preparing teachers: videotape program. The SCIS Videotape Project, carried out with the Associated Colleges of the Midwest, is housed at Carleton College, Northfield, Minn. Tapes of SCIS in public schools are available for use in teacher preparation by interested school districts and colleges.

PROJECT EVALUATION:

1. Has the effectiveness of your materials been evaluated: Not answered.

2. Published research studies: Bruce, Larry R., "A Study of the Relation Between the SCIS Teacher's Attitude Toward the Teacher–Student Relationship and Question Types," *Journal of Research in Science Teaching*, vol. 8, no. 2, pp. 157–164.

3. Brief abstract of in-house or unpublished research; Supervised field tests of the first two evaluation supplements are currently underway in school systems in nine different states. The emphasis in this intensive field test is on the supplements themselves, their design and usefulness in the classroom as a valuable adjunct to the teaching program. The result of the field tests will provide the input for the revisions necessary in the two published supplements, and information obtained will also be used in the design and production of supplements for other units.

4. Evaluative data available to interested individuals: Not answered.

PROJECT PUBLICITY:

1. Berger, Carl and Robert Karplus, "Models for Electric and Magnetic Interactions," *Science and Children*, vol. 6, no. 1 (February 1968), pp. 43–49.

2. Conard, David and Herbert D. Thier, "The Life Sciences—A Short Course for Teachers," *The Instructor*, vol. 78 (January 1969), pp. 63–68.

3. Fishleder, Jack, "The Science Curriculum Improvement Study (SCIS)," *Science for Society—Education Review*, vol. 1, no. 3 (September 1971), pp. 5–6.

4. Karplus, Robert and Herbert D. Thier, "The Science Curriculum Improvement Study," *The Instructor*, vol. 74 (January 1965), pp. 43–84.

5. Karplus, Robert and Herbert D. Thier, *A New Look at Elementary School Science* (Chicago: Rand McNally & Company, 1967).
6. Lawson, Chester A., "The Life Science Program of the Science Curriculum Improvement Study," *The American Biology Teacher*, vol. 29, no. 3 (March 1967), pp. 185–190.
7. Lawson, Chester A., "Ecology and Children," *The American Biology Teacher*, vol. 35, no. 1 (January 1971), pp. 22–25.
8. Rowe, Mary Budd, "Science, Silence and Sanctions," *Science and Children*, vol. 6, no. 6 (March 1969), pp. 11–13.
9. Thomson, Barbara S. and Alan M. Voelker, "Programs for Improving Science in the Elementary Schools—Part II, SCIS," *Science and Children*, vol. 7, no. 8 (May 1970), pp. 29–37.

BRIEF SUMMARY OF PROJECT ACTIVITIES
SINCE 1970 REPORT:
SCIS has continued with the publication of the program in final edition and, as of the summer of 1972, all units will have been published in final edition. The SCIS Evaluation Program has been developing evaluation supplements to be used by classroom teachers (see item T).

PLANS FOR THE FUTURE:
All grade levels of the physical and life science programs will have been published in final edition by the summer of 1972. In addition to the twelve main units of the program (see item L), optional units may be developed to further the use of the program in individualized classrooms and a kindergarten program may be published. A final edition of the *SCIS Elementary Science Sourcebook*, combining material in the trial edition of the primary grade sourcebook and that of the upper-grade sourcebook now being prepared, is planned. Other aspects of the Teacher Education Program will be receiving special attention in the final phases of the project. Continued emphasis will be placed on the development of SCIS evaluation techniques.

Creative Aspects

The refinement of units through testing and tryout, concomitant with teacher training workshops over a ten-year span has added a dimension of greater flexibility to the program which could elicit creative development. Within the parameters of structure, process-oriented concepts are stressed, exploratory teaching encouraged, and open-ended activities developed. The opportunity for creative response becomes apparent when children observe or manipulate selected material freely and when "invention lessons" give way to "discovery lessons." A creative teacher could modify the units towards a creative frame of reference and generate creative growth in children.

ADAPTING SCIENCE MATERIALS FOR THE BLIND (ASMB)

PROJECT DIRECTOR:
Dr. Herbert D. Thier, Research Educator, Lawrence Hall of Science, University of California, Berkeley, Calif. 94720. (415) 642-4541.
Dr. Robert Knott, Assistant Professor, Biology Department, State University of New York, Stonybrook, L.I., N.Y.

PROJECT HEADQUARTERS:
1. Contact: Dr. Herbert Thier.
2. Special facilities or activities available for visitor viewing: Adapted materials, general information, research findings.

PRINCIPAL PROFESSIONAL STAFF:
Dr. Robert Knott, Assistant Director; Dr. Marcia Linn, Evaluation; Mr. Marshall Montgomery, Equipment Design; Mrs. Christina Kageyama, Teacher; Mr. Ross Huckins, Teacher; Mrs. Judy Olsen, Secretary.

PROJECT SUPPORT:
1. Funding agencies: Title III ESEA, State of California.
2. Associated agencies: Alameda County Public Schools, Lawrence Hall of Science; California School for the Blind.

PROJECT HISTORY:
1. Principal originator: Dr. Herbert D. Thier, Assistant Director, Science Curriculum Improvement Study; Dr. Everett Wilcox, Superintendent, California State School for the Blind; Dr. Daniel Johnson, Alameda County School District.
2. Date and place of initiation: August 1969; Lawrence Hall of Science, University of California, Berkeley; California State School for the Blind, Berkeley.
3. Evolution and development of the project: Interest by the California School for the Blind staff in the SCIS materials lead to the formulation of a plan to adapt the SCIS materials to the needs of blind and partially sighted children.

PROJECT OBJECTIVES:
1. Overall project purpose: A science curriculum is being designed for blind and partially sighted elementary school children by adapting the materials of the Science Curriculum Improvement Study. Field trials and evaluative studies are under way at the

California State School for the Blind, Berkeley; Proctor Elementary School, Castro Valley; and the Francis Blend Elementary School, Los Angeles.
2. Specific objectives:
   (a) To adapt and field test the teacher's guides, student manuals, and equipment kits of the Science Curriculum Improvement Study so as to make them useful and meaningful for blind and partially sighted children.
   (b) To design, develop, and field test necessary new equipment to enable blind children to have laboratory experiences in science.
   (c) To design an evaluation program which helps measure the learning of blind children in a laboratory-centered science program.

UNIQUE CHARACTERISTICS OF THE PROJECT:
The project is intended to provide blind and partially sighted children with laboratory-centered experiences in science. The adaptations are intended to allow the child to participate in the regular classroom situation. The materials are also useful in the special class for blind children.

SPECIFIC SUBJECTS, GRADE, AGE AND ABILITY LEVELS:
Life and physical science for blind and partially sighted elementary school pupils. Also useful in nongraded school situations for blind and partially sighted children.

MAIN METHODS OF INSTRUCTION USED
IN THE PROJECT:
Independent study, laboratory investigations, discussion sessions, and field experiences.

PRESENT COMMERCIAL AFFILIATIONS:
Adapting Science Materials for the Blind is an adaptation of the work of the Science Curriculum Improvement Study. The materials of the Science Curriculum Improvement Study are distributed by the Rand McNally & Co., Chicago, Ill. Current plans do not include the commercial production of the adapted materials. Prototypes will be available through the project.

DESCRIPTION OF MATERIALS ALREADY PRODUCED:
1. *Material Objects* Teacher's Guide Adaptations.
2. *Material Objects* Equipment Kit Adaptations.
3. *Organisms* Teacher's Guide Adaptations.
4. *Organisms* Equipment Kit Adaptations.
5. *Interaction and Systems* Teacher's Guide Adaptations.
6. *Interaction and Systems* Student Manual (braille).
7. *Interaction and Systems* Equipment Kit Adaptations.
8. *Life Cycles* Teacher's Guide Adaptations.
9. *Life Cycles* Equipment Kit Adaptations.

10. *Subsystems and Variables* Teacher's Guide Adaptations.
11. *Subsystems and Variables* Student Manual (braille).
12. *Subsystems and Variables* Student Manual (large print).
13. *Subsystems and Variables* Equipment Kit Adaptations.
14. *Environments* Teacher's Guide Adaptations.
15. *Environments* Student Manual (braille).
16. *Environments* Student Manual (large print).
17. *Environments* Equipment Kit Adaptations.
18. *Energy Sources* Teacher's Guide Adaptations.
19. *Energy Sources* Equipment Kit Adaptations.
20. *Energy Sources* Student Manual (braille).
21. *Energy Sources* Student Manual (large print).
22. *Communities* Teacher's Guide Adaptations.
23. *Communities* Student Manual (braille).
24. *Communities* Equipment Kit Adaptations.
25. *Communities* Student Manual (large print).
26. "Laboratory Science for Visually Handicapped Elementary School Children." Reprint from *New Outlook for the Blind*.

MATERIALS AVAILABLE FREE:
Item 26.

MATERIALS PURCHASABLE:
Contact project headquarters for current availability and cost of materials developed.

ADDITIONAL MATERIALS BEING DEVELOPED:
1. *Populations* Teacher's Guide and Equipment Kit Adaptations.
2. *Relative Position and Motion* Teacher's Guide, Student Manual, and Equipment Kit Adaptations.
3. *Models: Electric and Magnetic Interactions* Teacher's Guide, Student Manual, and Equipment Kit Adaptations.
4. *Ecosystems* Teacher's Guide, Student Manual, and Equipment Kit Adaptations.

LANGUAGE IN WHICH MATERIALS:
1. Were originally written: English.
2. Have been or will be translated: Not answered.

COUNTRIES IN WHICH MATERIALS ARE USED:
United States.

PROJECT IMPLEMENTATION:
Field trials and evaluative studies are underway. For the name and location of selected schools where the program is in use, see SCIS listing.

TEACHER PREPARATION:
Not answered.

PROJECT EVALUATION:
1. Has the effectiveness of materials been evaluated: Yes, internally.
2. Pertinent published research studies: "Effective Adaptation of an Experimental Science Curriculum for the Visually Impaired" by Marcia Linn, Ph.D. Submitted to *Exceptional Children*.
3. Brief abstract of in-house or unpublished research: Adapting existing curricula is an efficient way to provide up-to-date materials for special learners. Also, adaptations permit the integration of certain children, such as the visually impaired, into regular classes. Adaptation and evaluation of a materials-centered experiential curriculum for visually impaired children is described. Classroom trials of two of the adapted units revealed that visually impaired students made significant gains in understanding both content and process objectives of the units.
4. Evaluative data available to interested individuals: Contact Dr. Marcia Linn, Evaluator, ASMB, Lawrence Hall of Science, University of California, Berkeley, Calif. 94720.

PROJECT PUBLICITY:
1. Linn, Marcia, "Effective Adaptation of an Experimental Science Curriculum for the Visually Impaired," *Exceptional Children* (in process).
2. Thier, Herbert D., "Laboratory Science for Visually Handicapped Elementary School Children," *The New Outlook* (June 1971), pp. 190–194.
3. "Adapting Science Materials for the Blind," *SCIS Newsletter*, no. 20 (Spring 1971), pp. 4–5.
4. "Lab Science for Visually Handicapped Children," Lawrence Hall of Science Kaleidoscope (January–February 1972).

BRIEF SUMMARY OF PROJECT ACTIVITIES SINCE 1970 REPORT:
A new project.

PLANS FOR THE FUTURE:
Not answered.

Creative Aspects

What has been said of the previous curriculum projects is also true of this one. The use of these units will not insure the attainment of creative objectives unless the teachers explicitly teach for them; however, adapting science materials for the blind has been a creative adventure for both pupil and teacher. Much experimentation involves structure vs. spontaneity.

MINNESOTA MATHEMATICS AND SCIENCE TEACHING PROJECT (MINNEMAST)

PROJECT DIRECTOR:
James H. Werntz, Jr., Professor of Physics, Director, Center for Educational Development, University of Minnesota, Minneapolis, Minn. 55455. (612) 373-4537.

PROJECT HEADQUARTERS:
1. Contact: Minnemath Center, University of Minnesota, 720 Washington Avenue, S.E., Mineapolis, Minn. 55455.
2. Special facilities or activities available for visitor viewing: None.

PRINCIPAL PROFESSIONAL STAFF:
M. R. Boudrye, Research Associate, Administrator.

PROJECT SUPPORT:
1. Funding agencies: University of Minnesota.
2. Associated agencies: Formerly funded by the National Science Foundation.

PROJECT HISTORY:
1. Principal originator: Paul C. Rosenbloom, Professor of Mathematics.
2. Date and place of initiation: 1961; University of Minnesota.
3. Project terminated: September, 1970.

PROJECT OBJECTIVES:
1. Overall project purpose: To produce coordinated mathematics and science curriculum for grades K–6.
2. Specific objectives: To develop process acquisition, attitudinal changes, and scientific literacy.

UNIQUE CHARACTERISTICS OF THE PROJECT:
Broad spectrum of elementary school children of varying capacities and backgrounds.

SPECIFIC SUBJECTS, GRADE, AGE AND ABILITY LEVELS:
Coordinated mathematics and science, grades K–3; college level, teacher preparatory.

MAIN METHODS OF INSTRUCTION
USED IN THE PROJECT:
Independent study, laboratory investigations, seminars, and discussion sessions.

PRESENT COMMERCIAL AFFILIATIONS:
Textbook in mathematics: *Ideas in Mathematics* (Philadelphia: W. B. Saunders Co., 1970).

FIGURE 6-4. *A grid is a useful mathematical tool to illustrate geographical distances in the study of animal migration. (SCIS Photo)*

DESCRIPTION OF MATERIALS ALREADY PRODUCED:
1. Minnemath Reports (terminated 1969).
2. Coordinated units: 1–29 for grades K–3.
3. Overview.
4. Living Things in Field and Classroom.
5. Extending Man's Senses.
6. Ideas in Mathematics.
7. Questions and Answers about Minnemast.

MATERIALS AVAILABLE FREE:
Item 7 only. Please address the project headquarters.

MATERIALS PURCHASABLE:
Items 2–5, information available by writing project headquarters.
Item 6 from W. B. Saunders Co., Philadelphia, Pa.

ADDITIONAL MATERIALS BEING DEVELOPED:
Pre-service and in-service teacher aids.

LANGUAGE IN WHICH MATERIALS:
1. Were originally written: English.
2. Have been or will be translated: None.

COUNTRIES IN WHICH MATERIALS ARE USED:
United States and Canada.

PROJECT IMPLEMENTATION:
1. Total number of teachers using any of the materials: 200.
2. Total number of students using any of the materials: 5,000+.
3. Total number of schools using any of the materials: 125.
4. Number of teachers who have adopted the entire program: 20 school systems.
5. Number of students involved: 6,000.
6. Number of schools involved: 125.
7. The total stated in 1, 2, 3, 5, and 6 are estimated.
8. Name and location of selected schools where this program is in use: St. Paul, Minn.; West St. Paul, Minn.; South Hadley, Mass.; Pittsfield, Mass.; Newton, N.J.; Quincy, Mass.; Redlands, Calif.

TEACHER PREPARATION:
1. Consultant services available for teachers using the materials: Write to the Center at address in C–1.
2. Activities conducted for pre-service and in-service teacher training: Summer workshops, supported by National Science Foundation, in various areas. Information available from NSF, Student and Curriculum Improvement Section, Washington, D.C. 20550.
3. Available pre-service and/or in-service teaching materials for science educators to use in preparing teachers: Pre-service and in-service materials were planned, and some early development completed. No funds have been available for completing these materials and early phases are no longer available for distribution.

PROJECT EVALUATION:
1. Has the effectiveness of the materials been evaluated: Yes, internally.
2. Published research studies:
   (a) Hively, W., H. Patterson, and Sara H. Page, "A Universe-Defined System of Arithmetic Achievement Tests," *Journal of Educational Measurement*, vol. 5, no. 4 (Winter 1968), p. 275.
   (b) Johnson, P. E., "On the Communication of Concepts in Science," *Journal of Educational Psychology*, vol. 60 (1969), pp. 32–40.
   (c) Murray, F., "Reversibility Training in the Acquisition of Length Conservation," *Journal of Educational Psychology*, vol. 59, no. 2 (1968), pp. 82–87.
   (d) Murray, F., "Operational Conservation of Illusion-Distorted Length," *British Journal of Educational Psychology*, vol. 38, part 2 (June 1968), pp. 189–193.
3. Brief abstract of in-house or unpublished research:
   (a) Reports on the direct evaluation of most of the K–3 units have been completed. These reports contain a detailed

description of the test domain for the unit and a summary of the results obtained during the field test of the unit.

(b) *The MINNEMAST Experiment with Domain Referenced Achievement Testing Systems.* A detailed description of the evaluation procedures used in the MINNEMAST evaluation project.

(c) *A Curriculum Evaluation and Revision Based on Domain Referenced Achievement Test System.* This paper describes how an individual unit (Unit 2) was evaluated and revised based upon the results of that evaluation. It also presents the results of a subsequent evaluation.

(d) *The Use of Sample Test Items as Objectives for Instruction—The Effects Upon the Teacher and Upon the Learner.* This paper describes a study in which six kindergarten teachers were provided with sample test items for a MINNE-MAST unit while a matched sample of six other teachers were provided with the unit only. The study sheds some light on the role of objectives in instruction.

(e) *Future Uses of Domain Referenced Achievement Testing Systems.* This paper outlines some of the potential uses for Domain Referenced Achievement Testing Systems. It also points to some of the pitfalls in those applications.

(f) *An Introduction to Domain Referenced Achievement Testing.* An overview of the psychological basis for the evaluation model utilized in the MINNEMAST project. The paper also includes a glossary of terms as utilized in the testing model.

(g) *The Experimental Analysis of Educational Objectives.* Ph.D. Thesis, University of Minnesota, George Rabehl. The paper represents the philosophical and scientific rationale for casting the formulation of educational objectives into an experimental context. It shows that the specification of relevant and irrelevant conditions is not a once-and-for-all activity but requires instead a continuing self-corrective process involving the steps of hypothesis, application, analysis, and a reformulation of educational intent. What is achieved is a framework for analyzing, describing, and comparing curricular materials; for making inferences from student performances beyond a finite set of items; and finally a basis for proposing and interpreting psychological studies in terms of the actual characteristics of educational requirements.

(h) *A Comparison of Two Conceptual Frameworks for Teaching the Basic Concepts of Rational Numbers.* Ph.D. Thesis, University of Minnesota, Donald Sension. This paper compares the effects of two physical models for teaching fraction concepts on student performance. It utilizes a Domain Reference Achievement Testing System.

(i) *An Investigation of the Effectiveness of Independent Study of Novel Mathematics Material in the Elementary School.* Ph.D. Thesis, University of Minnesota, Lester Becklund. The paper presents the results of a study which examined the role of the teacher in presenting some novel mathematics. A MINNE-MAST game unit on vectors and transformations was used.

(j) *Arithmetic Achievement Test Performance of MINNE-MAST Mathematics Pupils in the Third and Fourth Grades.* This paper presents a summary of the results of a two-year study of the performance of pupils in the MINNEMAST mathematics program on selected arithmetic achievement tests.

(k) *The Relationship Between Concepts of Conservation of Length and Number.* The purpose of this study was to describe the relationship between attainment of concepts of conservation of length and number. The concepts were embodied in a compound number–length task. Two aspects of performance were investigated: 1) the comparative performance of solvers and nonsolvers on conservation of number and conservation of length, and 2) the stability of performance characteristics across the age span sampled. Fifty-five children, 21 females and 34 males, ages 6 through 9 years, participated in the study.

PROJECT PUBLICITY:

1. Ahrens, R. B., "MINNEMAST—The Coordinated Science and Mathematics Program," *Science and Children,* vol. 65 (December 1965), pp. 811–814.
2. Bray, Edmund C., "MINNEMAST, An Elementary Math–Science Program," *School Science and Mathematics* (June 1969).
3. Bray, Edmund C., ('The MINNEMAST Elementary Mathematics–Science Program," *The Physics Teacher* (May 1968).
4. Maxwell, Graham, "Some Notes and Comments on the Minnesota Mathematics and Science Teaching Project," *The Australian Mathematics Teacher* (March 1969).
5. Rising, Gerald R., "Research and Development in Mathematics and Science Education at the Minnesota School Mathematics and Science Center and the Minnesota National Laboratory," *School Science and Mathematics,* vol. 65 (December 1965), pp. 811–814.
6. Rosenbloom, P. C., *Journal of Research in Science Teaching* (1963), pp. 276–280.
7. Subarsky, Zachariah, "Curriculum Construction for K–6 Science and Math—a Strategy," *Science and Children* (November 1968).
8. Subarsky, Zachariah, "The Systems Concept in Science," *The Instructor* (January 1968).
9. Victor, Laurence, "Systems: An Organizing Principle for Science Curricula," *Science and Children* (January–February 1968), pp. 17–20.
10. Werntz, James H., "A Style of Understanding," *Nature and Science,* vol. 4, no. 12 (March 13, 1967).

BRIEF SUMMARY OF PROJECT ACTIVITIES
SINCE 1970 REPORT:
Preparation for sale of printed materials and laboratory kits.

PLANS FOR THE FUTURE:
Continued availability of materials. Write to the Center.

Creative Aspects

The project has made more significant progress with the development of mathematics than it has with science materials. It is difficult now to make any thorough evaluation of the program. The materials produced thus far are inquiry-oriented and if taught from the viewpoint of developing creative endeavor would undoubtedly contribute to this objective. The project, particularly in the mathematical units, borrows extensively from the work of Dr. Jean Piaget, the Swiss psychologist who has done so much to reveal the emergence of intelligence and cognitive abilities as a child progresses to maturity. MINNEMAST has on the staff Dr. Lydia Muller-Willis, who was trained under Dr. Piaget at the Institut des Sciences de L'Education in Geneva, Switzerland. She undoubtedly had a major influence in giving the project its psychological foundation and direction.

THE ELEMENTARY SCIENCE PROJECT (ESP) (HOWARD UNIVERSITY)

This project has tried to provide science experiences for disadvantaged children K–6 and their parents. The purpose of such a program is to help to overcome social and personal handicaps. Units completed are *Air Has Pressure, Air and Water, Changing Air Pressure, Gravity Flow System, Heat, How Seeds Become Plants, Metals, Mirrors, Pressure, Static Electricity, Space Materials, Sound, Surface Tension, Taste, The Magnifying Glass, The Suction Cup*, and *Magnets*.

Creative Aspects

This project has not been expressly written for the development of creative objectives. With proper direction it could contribute to the development of creative potential for the disadvantaged and may provide creative outlets that can contribute particularly to this group's mental health.

CONCEPTUALLY ORIENTED PROGRAM IN
ELEMENTARY SCIENCE (COPES)

PROJECT DIRECTORS:
Professor Morris H. Shamos, Professor of Physics; and Professor
J. Darrell Barnard, Professor of Science Education, New York
University, 4 Washington Place, New York, N.Y. 10003.
(212) 598-3735.

PROJECT HEADQUARTERS:
1. Contact: Project directors.
2. Special facilities or activities available for visitor viewing:
Teaching materials production center; complete collection of
laboratory equipment used in the COPES teaching materials.

PRINCIPAL PROFESSIONAL STAFF:
Morris H. Shamos, Director; J. Darrell Barnard, Associate
Director; Janice A. Cutler, Assistant Director; Philip R. Merrifield,
Head, Evaluation Team; Arnold H. Diamond, Evaluation
Specialist; Dean R. Casperson, Physicist and Science Educator;
Joseph H. Rubinstein, Biologist; Lois Arnold, Editor; Alvin
Hertzberg, Elementary School Principal and Science Specialist.

PROJECT SUPPORT:
1. Funding agencies: U.S. Office of Education.
2. Associated agencies: New York University.

PROJECT HISTORY:
1. Principal originators: Morris H. Shamos and J. Darrell
Barnard.
2. Date and place of initiation: September 1965; New York
University.
3. Evolution and development of the project: The need for a
highly structured sequentially organized K–6 science program
was highlighted as an outcome of a three-day conference on
elementary school science conducted by New York University
scientists, psychologists, and educators in 1962. As a consequence
of this conference, Morris H. Shamos, and J. Darrell Barnard,
developed a plan designed to produce a conceptually oriented
program in elementary school science (COPES). With administrative support from the Deans of the School of Education and the
Graduate School of Arts and Science, the plan was generally
accepted as an all-university project.
A two-year pilot study to test the feasibility of a conceptual
scheme approach was eventually funded by the Office of Education in 1965. The success of the pilot study in 1967, dealing
with one conceptual scheme—the conservation of energy—led

to the ultimate development of an elementary school science program based upon five conceptual schemes.

PROJECT OBJECTIVES:
1. Overall project purpose: To develop a K–6 science curriculum based on the conceptual schemes approach.
2. Specific objectives: To develop an elementary science curriculum based upon selected "great ideas" or conceptual schemes in science. The ultimate goal is to help develop a scientific literacy by developing an understanding of the nature of matter (both animate and inanimate) in terms of a few basic conceptual schemes. Each concept, each conceptual scheme, is presented in a K–6 structured learning sequence with the purpose of contributing to this understanding. The concepts are organized in a hierarchy which is both scientifically and pedagogically logical. The order of the sequence is in the form of a "spiral" development. The five conceptual schemes selected to form the core of the COPES curriculum are (in hierarchical order): 1) The Structural Units of the Universe; 2) Interaction and Change; 3) Conservation of Energy; 4) Degradation of Energy; and 5) The Statistical View of Nature (or Order from Disorder). All five schemes are being developed concurrently.

The K–2 portion of the curriculum comprises those manipulative and conceptual skills which lay a foundation for the main portions of the five conceptual skills which effectively should start at grade 3. Here too, the sequence of the K–2 program is in the form of a "spiral" development linking its major content sections.

The COPES curriculum is action-centered. Almost all activities require exploration of a nonreading nature to be carried out by individual or small groups of students. It is also a fundamental principle of COPES that as the major and supporting science concepts are being developed within the structured sequences, basic skills, where appropriate to the teaching materials, must be concurrently developed and refined. The learning, understanding, and appreciation of science cannot proceed properly without these basic skills (or processes of science). Although the materials are designed to involve children in various methods of investigation, the primary objective is an understanding of basic concepts.

It is expected that COPES will form the major portion (about 80 percent) of an elementary science curriculum, the remainder being devoted to applications or projects of the individual school's or teacher's choosing. The philosophy of the COPES program can be found in its descriptive brochure (March 1971).

No material is being written for the children. The curriculum is presented in the form of a series of Teacher's Guides. Each guide includes groups of "minisequences" of teaching activities interrelated to develop a progression of concepts related to a major concept or topic. Contained within each guide for each grade are sets of assessments, one for each minisequence or topic. Each set consists of 1) group screening assesments designed to determine how well the children have mastered the concepts of the minisequence and 2) individual assessments designed as additional learning experiences for children falling short of the teacher's expectations on the group assessments.

UNIQUE CHARACTERISTICS OF THE PROJECT:
The curriculum has been prepared for a broad spectrum of socio-economic and cultural backgrounds. Since it makes little demands upon the reading ability of children it can be used effectively in classes where children have reading difficulties. Its content is acultural and has been used effectively in bilingual (Spanish–English) schools. Its concepts are developed in an educational progressive manner and therefore have been used effectively in audio-tutorial instructional programs. Because of the uniquely different approach to learning science concepts it also challenges the above-average child. The Teacher's Guides suggest ways in which teachers can adapt the materials to the various ability levels of children.

SPECIFIC SUBJECTS, GRADE, AGE AND ABILITY LEVELS:
All areas of science have been developed for K–6 (ages 5–12), although it has been used and is usable through grade 16. Evidence so far is that it is suitable for all ability levels.

MAIN METHODS OF INSTRUCTION
USED IN THE PROJECT:
Laboratory investigations and teacher directed discussion and interpretation.

PRESENT COMMERCIAL AFFILIATIONS:
One minisequence, suitable for grades 3 and above, has been published by American Science and Engineering, 20 Overland Street, Boston, Mass. 02215.
Teacher's Guides are being published and distributed by The Center for Field Research and School Services, New York University, 51 Press Building, Washington Square, New York, N.Y. 10003.

DESCRIPTION OF MATERIALS ALREADY PRODUCED:
1. Newsletter #1, 2, and 3 (out of print).
2. Newsletter #4 (March 1970).
3. A pilot project to develop an elementary science sequence, August 1967.
4. Descriptive brochures: October 1966, March 1969, November 1969, March 1971.
5. Teacher's Guide for a Conservation of Energy Sequence.
6. Water-Mix Experiments (booklet).

7. Teacher's Guide for Kindergarten–Grade One Sequence.
8. Teacher's Guide for Grade Two.
9. Teacher's Guide for Grade Three.
10. K–1 Assessment Kit.
11. Grade 2 Assessment Kit.

MATERIALS AVAILABLE FREE:
Item 2 available from COPES Project, New York University, 4 Washington Place, New York, N.Y. 10003.
Item 3 available only through USOE.
Item 4 (March 1971 only) available from COPES Project.

MATERIALS PURCHASABLE:
Item 5. Available from Center for Field Research, New York University, 51 Press Bldg., Washington Square, New York, N.Y. 10003. ($5.35)
Item 6. Available from American Science & Engineering, 20 Overland Street, Boston, Mass. 02215. ($3.50)
Item 7. Available from Center for Field Research. ($7.00)
Item 8. Available from Center for Field Research. ($5.50)
Item 9. Available from Center for Field Research. (Cost not established.)
Item 10. Available from Center for Field Research. ($2.10)
Item 11. Available from Center for Field Research. ($1.00)
Total K–2 package. Available from Center for Field Research. ($14.00)

ADDITIONAL MATERIALS BEING DEVELOPED:
Teacher's Guides for Grades 4, 5, and 6.

LANGUAGE IN WHICH MATERIALS:
1. Were originally written: English.
2. Have been or will be translated: None for publication.

COUNTRIES IN WHICH MATERIALS ARE USED:
United States only.

PROJECT IMPLEMENTATION:
1. Total number of teachers using any of the materials: 100.
2. Total number of students using any of the materials: 2,500.
3. Total number of schools using any of the materials: 50.
4. The totals stated in 1, 2, and 3 are estimated.
5. Name and location of selected schools where the program is in use: Old Bethpage School, Round Swamp Road, Old Bethpage, N.Y.; Theodore Roosevelt School, West Main Street, Oyster Bay, L.I., N.Y. 11771; Schwarting School, Flower Road and Jerusalem Avenue, North Massapequa, N.Y. 11758; some Montgomery County, Maryland schools; New York City schools: P.S. 2; P.S. 41; and P.S. 151.

TEACHER PREPARATION:
1. Consultant services available for teachers using materials: by direct contact with the project headquarters, at present.
2. Activities conducted for pre-service and in-service teacher training: a full year in-service course was prepared. Short term workshops are given in various parts of the country which have been financed by the Project or requesting agency. At the end of 1972 it is expected that more information will be available on teacher preparation as the project enters its final testing stage.
3. Available pre-service and/or in-service teaching materials for science educators to use in preparing teachers: no special materials available at present. A package will be prepared for the final testing phase. The Teacher's Guides themselves can be used. For cost see "Materials Purchasable" above.

PROJECT EVALUATION:
1. Has the effectiveness of the materials been evaluated: Yes, internally.
2. Pertinent published research studies: Morris H. Shamos and J. Darrell Barnard, *A Pilot Project to Develop an Elementary Science Sequence*, U.S. Office of Education, Project No. H-281 (New York: New York University, 1967).
3. Brief abstract of in-house or unpublished research:
   (a) Graeber[5] compared a typical overall approach to the teaching of a science methods course for prospective elementary school teachers with an experimental approach based upon the COPES rationale. The experimental approach concentrated upon activities as prescribed in the COPES *Teacher's Guide for a Conservation of Energy Sequence* and taught exclusively by involving the prospective teachers in the same type of investigations as recommended for use with children. The positive statistically significant difference in favor of the experimental group obtained when testing the teaching performance of students involved in the study would support the premise that the experimental approach (as used in this study) is not only affective in developing positive teacher attitude (as measured by a paper and pencil test) but also affects the actual teaching performance.
   (b) Netburn[6] developed and tested the relative effectiveness of an audio-tutorial programmed method of teaching with the

5. Mary Graeber, "A Comparison of Two Methods of Teaching an Elementary School Science Methods Course at Hunter College," unpublished doctoral thesis, New York University, 1971.
6. Allan N. Netburn, "A Comparison of the Effectiveness of Two Methods of Presenting Science Experiments to Children of the Fourth Grade in a Northeastern Suburb," unpublished doctoral thesis, New York University, 1971.

COPES teacher-directed method of teaching the same selected minisequence from the COPES curriculum. He found that children learned as well by the audio-tutorial method as the teacher-directed method. However, the average time required to complete the minisequence by the audio-tutorial method was 20 percent less than by the prescribed teacher-directed method.

(c) Nevarez[7] compared three methods of oral presentation of a selected minisequence of COPES activities to Spanish-speaking children. By one method only English was used, by the second only Spanish, and by the third a bilingual method (English and Spanish) was used. Children taught science by the simultaneous use of English and Spanish as the medium of oral presentation achieve more than those taught exclusively in English; children taught science by the simultaneous use of English and Spanish as the medium of oral presentation achieve more than those taught exclusively in Spanish; and children taught science exclusively in Spanish as the medium of oral presentation achieve more than those taught exclusively in English.

(d) Shah[8] found in his study of the COPES Tests used in the pilot study dealing with the conservation of energy that: 1) items discriminated better than by chance, 2) items could not be demonstrated to constitute a scale, such as a Guttman Scale, 3) criterion-related validity of the tests can be demonstrated, and 4) the higher the concept in the hierarchy of science concepts in the conceptual scheme under investigation —which an item in the COPES Test of Science Concepts is intended to measure or represent—the more difficult, on the average, the item will tend to be.

(e) Sher[9] Aptitude measures based on Guilford's Structure-of-Intellect model were developed for elementary school children. These were used to study the mediation of achievement by children's abilities in third and fourth grade classes which studied the COPES thermal energy sequence within the Conservation of Energy. The study of children's learning as a function of teacher training and learner's aptitudes disclosed

7. Miguel A. Nevarez, "A Comparison of Three Methods of Oral Presentation of Science Activities to Fourth Grade Spanish-Speaking Children," unpublished doctoral thesis, New York University, 1971.
8. Rashid Ahmed Shah, "The Structure and the Criterion-related Validity of the *COPES Test of Critical Terms* and the *COPES Test of Science Concepts*," unpublished doctoral thesis, New York University, 1969.
9. Abigail B. Sher, "Using Aptitude Measures as Predictors of Differential Achievement" (paper presented at AERA Convention, New York City, February 4, 1971).

the statistically significant contribution of aptitudes in the domain of productive thinking about both figurally and verbally mediated ideas.

(f) Woodruff assessed children's concepts by an oral interview technique and compared them with assessments of the same concepts by the COPES Test of Science Concepts. This was done after the children had been taught the lower levels of the conservation of energy sequence. He found that in many instances children could explain concepts which the results of the written tests indicated they did not possess. Children often found the vocabulary and sentence structure of the written tests to be too complex even though all test items had previously been tried out with children and revised before they were used in the pilot study. Woodruff's study has resulted in a revision of our approach to the assessment of concepts in the COPES curriculum.

4. Evaluative data available to interested individuals: None at present.

PROJECT PUBLICITY:

1. Barnard, J. Darrell, "COPES: The New Elementary Science Program," *Science and Children,* vol. 9 (November 1971), pp. 9–11.

2. Barnard, J. Darrell, "The Conceptual-Scheme Relation in Science Education," *Education Quarterly,* New York University, 1971, pp. 24–30.

3. Hill, Katherine E., "Science in the Elementary School: A Look Ahead," *Science and Children,* vol. 6 (January–February 1969), pp. 28–33.

4. Cutler, Janice A., "Heat and Temperature," *Science and Children,* vol. 3 (November 1968), pp. 36–42.

5. Shamos, Morris H., "The Role of Major Conceptual Schemes in Science Education," *The Science Teacher,* vol. 33, no. 1 (January 1966), pp. 27–30.

6. Victor, Edward, "Controversial Aspects of the Elementary Science Curriculum Projects," *Science and Children,* vol. 5 (October 1967), pp. 27–31.

7. Hurd, Paul D., and James Gallagher, "Conceptually Oriented Program in Elementary Science," *New Directions in Elementary Science Teaching* (Belmont, Calif.: Wadsworth Publishing Co., 1968), pp. 52–57.

8. Anon., "Scientific Literacy: The COPES Approach," *The Indicator:* Chemical Education Today, New York and North Jersey American Chemical Society News', vol. 50, no. 1 (January 26, 1969), pp. 28–30.

9. Wailes, James R., *Elementary School Science Experimental Projects,* University of Colorado, Boulder, Colo. (revised August 1969), pp. 6, 7.

10. Cutler, Janice A., "Background of the COPES Project," *Project Report: Conceptual Schemes in Science: A Basis for Curriculum Development,* Charles R. Botticelli, Project Director, National Science Teachers Association, Washington, D.C. (1968), pp. 38–43.

SUMMARY OF PROJECT ACTIVITIES SINCE 1970 REPORT:
1. The vertical development of concepts and designation of activities for each of the five conceptual schemes completed.
2. Selected activities were tested in the COPES Laboratory School and local cooperating schools.
3. Activities prerequisite for all five conceptual schemes were identified and Teacher's Guides for K, grade 1, and grade 2 were written and published.
4. The concepts to be taught in grades 3 to 6 were identified and organized into a series of minisequences for each grade level.
5. Teaching activities were designed to develop the above concepts and were then arranged in a hierarchy of minisequences.
6. By the activities listed in 4 and 5 above, all five conceptual schemes are developed concurrently at each grade level.
7. Teacher's Guide for Grade 3 written and published.
8. Teacher's Guides for Grades 4, 5, and 6 are available.
9. Assessment materials for each minisequence in each grade level have been written and are being published as a part of each Teacher's Guide.
10. A design for field testing COPES materials has been developed.

PLANS FOR THE FUTURE:
Plans for the immediate future call for field testing of COPES materials in a number of elementary schools across the country. Results will not only be used in determining the adaptability of COPES materials to a variety of school situations but also as bases for revising the present editions of the Teacher's Guides.

Creative Aspects

The COPES curriculum is action centered and almost all activities require exploration of a nonreading nature to be achieved by individuals or small groups. In spite of a highly structured schema, the project suggests dimensions indicating a creative process function. For example, before entering the major threads of the sequence, K–2 children will be taught presequence materials that include the early concepts and skills needed for the development of the major concepts in the sequence on a broad spiral. The concepts are introduced in several ways—first on an intuitive basis and finally in more highly developed activities. Here again the teacher will be the prime determiner of creativity in the program.

INDIVIDUALIZED SCIENCE (FORMERLY INDIVIDUALLY PRESCRIBED INSTRUCTION IN SCIENCE—IPI SCIENCE)

PROJECT DIRECTOR:
Dr. Leopold E. Klopfer, Director, Individualized Science Learning Research and Development Center of the University of Pittsburgh, Pittsburgh, Pa. 15213. (412) 683–8640.

PROJECT HEADQUARTERS:
1. Contact: Project director.
2. Special facilities of activities available for visitor viewing: Oakleaf Elementary School—implementation of levels A, B, C, D, E, and F.

PRINCIPAL PROFESSIONAL STAFF:
Dr. Audrey Champagne, Research Associate; Sister Mary Hughes, Graduate Research Assistant; Dr. Leopold Klopfer, Director; Ronald Lupish, Research Assistant; Martina Magenau, Graduate Research Assistant; Catherine McCann, Research Assistant; Dr. Albert Nous, Research Associate; June Pittman, Senior Research Assistant; Savithri Srinivasan, Research Assistant; Victor Weber, Consultant.

PROJECT SUPPORT:
1. Funding agencies: Learning Research and Development Center (organizational agency), U.S. Office of Education; Imperial International Learning Corporation.
2. Associated agencies: Research for Better Schools.

PROJECT HISTORY:
1. Principal originators: Robert Glaser, John Bolvin, Joseph Lipson.
2. Date and place of initiation: 1964; University of Pittsburgh.
3. Evolution and development of the project: The project has evolved from the original efforts to individualize elementary school science instruction by the Learning Research and Development Center, working in cooperation with the Oakleaf School, a public elementary school in the Baldwin-Whitehall District. While the early versions of the program were based on the model of Individually Prescribed Instruction, the program presently being developed encompasses individualization on a much broader basis.

PROJECT OBJECTIVES:
1. Overall project purpose: The development of a complete individualized science program which will serve every student

from his entry into the elementary school to the beginning of high school.

2. Specific objectives: The five goals of the Individualized Science program are attuned to the needs and interests of the student, to the development of the child, and to the circumstances of the 1970s. The program utilizes a variety of learning resources to achieve these five goals.

(a) *Student Self-Direction Goal* The student views the learning process as primarily self-directed and self-initiated.

(b) *Student Co-Evaluation Goal* The student plays a major role in evaluating the quality, extent, and rapidity of his learning.

(c) *Affective Goal* The student displays informed attitudes toward his study of science, scientific inquiry, and the scientific enterprise.

(d) *Inquiry Goal* The student is skillful in using the processes of scientific inquiry, and he is able to carry out inquiries.

(e) *Scientific Literacy Goal* The student acquires a foundation of scientific literacy.

Individualized Science does not emphasize any one of these goals over another but, rather, provides for student growth in all five areas.

UNIQUE CHARACTERISTICS OF THE PROJECT:

Individualized Science is organized into ten developmental levels (levels A through J). Although the units included in each of these levels provide for roughly one year of work, individual students in any given school grade are usually involved in different units within a level or on different levels. A "Mainstream," which runs through the ten levels provides a common core of science learning for all students. Every student is expected to achieve mastery of the skills and content in the sequential Mainstream units. Alternative Pathway activities and units arise from potential branches of curiosity which the student may experience as he proceeds through the Mainstream units. Alternative Pathway activities and units are optional, and they increase in number and length as the student progresses through the levels of Individualized Science.

The program contains integrated management procedures to facilitate handling of the wide variety of learning resources necessary for individualization. These procedures reduce the teacher's administrative chores and contribute to the student's development as an independent learner. (See goals I and II in section (b) above.)

Research evidence thus far obtained on the early levels of Individualized Science indicates that the program is suitable for students from a broad range of socioeconomic, cultural, and intellectual backgrounds.

SPECIFIC SUBJECTS, GRADE, AGE AND ABILITY LEVELS:
The subject studied is general science, with major emphases placed on science as inquiry and on the individual's needs for knowledge and understanding which are relevant to current societal issues and relevant to himself.

School grades K or 1 through 8; all ages and abilities within the respective groups (after all, it's an individualized program).

MAIN METHODS OF INSTRUCTION
USED IN THE PROJECT:
Independent study, laboratory investigations, seminars, discussion sessions, Men and Ideas filmstrips, individual lessons, individual taped lessons, mini-explorations, directed readings in science, and science learning games.

PRESENT COMMERCIAL AFFILIATIONS:
Imperial International Learning, Box 548, Kankakee, Ill. 60901.

DESCRIPTION OF MATERIALS ALREADY PRODUCED:
Student materials for each unit include a variety of learning resources: individual lessons, directed readings in science, student activities, learning games, mini-explorations, etc. Each unit's materials also include a teacher's manual and a management system. Materials produced: levels A through D Mainstream units, in field testing stage; levels E through G Mainstream and Alternative Pathway units, in prototype testing stage.

1. Level A Units
   (a) *Simpson* (sorting).*
   (b) *Galileo* (observing).*
   (c) *Michelson* (measuring).*
2. Level B Units
   (a) *Burbank* (classifying).*
   (b) *Hooke* (forces).*
   (c) *Curie* (physical states).*
3. Level C Units
   (a) *Lagrange* (metric measurement).*
   (b) *Vesalius* (systems).*
   (c) *Black* (chemical systems).*
4. Level D Units
   (a) *Lavoisier* (burning).*
   (b) *Dalton* (atoms and molecules).*
   (c) *Haldane* (breathing).*
   (d) *Comstock* (recognizing plants).
5. Level E Units
   (a) *Joule* (energy).*
   (b) *Beaumont* (digestion).*

* These units comprise the basic science core which each student is expected to study. Alternative Pathway units are optional explorations which are available to the student.

    (c) *Voit* (nutrition).*
    (d) *Copernicus* (solar system).
    (e) *Volta* (electricity).
    (f) *Archimedes* (machines).
    (g) *Linnaeus* (plant growth).
6. Level F Units
    (a) *Powell* (water).*
    (b) *Harvey* (circulation).*
    (c) *Watt* (thermodynamics).
    (d) *Kepler* (optics).
    (e) *Drew* (blood).
    (f) *Arrhenius* (chemical solutions).
    (g) *Audubon* (birds).
7. Level G Units
    (a) *Borelli* (motion).*
    (b) *Quetelet* (variation).*
    (c) *Newton* (motion).
    (d) *Helmholz* (nervous system).
    (e) *Fraunhofer* (spectra).
    (f) *Foucault* (pendulums).
    (g) *James* (memory).
    (h) *Boyle* (fluids).

MATERIALS AVAILABLE FREE:
Individualized Science Newsletter—contact Project Director.
Individualized Science brochure—contact Imperial International
Learning, Box 548, Kankakee, Ill. 60901.

MATERIALS PURCHASABLE:
Commercial availability in Spring 1973 of items 1 and 2; from
Imperial International Learning, Box 548, Kankakee, Ill. 60901.

ADDITIONAL MATERIALS BEING DEVELOPED:
1. Level H Units
    (a) *Leuwenhoek* (microorganisms).*
    (b) *Haekel* (reproduction).*
    (c) *Darwin* (evolution).*
    (d) *Schwann* (cells).
    (e) *Mendel* (genetics).
    (f) *Turner* (insects).
    (g) *Hertz* (electronmagnetic waves).
    (h) *Cannon* (astronomy).
2. Level I Units
    (a) *Cowles* (food chains).*
    (b) *Bjerknes* (weather).*

* These units comprise the basic science core which each student is expected to study. Alternative Pathway units are optional explorations which are available to the student.

  (c) *Clements* (bioecology).*
  (d) *Lyell* (geology).
  (e) *Einstein* (frames of reference).
  (f) *Saussure* (plant respiration).
  (g) *Bohr* (atomic structure).
  (h) *Cori* (biochemistry).
 3. Level J Units
  (a) *Hauser* (populations).
  (b) *Commoner* (pollution).
  (c) *von Braun* (space exploration).

LANGUAGE IN WHICH MATERIALS:
1. Were originally written: English.
2. Have been or will be translated: None as yet.

COUNTRIES IN WHICH MATERIALS ARE USED:
United States.

PROJECT IMPLEMENTATION:
The first parts of the program are being field tested.
1. Total number of teachers using any of the materials: 35.
2. Total number of students using any of the materials: 900.
3. Total number of schools using any of the materials: 6.
4. The totals stated in 1, 2, and 3 are definitive.
5. Name and location of selected schools where the program is in use: Oakleaf School, Frick School, Pittsburgh, Pa.; Richland School, Quakertown, Pa.; Gray School, Wilmington, Del.; Hillside School, Berwyn, Pa.; and Aroma Park School, Kankakee, Ill.

TEACHER PREPARATION:
1. Consultant services available for teachers using the materials: in development stage at Research for Better Schools, Inc., 1700 Market Street, Philadelphia, Pa. 19103.
2. Activities conducted for pre-service and in-service teacher training: none as yet; developmental work at Research for Better Schools.
3. Pre-service and/or in-service teaching materials for science educators to use in preparing teachers: none as yet; in development at Research for Better Schools for publication by Imperial International Learning.

PROJECT EVALUATION:
1. Has the effectiveness of your materials been evaluated? Yes, by Research for Better Schools, Inc.
2. Pertinent published research studies: "The Development of a Computer-Based Management Program for Use with Adaptive Instructional Systems," Richard E. Sass, University of Pittsburgh, 1970 (unpublished Ph.D. dissertation).

* These units comprise the basic science core which each student is expected to study. Alternative Pathway units are optional explorations which are available to the student.

3. Brief abstract of in-house or unpublished research: Systematic collecting of data on the content, manageability and clarity of Individualized Science materials are an integral part of the development of the program. Members of the Individualized Science staff observe the program in the prototype testing classroom. Students' completed test papers are kept for detailed analysis. Teachers' suggestions and comments as well as staff evaluations are noted. Periodic research reports have involved detailed analyses of these data. Staff members have undertaken such research prior to revising Individualized Science materials, and a number of graduate students and Ph.D. candidates have done research on some aspect of the Individualized Science program.

4. Evaluative data available to interested individuals: Two Graduate Research Assistants are currently compiling data for individual case studies on 15 percent of Pittsburgh (Oakleaf and Frick schools) students using Individualized Science.

PROJECT PUBLICITY:
1. Leopold E. Klopfer, "IPI Science: A Teaching Revolution in the Making," *Science Activities*, vol. 1, no. 1 (1969).
2. Joseph I. Lipson, "An Individualized Science Laboratory," *Science and Children*, vol. 4, no. 4 (December 1966). (ED-013-664.)
3. Leopold E. Klopfer, "Individualized Science in Focus," *Science Activities*, vol. 6, no. 3 (November 1971).
4. Leopold E. Klopfer, "Individualized Science: Relevance for the 1970s," *Science Education*, 55 (1971).

SUMMARY OF PROJECT ACTIVITIES SINCE 1970 REPORT:
1. Reorganization of levels A and B after field testing.
2. Development and publication contract with Imperial International Learning.
3. Preparation of levels D through G units.

PLANS FOR THE FUTURE:
Second conference with Science Education Advisory Group, Spring 1972. Continued development, testing and revision of materials. Projected commercial availability of total program in late 1975 or early 1976. First two levels are scheduled for release in Spring 1973.

Creative Aspects

No explicit provision is made for creative development. However, the individualized orientation from K–8 affords wide latitude for the teacher to provide opportunity for creative activity.

SCIENCE FOR THE SEVENTIES (SFTS)

PROJECT DIRECTOR:
Dr. Irvin T. Edgar, Science Education Adviser, Bureau of General and Academic Education, Box 911, Harrisburg, Pa. 17126. (717) 787-7320.

PROJECT HEADQUARTERS:
1. Contact: Project director.
2. Special facilities or activities available for visitor viewing: None.

PRINCIPAL PROFESSIONAL STAFF:
William H. Bolles, Science Education Adviser and John J. McDermott, Science Education Adviser.

PROJECT SUPPORT:
1. Funding agencies: Commonwealth of Pennsylvania.
2. Associated agencies: The Clarion Foundation, Clarion, Pa.

PROJECT HISTORY:
1. Principal originators: Francis Alder, Elementary Science Coordinator, Keystone Oaks School District. Dr. Dorothy Alfke, Professor, Elementary Science Department, The Pennsylvania State University. Dr. Roy W. Allison, Professor, Elementary Science Education, The Pennsylvania State University, Capitol Campus. Dr. James Currie, Professor, Edinboro State College. William H. Bolles, Science Education Adviser, Pennsylvania Department of Education. Dr. William Chamberlain, Professor, Science Education, Clarion State College. Dr. Thomas V. Come, Professor, Elementary Education Department, Edinboro State College. Carl E. Heilman, Coordinator, Division of Science and Mathematics, Pennsylvania Department of Education. John J. McDermott, Science Education Adviser, Pennsylvania Department of Education. Dr. Duane Smith, Professor, Elementary Education, The Pennsylvania State University, Capitol Campus. Dr. Paul W. Welliver, Professor, Pennsylvania State University.
2. Date and place of initiation: July 1968; Harrisburg, Pa.
3. Evolution and development of the project: SFTS was begun in 1968 with the writing of the Guide and two representative lessons. Additional lessons were added, a descriptive film produced, and plans for additional media use have been initiated.

PROJECT OBJECTIVES:
1. Overall project purpose: This project has produced materials to provide direction for elementary teachers in teaching science through the provision of illustrative science materials. It provides a variety of activities and procedures to be adapted by the teacher

to suit the individual classroom. The aims of this project are to develop students who are scientifically literate and who have sound problem-solving strategies.

2. Specific objectives:

(a) The student will measure with English units and metric units to solve problems concerning length, area, volume, and weight.

(b) The student will formulate and ask questions of his environment. He will use questions to describe, clarify, analyze problems, and to provide direction for problem solving.

(c) The student will solve problems by gathering information, working independently, using equipment and materials, observing purposefully, and drawing appropriate conclusions based on these findings.

(d) The student will explain basic conceptual schemes of the material world using personal experiences acquired through various activities as the basis for his explanation.

(e) The student will identify examples of scientific hypotheses and theories as evidence that man's interpretation of truth changes as his knowledge increases.

(f) The student will demonstrate competency in the use of the processes of science by: (1) observing, (2) classifying, (3) communicating, (4) measuring, (5) inferring, (6) formulating hypotheses, (7) interpreting data, (8) controlling variables, and (9) experimenting.

(g) The student will demonstrate his competency with textbooks or reference books using the table of contents, the index, and the glossary to obtain information.

(h) The student will discriminate between evidence and proof, fact and theory, observation and inference, summation and analysis.

(i) The student will construct quantitative and qualitative records that can be used as evidence for reaching tentative conclusions.

(j) The student will pursue problems for study and state the methods for gaining the solutions to these problems.

(k) The student will demonstrate a desire to learn and a curiosity for the unknown by formulating and performing self-motivated investigations.

(l) The student will defend a point of view by making use of supporting evidence.

UNIQUE CHARACTERISTICS OF THE PROJECT:

SFTS is designed for use in elementary schools. Lessons are designed for primary or intermediate classes specifically while the Guide is designed for general use by elementary teachers. The materials provide assistance to schools, administrators, and teachers in improving their present elementary science program.

SPECIFIC SUBJECTS, GRADE, AGE AND ABILITY LEVELS:
Primary Grade Level:
1. Investigating Magnets.
2. Investigating Observation and Description.
3. Investigating Flowers and Fruits.
4. Investigating Siphons.
5. Investigating Static Electricity.
Intermediate Grade Level:
6. Investigating Static Electricity.
7. Investigating Splashes.
8. Investigating Drop Designs.
9. Investigating Astronomy.
10. Investigating Liquid Surfaces in Containers.
11. Investigating Bouncing Objects.

MAIN METHODS OF INSTRUCTION
USED IN THE PROJECT:
Laboratory investigations, discussion sessions, and field experiences.

PRESENT COMMERCIAL AFFILIATIONS:
The Clarion Foundation, Clarion, Pa.

DESCRIPTION OF MATERIALS ALREADY PRODUCED:
See section I above.

MATERIALS AVAILABLE FREE:
Materials are available free to Pennsylvania teaching or administrative personnel.

MATERIALS PURCHASABLE:
Non-educators and nonstate residents may purchase the items 1–11 from the Clarion Foundation, Clarion, Pa.

ADDITIONAL MATERIALS BEING DEVELOPED:
Additional lessons are under development.

LANGUAGE IN WHICH MATERIALS:
1. Were originally written: English.
2. Have been or will be translated: Not answered.

COUNTRIES IN WHICH MATERIALS ARE USED:
United States and Korea.

PROJECT IMPLEMENTATION:
1. Total number of teachers using any of the materials: 3,000 (estimated).
2. Total number of students using any of the materials: Unknown.
3. Total number of schools using any of the materials: Unknown.
4. Name and location of selected schools where program is in use: Trial schools are being identified and their locations may eventually be obtained from the project director.

TEACHER PREPARATION:

1. Consultants for SFTS are listed in the SFTS Guide.
2. Activities conducted for pre-service and in-service teacher training: An SFTS workshop is held annually at Shippensburg State College, Shippensburg, Pa., in June. The cost per teacher is approximately $50.00. A minimum of three developmental conferences are held yearly in February, April, and November.
3. Available pre-service and/or in-service teaching materials for science educators to use in preparing teachers: The SFTS teaching materials may be used for this purpose.

PROJECT EVALUATION:

1. Has the effectiveness of your materials been evaluated: Yes, internally.
2. Published research studies: Not answered.
3. Brief abstract of in-house or unpublished research: SFTS lessons are used and analyzed by the lesson developer, pre-service teachers and students, and in-service teachers and students.
4. Evaluative data available to interested individuals: None.

PROJECT PUBLICITY:

1. Science for the Seventies—Pennsylvania Clearinghouse on Methodology in Elementary Sciences 1968.
2. Science for the Seventies—Pennsylvania Clearinghouse on Methodology in Elementary Sciences 1969.

SUMMARY OF PROJECT ACTIVITIES SINCE 1970 REPORT:
Not answered.

PLANS FOR THE FUTURE:
Additional material under development.

Creative Aspects

The teacher is the key to creative endeavor. This program may become highly structured if the teacher is so inclined; or creative, if the teacher has the skill to break out of the behavioral straitjacket and provide the freedom in problem-solving activities required to generate creativity.

MODEL EDUCATIONAL PROGRAM IN ECOLOGY, KINDERGARTEN THROUGH ADULT EDUCATION

PROJECT DIRECTORS:
David P. McLaren, Instructional Specialist, 450 North Grand Avenue, Los Angeles, Calif. 90012. (213) 687-4285.

Sid Sitkoff, Instructional Specialist, North Field Service Center, 8111 Calhoun Avenue, Panorama City, Calif. 91402. (213) 782-0350.

PROJECT HEADQUARTERS:
1. Contact: Grant Cary, Ecology Coordinator, Laurel Ecology Center, 1044 North Hayworth, Los Angeles, Calif. 90046. (213) 656-7457.
2. Special facilities or activities available for visitor viewing: Laurel Ecology Center, 1044 North Hayworth Avenue, Calif. 90046 and Placerita Canyon Nature Center, 19152 West Placerita Canyon, Newhall, Calif. 91321.

PRINCIPAL PROFESSIONAL STAFF:
Grant Cary, Ecology Coordinator (directs activity of Project); Deloy A. Stromme, Ecology Center Specialist; Floraline Stevens, Project Evaluator; Shirley Leon, Resource Consultant; and William Wilson, Resource Teacher.

PROJECT SUPPORT:
1. Funding agencies: ESEA Title III.
2. Associated agencies: None.

PROJECT HISTORY:
1. Principal originators: Project directors.
2. Date and place of initiation: July 1971; Los Angeles Unified School District, Los Angeles, Calif.
3. Evolution and development of the project: Preliminary proposal was submitted in April 1971 and planning grant requested in May 1971. Final proposal completed in May 1971 and grant received in June 1971.

PROJECT OBJECTIVES:
1. Overall project purpose: To develop, implement, and monitor a comprehensive program in ecology (environmental education) from kindergarten through adult education.
2. Specific objectives:
 (a) Development of a sequentially developed program in environmental education. Establishment of an ecology center complex (Laurel Ecology Center, located at 1044 North Hayworth, Los Angeles).
 (b) Preparation of instructional materials for pupil and teacher use.
 (c) Development of two mobile ecology laboratories.
 (d) Enrichment of the total curriculum as it relates to environmental education.
 (e) Development of a television series on ecology at elementary–secondary levels.
 (f) Establishment of evaluative procedures for assessing the effectiveness of all components.

UNIQUE CHARACTERISTICS OF THE PROJECT:
1. Laurel Ecology Center Complex. The unique features of this
complex enable it to:
   (a) Serve a coordinating function for evaluating, collating,
and distributing materials from public and private agencies.
   (b) Provide indoor and outdoor laboratory experiences for
students bused to the center.
   (c) Establish a program for leadership and teacher staff
development emphasizing the content areas and teaching the
program for specific classroom needs of a student population
representing a wide range of educational, language, and
societal backgrounds.
   (d) Develop written and multisensory type pupil materials
such as kits and models which emphasize student investigation
of environmental problems.
   (e) Coordinate visitation program of resource personnel to
schools.
2. Learning Activity Modules (LAM) make up a unique approach
to concept development in the project. The Modules utilize a
systems approach to instruction.
All components of the instructional program in concept development are provided the classroom teacher. These include student
reading material designed for the reading level and interests of
the pupil; complete teacher's handbook with background information; teaching suggestions, reference to agencies and organizations supporting environmental education, and suggested
methodology; materials supporting individual pupil investigations,
such as all laboratory hardware and software, and study kits for
outdoor laboratory use; multimedia such as audio-visual materials,
including sound tape cassettes, filmstrips, 8mm film loops, slides,
simple models, and specimen displays; raw materials for constructing audio-visual materials, field trips which involve a
pre-trip preparation, directed experiences on the field trip, and
follow-up classroom activities related to the field trip.

SPECIFIC SUBJECTS, GRADE, AGE AND ABILITY LEVELS:
The Project's curricular framework draws on *Ekistics: A Handbook for Curricular Development in Conservation and Environmental Education* for its overall major conceptual structure. The
handbook was developed through the California State Department
of Education. An interdisciplinary design utilizes several subject
areas including the social sciences, science, health, and the
humanities. The teaching strategy employed by the teacher may
draw on any or all disciplines during a given lesson. It is the
intent of this project to directly involve the student in an investigative approach to environmental education where his activities
lead to conceptual understandings or identified in the overall
framework. Further it is intended that the objectives be accom-

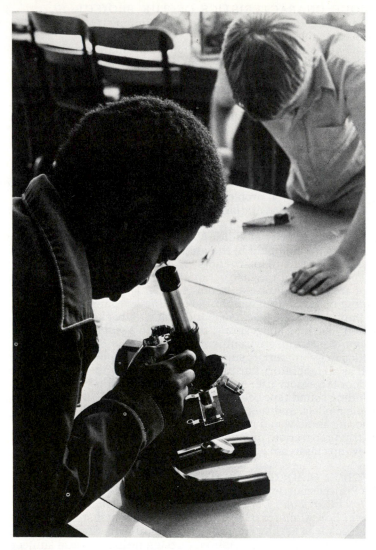

FIGURE 6-5. *Instruments extend man's discrimination in measurement. Early experiences with observation, measurement, and data gathering are vital in science education. (Photo from Los Angeles Unified Schools—A Model Educational Program in Ecology, ESEA Title III)*

plished within the existing curriculum organization rather than as a separate, additional time block. Grade levels include kindergarten through grade 12—pupils of age 5 through age 12. Pupil material is designed to correspond with the actual reading level of the pupil regardless of age or grade level of placement.

MAIN METHODS OF INSTRUCTION USED IN THE PROJECT: Independent study, programmed instruction, laboratory investigations, lectures, seminars, discussion sessions, computer assisted instruction, field experiences, audio-tutorial and production of environmental education audio-visual material by pupils.

PRESENT COMMERCIAL AFFILIATIONS: None.

DESCRIPTION OF MATERIALS ALREADY PRODUCED:
1. Project descriptive brochure.
2. Learning Activity Modules for kindergarten through grade 4 (see above under "Unique Characteristics").
3. Instructional bulletins.
4. Schedule and sequence of project development.

MATERIALS AVAILABLE FREE:
Items 1 and 4.

MATERIALS PURCHASABLE:
None.

ADDITIONAL MATERIALS BEING DEVELOPED:
Learning Activity Modules, Grades 5 and 6, to be in classrooms February, 1972. Learning Activity Modules, High and Junior High Schools, to be completed school year 1972–73.

LANGUAGE IN WHICH MATERIALS:
1. Were originally written: English.
2. Have been or will be translated: Elementary learning activity modules include material in Spanish. Sample student material in Spanish available from Project Coordinator.

COUNTRIES IN WHICH MATERIALS ARE USED:
United States.

PROJECT IMPLEMENTATION:
The material is not available as an entire program.
1. Total number of teachers using any of the materials: 75 to extend to 1,700 (1974).
2. Total number of students using any of the materials: 3,600 to extend to 35,000 (1974).
3. Total number of schools using any of the materials: 75 to extend to 650 (1974).
4. The totals stated in 1, 2, and 3 are definitive for school year 1971–72 and a close estimate for year 1974.

5. Name and location of selected schools where the program is in use: Elementary schools at Castle Heights, 9755 Cattaraugus Avenue, Los Angeles, Calif.; Grape Street, 1940 E. 111th Street, Los Angeles, Calif.; Marvin Avenue, 2411 Marvin Avenue, Los Angeles, Calif.; Ann Street, 126 Bloom Street, Los Angeles, Calif.; Compton Avenue, 1515 E. 104th Street, Los Angeles, Calif.; Murchison, 1501 Murchison Street, Los Angeles, Calif.; Toluca Lake, 4840 Cahuenga Blvd., North Hollywood, Calif.; Rio Vista, 4235 Satsuma Avenue, North Hollywood, Calif.

TEACHER PREPARATION:
1. Consultant services available for teachers using the materials: At the Laurel Ecology Center, (213) 656-7457, contact Leroy A. Stromme, William L. Wilson, or Shirley Leon.
2. Activities conducted for pre-service and in-service teacher training: Comprehensive Staff Development. Concentrated staff development has begun by releasing teachers to attend comprehensive inservice training. Teachers release time is accomplished through project funds. No local funds available. Release time costs approximately $60.00 per teacher per day.
3. Available preservice and/or inservice teaching materials for science educators to use in preparing teachers: Actual Learning Module materials are used in pre-service and in-service training. These are not available for outside purchase.

PROJECT EVALUATION:
1. Has the effectiveness of the materials been evaluated: Yes, internally and by Educational and Community Consultants and Planners, Inc., San Francisco, Calif.
2. Pertinent published research studies: None.
3. Brief abstract of in-house or unpublished research: All in-house and outside agency evaluations are submitted to the U.S. Office of Education.
4. Evaluative data available to interested individuals: Evaluation will be available as released by the U.S. Office of Education.

PROJECT PUBLICITY:
None.

SUMMARY OF PROJECT ACTIVITIES SINCE 1970 REPORT:
Not previously listed.

PLANS FOR THE FUTURE:
Future development includes expansion of services to sixteen high schools and their feeder junior high and elementary schools during the third year of project development. The establishment of four ecology centers for 1974. Development of two mobile ecology laboratories by 1974. A total implementation of the program throughout the Los Angeles Unified School District serving sixty-two high schools, seventy-five junior high schools and 449 elementary schools by 1975.

Creative Aspects

This program has an ecological theme whose configuration is especially adaptable to creative teaching and learning. However, if creative awareness is lacking, the systems approach might conceivably lead to prescriptive teaching.

PROJECT IN-STEP (IN-SERVICE TEACHER EDUCATION PROGRAM)

PROJECT DIRECTOR:
John C. Thurber, Director, Inservice Education, Palm Beach County Schools, P.O. Box 2469, West Palm Beach, Fla. 33402. (305) 683-0050.

PROJECT HEADQUARTERS:
1. Contact: Project Director.
2. Special facilities or activities available for visitor viewing: Previewing of project-produced videotapes or kinescopes.

PRINCIPAL PROFESSIONAL STAFF:
John C. Thurber, Director; Allen L. Carnahan, Instructor; Karl L. Combs, Instructor; J. Georgann Hall, Instructor; Merton P. Baker, Instructor; Sam J. Barbaro, TV Producer; Robert Evans, Program Statistician; Alice O. Williamson, Secretary.

PROJECT SUPPORT:
1. Funding agencies: U.S. Office of Education—Title III ESEA (P.L. 89-10)
2 Associated agencies: Not answered.

PROJECT HISTORY:
1. Principal originators: John C. Thurber, Dr. Rodney A. Lane, Dr. Harold M. Harmes, Robert Binger, Robert Westbrook.
2. Date and place of initiation: July 1, 1968; Palm Beach, Fla.
3. Evolution and development of the project: Phases I and II— development of an individualized, multimedia approach to in- service teacher education. The vehicle used for development of model was AAAS Science. Phase III—implementation of the model developed in Phases I and II in a program for development of teaching strategies.

PROJECT OBJECTIVES:
1. Overall project purpose: Development, implementation, field testing, and revision of an individualized, multimedia model for in-service teacher education.

2. Specific objectives:
   (a) Development of an individualized program for training teachers in *Science—A Process Approach*. The complete program is available for this course.
   (b) Development of an individualized, multimedia, modular program in teaching strategies. The complete program is now available for this course.

UNIQUE CHARACTERISTICS OF THE PROJECT:
These programs or the model developed can be used to effect teacher training for a large number of teachers at low cost. The Phase III program in teaching strategies can be made applicable to any content area and also to effective programs. In a large group, individual teachers can still be working towards own goals.

SPECIFIC SUBJECTS, GRADE, AGE AND ABILITY LEVELS:
Phases I and II—teachers of elementary science; Phase III—teachers of any and/or all subjects, grades, age and ability levels as well as administrators.

MAIN METHODS OF INSTRUCTION
USED IN THE PROJECT:
Independent study, programmed instruction, laboratory investigations, seminars, discussion sessions, videotapes, action handbook, and kinescopes.

PRESENT COMMERCIAL AFFILIATIONS:
A program in in-service education systems based upon the concept of the IN-STEP model is available through Interactive Education, Inc., a Prentice-Hall company, 2525 Old Okeechobee Road, West Palm Beach, Fla. 33401.

DESCRIPTION OF MATERIALS ALREADY PRODUCED:
IN-STEP, PHASES I AND II.
Videotape series (tape length—25 minutes).
 1. Introductory to IN-STEP.
 2. Philosophy and Mechanics of *Science—A Process Approach*.
 3. Behavioral Objectives I.
 4. Behavioral Objectives II.
 5. Implementation I.
 6. Implementation II.
 7. Observing I—(Process Rationale).
 8. Observing II—(Sample Lesson).
 9. Classifying I—(Process Rationale).
10. Classifying II—(Sample Lesson).
11. Using Space–Time Relationships I—(Process Rationale).
12. Using Space–Time Relationships II—(Sample Lesson).
13. Communicating I—(Process Rationale).
14. Communicating II—(Sample Lesson).

15. Measuring I—(Process Rationale).
16. Measuring II—(Sample Lesson).
17. Inferring I—(Process Rationale).
18. Inferring II—(Sample Lesson).
19. Predicting I—(Process Rationale).
20. Predicting II—(Sample Lesson).
21. Formulating Hypotheses I—(Process Rationale).
22. Formulating Hypotheses II—(Sample Lesson).
23. Controlling Variables I—(Process Rationale).
24. Controlling Variables II   (Sample Lesson).
25. Interpreting Data I—(Process Rationale).
26. Interpreting Data II—(Sample Lesson).
27. Defining Operationally—(Process Rationale and Lesson).
28. Using Numbers—(Process Rationale and Lesson).
29. Experimenting I—(Process Rationale).
30. Experimenting II—(Sample Lesson).
Other Items:
31. Kinescope copies of the videotape series.
32. Action Handbook (correlated with videotape series) involves participants in psychomotor activities, before, after, and sometimes during viewing of tape series in order to aid in development of cognitive skills.
33. Self-Study Programmed Text includes material on: philosophy of contemporary science education in the elementary schools emphasizing AAAS, the format of AAAS material, behavioral objectives, and each of the basic and integrated processes.
34. Elementary Science Teachers Inventory (pre- and post-test).
35. Teacher Attitude Survey Questionnaire.
36. Student Tests of Process Acquisition: a) Observation, b) Measurement.
37. Q-Sort student attitude survey on I.B.M. cards for easy scoring.
38. Footprints from IN-STEP (newsletter).
39. Evaluation Report—Phase I.
40. Evaluation Report—Phase II.
IN-STEP, PHASE III.
Videotape series with description of content—tape length approximately 25 minutes.
41. Psychological Foundations—rationale for the role of innovation in the curricula of the "seventies."
42. Systems Approach—rationale for using a systems approach in designing an instructional program.
43. Behavioral Objectives—use of behavioral objectives in designing an instructional system.
44. Educational Taxonomies—how to use educational taxonomies when planning an instructional sequence.
45. Behavioral Hierarchies—how to recognize and construct a behavioral hierarchy.

46. Educational Needs Assessment I—rationale for conducting an educational needs assessment.

47. Educational Needs Assessment II—how to conduct an educational needs assessment.

48. Instructional Systems—how to develop an instructional system.

49. Instructional Techniques—how to develop and recognize appropriate (equivalent and analogous) educational tasks.

50. Feedback and Evaluation—techniques for evaluating an instructional system.

Other Items:

51. Kinescope copies of the videotape series.

52. Action Handbook Phase III—correlated with each videotape–kinescope (items 41–50).

53. Self-Study Programmed Text Phase III—one chapter on each of items 41–50.

54. Teacher Survey.

55. Evaluation Report—Phase III.

MATERIALS FREE:

Items 32–40 (Phase I and II) and items 52–55 (Phase III).

MATERIALS PURCHASABLE:

Items 1–31 and 41–50. These may be leased for $50.00 a tape or kinescope for one week (approximately $1500 for Phases I and II lessons, and $500 for Phase III lessons). In some cases a set of 2″ tapes may be supplied at no charge to systems desiring to duplicate at their own expense.

ADDITIONAL MATERIALS BEING DEVELOPED:
None.

LANGUAGE IN WHICH MATERIALS:

1. Were originally written: English.

2. Have been or will be translated: Possibly Spanish.

COUNTRIES IN WHICH MATERIALS ARE USED:

United States, Canada, Great Britain, and Lebanon. Being examined for use in Chile, Argentina, and Venezuela.

PROJECT IMPLEMENTATION:

1. Total number of teachers using any of the materials: 1,000+.

2. Total number of students using any of the materials: Indirectly 30,000+.

3. Total number of schools using any of the materials: 150+.

4. Number of teachers who have adopted the entire program: 1,000+.

5. Number of students involved: 30,000+.

6. Number of schools involved: 150+.

7. The basic totals stated in 1, 2, 3, 4, 5, and 6 are definitive, anything above is estimated.

8. Name and location of selected schools where the program is in use: Palm Beach County Schools, Fla. (contact John C. Thurber); Alachua County Schools, Fla. (contact J. Strickland); Toronto, Canada (contact D. M. Jolley).

TEACHER PREPARATION:
1. Consultant services available for teachers using the materials: Project staff is available for consultant services.
2. Activities conducted for pre-service and in-service teacher training: Workshops for AAAS Science, Implementation of AAAS, Utilization of AAAS materials, Behavioral Objectives, In-service training in Modern Staff Development Programs. Costs depend upon nature of workshop and number of staff involved.
3. Available pre-service and/or in-service teaching materials for science educators to use in preparing teachers: This project applies directly to the in-service education of teachers.

PROJECT EVALUATION:
1. Has the effectiveness of the materials been evaluated: Yes, internally and by the Florida State Department of Education.
2. Pertinent published research studies: Evaluation Report—Phase I, ERIC. Evaluation Report—Phase II, ERIC.
3. Brief abstract of in-house or unpublished research: The IN-STEP Model for in-service education is a successful method for in-service teacher education. The model and programs have been shown to be efficient, effective, and economical.
4. Evaluative data available to interested individuals: Yes. Contact Project Director.

PROJECT PUBLICITY:
Not answered.

BRIEF SUMMARY OF PROJECT ACTIVITIES
SINCE 1970 REPORT:
Development of IN-STEP PHASE III Program.

PLANS FOR THE FUTURE:
Phase out of federal funding. However, materials produced will continue to be available; concept and model can be built into any systems in-service or pre-service program. Consultant service available from Project Director.

Creative Aspects

The stress on individualization and the multimedia element suggests a creative approach to the in-service program but to achieve this depends on the way the program is conducted.

ALL ELEMENTARY CURRICULUM MATERIALS
CAN BE MADE MORE CREATIVE

Although the curriculum projects above are discovery oriented, this does not mean that they cannot be improved by making them more creative. In fact many of these projects have in their materials relatively convergent questions, some requiring only yes or no answers. For example, the Elementary Science Study, *Bone Picture Book* asks many convergent questions: Do these animals use their long tails? Does this animal run, walk, or hop? Is this a dinosaur skull? Do other skulls have cracks? How would you change these questions to make them more divergent and therefore allow for more creative answers? Teachers aware of the importance of asking divergent questions to stimulate creative thought can do much to improve not only these instructional aids but others as well.

SUMMARY

The Physical Science Study Committee, established in 1956, was the first National Curriculum Project. Its financial support and methods of operation in revising a curriculum were revolutionary. It received millions of dollars to carry out its work, had a national trial testing program for two years, and produced all the instructional materials needed for the teaching of physics. These instructional aids included texts, laboratory manuals, films, unique and inexpensive equipment, and supplemental readings. The PSSC's method of operation has been followed by other nationally supported curriculum developments in both secondary and elementary education.

All of the national curriculum projects have produced materials that stress 1) learning science as a process, 2) developing inquiry competencies, and 3) involving children in science activities. Many projects are actively attempting to develop an elementary science curriculum for all of the grades, notably, Minnemast, Science—A Process Approach, Conceptually Oriented Programs in Elementary Science (COPES) and Science Curriculum Improvement Study, and Model Education Program in Ecology. Several other projects have produced units that could be used as part of a school district's course of study. They include the

Elementary Science Study, Individualized Science, Science Curriculum Improvement Study, School Science Curriculum Project, Science for the Seventies, and Science Concept Development in the Elementary School Through Inquiry Training.

QUESTIONS

1. What do the new elementary science projects have in common with each other?

2. If you were to choose one of the new elementary curriculum projects to teach, which would you use and why?

3. What advantages and disadvantages are there in using some of the new elementary texts instead of the curriculum project materials?

4. Obtain one of the curriculum project's materials and show how you would adapt one of their lessons for creative teaching. Outline also how you could use it to destroy creativity.

5. Look over one of the new science text series and describe how you would use one of the unit activities contained in them to teach for creativity.

6. If you were going to evaluate a curriculum for creativity, what one item do you think would be highest on your criteria for judging it? Why?

7. "Science—A Process Approach" lists several behavioral objectives under the heading "integrative categories." Why do you think they have given them this heading?

8. What advantages are there in having an inquiry-oriented curriculum in science, and how would it complement the overall objectives of the school?

9. Why do you think modern curriculum projects do not stress creativity as an objective?

10. If you were selected to head a new curriculum project and you were to meet with your new staff of twenty people for the first time, what would you do to orient them to creative science?

CHAPTER VII

Improving Curriculum Projects —The Concern for Creativity in Curriculum Reform

> *If sheer volume of knowledge were sufficient for predictive purposes, the problem of identifying and developing creative potential would be near solution. If so, we could merely consider each student as a "spongehead" and do everything possible to pour knowledge into him so that he who absorbed the most knowledge would be the one who would create the most new things.*
>
> CALVIN TAYLOR

ELEMENTARY SCIENCE TEXTBOOK REVISION

Most elementary school districts have either developed or adopted a science curriculum, or are in the process of selecting one from current programs. The present science programs almost always include one of the many elementary science textbook series now available—in fact, in many school districts it *is* the science program.

Textbook publishers in recent years have made many changes to meet the objectives of modern science education and many can be rated as good as or better than the national studies programs just described. There has been great improvement in the quality of the science texts available for elementary grades. Attractive format, abundant illustrations, and handsome color printing are in marked contrast to the less inviting books of a decade or so ago.

Most of the texts have abandoned the dialogue technique or "Dick and Jane" approach as a means of enlivening the material, and authors have made significant progress in writing in a manner that reveals to young readers the fascination inherent in science. The authors are also better grounded in science content. Although inaccuracies still persist, attempts are now made to hold them to a minimum. Many of the books also reveal that the authors are familiar with what is known about how children learn. For example, the question-and-answer approach, usually absent in the earlier books, is now more common. Although inquiry is more apparent in current textbooks, few authors are courageous enough to omit the answers from the text and relegate them to the teacher's manual. Most texts today provide ample opportunity for developing scientific attitudes and critical and creative thinking through concept formation. However, the process approach heartily endorsed by scientists and educators has increasingly become reflected in current text series.

ON USING YOUR SCIENCE TEXTBOOK

Although textbooks should be inextricably tied in with curriculum, the evidence indicates that many teachers lack knowledge of the textbook's function in a modern science program. There is as great a variation in the use of textbooks as there are ways that science is taught by the individual teacher.

Except for an occasional reference, some classroom teachers seldom use the textbook. Others may use it merely for ideas for discussion and demonstration. Of course the majority of teachers rely heavily on the textbook to shape their science program—and it often becomes the mainstay of such a program. The latter may be especially true for teachers who lack confidence in their knowledge of content and who feel insecure in teaching science. If this is the case, science may become almost entirely a reading activity. One pupil will read a paragraph in a text, another will continue with a second paragraph, and so on until the unit is completed. The teacher may perform an occasional demonstration provided it is clearly described in the text and the material is available, but questions arising from the text may be discouraged if the teacher's background is inadequate. It is obvious what the implication may be to the learners: The pupil is challenged to experience only to the degree that the text guides or directs him to activity.

This points up the need for guidance in the proper use of texts. Complete reliance on learning science through the sole medium of "reading about science" leaves much to be desired. A skillful teacher attempts to maintain an equilibrium between reading and other learning activities and makes selections on the basis of what is best for the pupil in a given learning situation. Some authors, cognizant of good teaching practice, frequently suggest activities that heighten observation and experiment and go beyond the confines of the textbook to focus on the creative aspects of science learning. Reading is an important tool in learning science, and textbooks may insure a developmental program and serve a unique function in the learning process.

CRITERIA FOR SELECTING AND EVALUATING SCIENCE TEXTBOOKS

The task of selecting a science textbook series for a school system is an enormous responsibility requiring close adherence to carefully selected criteria. Listed below are some basic criteria that focus on the creativity factor in text selection:

1. Are the books discovery oriented? Do they have many activities and experiments for children to discover things that matter?
2. Are the lessons teaching not only basic concepts and principles of science but how to inquire as well?
3. Do they give considerable depth to a topic, or are the topics superficially covered, and do they contain mostly pictures? Creative activity is more likely to occur when the children have had many diverse experiences in an area of interest.
4. Do the texts emphasize science activity with reading as a vehicle to carry the process?
5. Do the activities allow for creative use of measuring and quantifying in a science problem?
6. Do the texts stimulate imagination, and is it likely that with the encouragement of the teacher children will come up with ideas for experiments? Are there opportunities for creative enterprise in the texts?[1]

Most published elementary science texts would have difficulty in scoring 100 percent on all of the above criteria. A creative teacher will supplement from any possible source—national

1. For further suggestions for evaluating texts see: Harry Milgrom, "Science Books—33 Keys to Evaluation," *Science and Children* (March 1964), pp. 16–17.

curriculum projects, teacher-prepared lessons, multiple series texts, courses of study, and a host of audio-visual aids.

Two different sets of criteria for selection of science textbooks of an earlier vintage are shown below. If you were revising these sets today to insure that science texts reflected the creative process, what changes would you make?

CRITERIA FOR SELECTION OF ELEMENTARY SCIENCE TEXTBOOKS, GRADES 1–6[2]

Publishers

Criteria						
I. Attractiveness and usability for teachers and pupils: 1. format—printing, size of type 2. size of book, open pages, amount of white space 3. binding, cover, durability 4. glossary table of contents, index, bibliography						
II. Qualification of authors: 1. background and experience, elementary science teaching, elementary supervision 2. publications on method and procedure, evidence of research						
III. Readability: 1. reading level with respect to concept development 2. sentence length and space between lines conducive to easy reading						

2. Developed by Albert Piltz and evaluated with the Book Selection Committee, Detroit Public Schools, Detroit, Michigan, 1959.

CRITERIA FOR SELECTION OF ELEMENTARY SCIENCE
TEXTBOOKS, GRADES 1–6 (continued)

Publishers

Criteria						
IV. Guides and teaching aids: 1. teacher manuals suitable to the inexperienced science teacher as well as the experienced science teacher 2. bibliography for teachers						
V. Visual aids: 1. quality, accuracy and sufficiency of diagrammatic drawing, pictures, charts, graphs and tables 2. up-to-dateness of diagrammatic drawings, pictures, charts, graphs and tables 3. contribution to the understanding of content						
VI. Provision for individual differences: 1. additional science experiences sufficient to keep the learner working to capacity						
VII. Basic philosophy: 1. content promotes scientific attitudes and the use of the scientific method 2. promotes understanding and application of the way scientists have influenced history with inventions and discoveries						

CRITERIA FOR SELECTION OF ELEMENTARY SCIENCE
TEXTBOOKS, GRADES 1–6 (continued)

Publishers

Criteria							
VIII. Readiness: 1. book so written that meanings are established before new concepts are introduced 2. skills are developed in terms of readiness							
IX. Developmental methods: 1. science concepts related to social applications such as health, safety, conservation, etc. 2. known method (scientific problem solving) used in in the solutions of new problems 3. book provides opportunity for the child to learn by doing 4. explanations of scientific principles made in short, simple, understandable language 5. pupils' thinking guides through thought-provoking questions, suggestions, and directions 6. pupils led to generalize about new experiences on the level of meaning and understanding 7. problems and subject matter left open-ended (no problem finite or subject matter all-inclusive)							

CRITERIA FOR SELECTION OF ELEMENTARY SCIENCE TEXTBOOKS, GRADES 1–6 (continued)

Criteria	Publishers					
8. stresses principles, and uses technology as application of principles						
X. Content: 1. progresses and expands through a building-up process which represents a continuous reorganization of past experience—leads to emphasis upon relationships 2. leads to understanding in other subject matter areas 3. leads to greater appreciations of human relationships 4. presents science as a body of organized facts based upon accepted scientific principles which will enable the child to draw generalizations concerning his environment 5. material up to date and related to the daily life of the child. Each unit sufficiently independent to allow for "incidental teaching"						
XI. Problem solving: 1. an inherent part of the regular quantity and variety of science experiences						

CRITERIA FOR SELECTION OF ELEMENTARY SCIENCE
TEXTBOOKS, GRADES 1–6 (continued)

Publishers

Criteria						
2. book provides abundant opportunity for children to explore and discover for themselves						
XII. Balance: 1. must exist between the physical and biological sciences						

CRITERIA FOR EVALUATION OF TEXTBOOKS IN SCIENCE[3]

Title of Textbook	Publisher	Basic or Supplementary	Grade

LOW TO HIGH

0   1   2   3   4
— — — — —

TO WHAT DEGREE DOES THE BOOK:

A. *Point of View*

    1. Present science from a developmental point of view, i.e., needs, interest and capacities of children?   — — — — —

    2. Focus on social values through the basic philosophy in science?   — — — — —

    3. Clearly delineate in the presentation the underlying point of view in science?   — — — — —

3. Developed by Albert Piltz for the Book Selection Committee of Los Angeles County, 1956.

CRITERIA FOR EVALUATION OF TEXTBOOKS (continued)

Title of Textbook	Publisher	Basic or Supplementary	Grade

LOW TO HIGH

	0	1	2	3	4

B. *Content and Concept Formation*

1. Present materials in science known to be significant to children? — — — — —
2. Offer a balance in content between the physical and life sciences? — — — — —
3. Give consideration to an appreciation of the work of scientists and their contribution to social living? — — — — —
4. Help children appreciate and interpret the world around them? — — — — —
5. Help children develop an understanding of science through a wide variety of experiences, which enable them to face and solve problems? — — — — —
6. Offer opportunities for developing a continuous and integrated sequence of science experiences? — — — — —
7. Gradually introduce and develop basic science concepts and principles? — — — — —
8. Recognize the dynamic drives of children by providing opportunities to manipulate, investigate, explore, and discover for themselves? — — — — —
9. Lead children to develop desirable behavior in health, economy, and safety? — — — — —
10. Encourage the child to go beyond the ideas and experiences shown in the book? — — — — —
11. Foster a scientific attitude and develop critical thinking, i.e., careful observation, open-mindedness, weighing evidence, suspending judgment until all the facts are in, seeing relationships, generalizing and making application? — — — — —
12. Provide situations in science for improving skill in problem solving? — — — — —
13. Stimulate original thinking and creativity? — — — — —

CRITERIA FOR EVALUATION OF TEXTBOOKS (continued)

Title of Textbook	Publisher	Basic or Supplementary	Grade

LOW TO HIGH

0   1   2   3   4

14. Point up science as an integral part of the democratic process? — — — — —
15. Incorporate science information to help build security in children? — — — — —
16. Indicate opportunities for developing responsible citizenship through science experiences? — — — — —
17. Present reliable information based on research? — — — — —
18. Suggest simple materials and equipment which are readily available? — — — — —
19. Lead children to construct equipment and improvise materials for experimentation? — — — — —

C. *Appropriateness to Maturity Levels*
1. Develop concepts commensurate with the capacities of children? — — — — —
2. Recognize the maturity levels of children in relation to the reading level? — — — — —
3. Use a direct, clear, and suitable style of of writing which is appropriate to the abilities of children? — — — — —

D. *Physical Features*
1. Utilize paper, print and margins for ease in reading? — — — — —
2. Include up-to-date, realistic, accurate, and appropriate illustrations? — — — — —
3. Present a table of contents easily used by children? — — — — —
4. Include a readily usable index? — — — — —
5. Provide a functional glossary? — — — — —

E. *Guide for Teachers*
1. Develop a point of view and give appropriate guidance in a teachers' manual? — — — — —
2. Provide specific helps in content procedures and sources of material by means of a teacher's manual? — — — — —

THE SCIENCE SUPERVISOR SHOULD ENCOURAGE TEACHERS TO BE CREATIVE

Creative development is not likely to occur unless children have freedom under the guidance and helpful direction of a teacher. And this is just as true of the teacher. She should be allowed freedom in selecting instructional materials within the framework of the objectives of the elementary school curriculum. Science supervisors need to encourage this freedom, inform teachers of the kinds of materials available, encourage testing of creative objectives, and provide examples of creative activities for all grade levels according to the teacher's interest and capability.

TRENDS IN ELEMENTARY SCIENCE TEACHING OF A PAST DECADE— HAVE THEY BEEN REALIZED?

In 1962, at a Conference of State Supervisors of Science at the U.S. Office of Education, Dr. Philip G. Johnson of Cornell University summarized the directions of change in elementary and junior high school science as follows:

1. From much subject matter to less.
2. From one problem-solving method to many relatively unstructured instructional methods.
3. From much use of one textbook in a series to the use of many books.
4. From emphasis on accumulating knowledge to an emphasis on how to find and create knowledge.
5. From facts and factual concepts to skill in inquiry as teaching goals.
6. From teacher selected concepts as teaching goals to concepts as they arise in confirming and rejecting hypotheses.
7. From the terms "elementary science" and "general science" to science.
8. From reliance on qualitative observation to stress on making and recording quantitative observations.
9. From films that stress a body of knowledge to films that report one or a series of experiments.
10. From science experiences as preparation for secondary school science to experiences for the basic education of all pupils.
11. From science as something to be learned from books to something that grows out of a series of experiments.

12. From a program based on topics, limited concepts, and experiments to one based on a more fundamental frame of reference.
13. From great attention to uses of science including technology to more attention to science.
14. From science built on a limited understanding of mathematics to science built on mathematics.[4]

Elementary teachers, administrators, and science supervisors should evaluate their own curricula in the light of these trends of a past decade. These might suggest that predictions do not always anticipate events such as the environmental crisis and the energy crisis—essential factors for improving and modernizing programs in science education today. The following two sections should be of assistance in this.

A SUGGESTED EVALUATION OF CURRICULUM MATERIALS FOR CREATIVITY

The following basic criteria are suggested to evaluate a curriculum for its contribution to creative science objectives:

1. Are there many experiments for the children to become actively involved in? Are the experiments non-cookbook in design? Do they allow for some freedom on the part of the pupil?
2. Are the activities designed around inquiry? The inquiry, however, should not be just for inquiry's sake but lead to discovering important concepts and scientific principles.
3. Do the activities provide opportunities for the child to develop the following skills?
   a. Recognize problems.
   b. Formulate hypotheses.
   c. Test hypotheses (by designing experimental situations).
   d. Interpret data and draw conclusions.
   e. Provide for and suggest methods of communicating information while allowing for creative involvement of the child.
   f. Indicate and develop opportunities for further experimentation. In other words, are the experiments open-ended? Does the child progressing through the curriculum become increasingly sophisticated in seeing the open-endedness of experiments? For example, in the primary grades when the

4. Philip G. Johnson, "Changing Directions in Elementary and Junior High School Science," *Supervision for Quality Education in Science* (Washington, D.C.: U.S. Government, October 1962).

child engages in an experiment to determine the necessity of light for plants, are suggestions made as to how he might determine whether plants would grow in other kinds of light? Do the early lessons in the curriculum give this type of guidance but, as they progress, reduce these props until in the upper grades the children are simply asked to suggest further problems arising out of their study or experimentation?

DESIGNING A SCIENCE CURRICULUM FOR CREATIVITY

In designing curriculum materials to develop creative potential in science, the following points should be considered in the context of our social milieu and in terms of programs which may be oriented to "behavioral" objectives or any other. These points have implication for a wide variety of practices.

1. Creative ability is present in all children but their modes of expression will vary. Children should have opportunities to express their individual differences in varied types of science activities requiring creative responses.
2. Inquiring actvities that require imagination, originality, formulations and testing of hypotheses, discovery of problems, making judgments, and communicating discoveries should be included in the curriculum. Schools generally have not designed curricular materials to help children discover problems. The necessity of this skill, however, is becoming increasingly important. The advent of the computer means that many problems will be solved by machine. This will free the individual from doing the routine and menial. However, the demand for individuals to recognize problems and state them for the machine to solve will become more paramount.
3. The more creative the curriculum materials, the more likely they are to stimulate creativity among the teachers and pupils. Teachers should be encouraged to innovate, and to deviate from prepared curriculum materials, especially if they discover a "teaching moment" when the class or some individual is particularly motivated to study a problem not included in the curriculum. These innovated activities, however, should contribute to the general objectives of the science curriculum. The curriculum materials should provide the basic foundation for science instruction but should not become the dictum to be followed by all classes at a designated time. When innovated activities arise from children's interest and achieve considerable success, they should be considered for incorporation into the curriculum for other teachers to use and test.

4. Teachers should be encouraged to modify and design curricular materials. Above all they should not look at the curriculum as static but as constantly undergoing change and improvement. A teacher who enjoys a particular area of science should be encouraged to work in this area to improve the curriculum and to make it more creative.
5. Team teaching can be used as a method of testing, evaluating, and designing creative materials. Team teaching provides an atmosphere for honest editing by teachers. The materials produced have the advantage of being created by several teachers, tested under the watchful eyes of these teachers, and evaluated. They are more likely to have value for other teachers in the district because of their empirical base with children of that community.

HOW AN ELEMENTARY SCHOOL ADMINISTRATOR CAN CONTRIBUTE TO CREATIVE ACTIVITY IN SCIENCE

An administrator is responsible for the educational program and often exerts a position of leadership in curriculum development and reforms. He should, therefore, be cognizant of the criteria for evaluating how well his school's curriculum contributes to creative science objectives such as those discussed above. Some other ways he can contribute to these objectives are listed below:

1. Encourage teachers to be creative and experimental. Inform them that to fail when using a new technique is no sin but not to try to improve is.
2. Evaluate curricular failures for indications of some good ideas.
3. Do not overload teachers with excessive duties.
4. Attempt to get feedback of creative work being done in classes.
5. Have faculty meetings where creative work is recognized and reported by teachers. Bring in teachers from other schools and districts to show what they do. Evaluate ideas for experimentation in these meetings.
6. Occasionally have brainstorming sessions on how the schools can be more creative in science and other subjects.
7. Encourage communication between administration and teachers as much as possible.
8. Attempt to be creative in the aid given the teacher. For example, if a teacher wishes to purchase equipment beyond the the budget's possibilities, try to construct or suggest ways of improvising the apparatus. Become actively involved in con-

FIGURE 7-1. *A teacher's direct experience with all components of a lesson plan is vital. Experiment "failures" are often crucial learning points. Also, most teachers are better equipped to adapt changes and additions for their class after having reviewed all strategies. (Photo from Los Angeles Unified Schools—A Model Educational Program in Ecology, ESEA Title III)*

structing some of this apparatus. By so doing, you contribute to better morale and demonstrate active concern for learning in the classroom.

9. Don't overemphasize committee work or require teachers to work in teams.

10. Assign one of your creative teachers to work with the new teachers to help them develop creative activities.

11. Give recognition to students' creative work. When teachers have pupils work on science projects and make apparatus, inform the local papers so that this may be publicized. Observe classes, and when you see some creative activity or the product of such activity, compliment the teacher and pupils on it.

12. Endeavor as much as possible to develop in the school a creative environment where there is freedom of expression and experimentation.

13. If you do not already have team teaching, experiment with the approach with teachers who would like to try it. Stress that one of the objectives of using team teaching is to produce more creative teaching and creative activities for children. Encourage these teachers to evaluate their teaching and

experiment to produce creative curriculum materials for use by other teachers.

SUMMARY

The publishers of science textbooks have also been active in updating their publications so that they better meet the objectives of modern science education, have adapted many of the national studies' innovative ideas, and have also pioneered in developing process and inquiry activities related to the learner. It is important, therefore, that the selection of a text series should be determined on the basis of how well it stresses student involvement in science experience and provides opportunities to nurture creative endeavor. There are presently certain trends evolving in elementary science teaching centered mainly around 1) humanizing science, 2) giving greater emphasis on teaching the processes of science, 3) the use of mathematics in science, 4) greater experimentation by children, 5) learning through inquiry, and 6) developing a consciousness for the social ends of education particularly in the environmental and ecological field.

None of the present elementary science courses of study, units, or text books are specifically designed to develop creativity. However, because some of them require imagination, intuition, formulating and testing of hypotheses, and divergent patterns of thinking, they can, under the proper leadership and encouragement be adapted to meet the objectives of creativity.

Lists of suggestions for the evaluation and production of a curriculum, plus ideas for administrators to stimulate creative activity in the school, are included in the chapter.

QUESTIONS

1. What criteria would you use in the selection of a text series to insure that creative elements were present?

2. How would you compare contemporary elementary science texts with national studies programs?

3. Why are texts needed in a modern science program?

4. How would you rate textbooks when compared to other instructional aids in a creative program of science?

5. Consult Dr. Philip Johnson's list of trends in science education of over a decade ago. Show how his predictions are valid or invalid today. Why?

6. As a newly hired science supervisor, you have discovered that the science curriculum needs revision. How would you go about revising it and why?

7. Most school districts have some creative teachers. If this is true, how can you explain why they haven't made much impact in changing the instruction in the districts?

8. As an administrator, how would you develop creative teaching?

9. As an administrator, how would you insure that your staff continues to become more sophisticated in teaching creatively from year to year?

10. How would you evaluate the program, Model Education Program in Ecology, in the light of modern curricular requirements?

CHAPTER VIII

Examples of
Creative Science Activity

*The moment of illumination brings the process of creation
to a climax. Suddenly the creator grasps the solution to his
problem—the concept that focuses all his facts, the thought
that completes the chain of ideas on which he is working.
In the moment of inspiration everything falls into place.*

GEORGE F. KNELLER

This chapter contains examples of teaching techniques to stimulate creative activity for several different grade levels. The suitability of these suggestions for any particular level will vary with the competency of the teacher and the abilities of the students.

These activities are only examples; there has been no effort to cover all the areas of science subject matter nor to develop conceptual schemes. We encourage teachers to use these examples merely as guides for their own teaching designs, since teacher-designed activities will be more likely to focus on specific objectives.

All of these examples are centered around some aspect of problem solving and are designed to evoke creativity in the student. In solving a problem a student can be both original and inventive; the degree will depend on the nature of the problem, its complexity and difficulty, and the resources involved. Problem solving takes many forms. It may require the student to classify, use space and time relationships, communicate information, infer, predict, formulate hypotheses, control variables, design experiments, interpret data, or construct models.

Discovering, recognizing, and seeing possibilities for problems arising out of an experiment are to be strongly encouraged, since the identification of problems is one of the most important attributes of the creative scientist. The teaching techniques included in this section should never become the cemented structure of a span of class time through which the children move in lockstep fashion. Such a procedure is the antithesis of creativity. The teacher should consider the needs, abilities, interest, and maturity of the children and select and adapt those activities which best meet his or her purposes. If some of the activities appear too sophisticated for the pupils, others should be substituted, or sufficient background provided to make them meaningful. Activities should not be used at random but rather fit the context of the overall objectives in the learning sequence. All in all, the teacher should benefit from the illustrations by gaining new insights into ways of converting traditional science to creative science.

Before thinking of specific techniques for improving creativity, it is good to renew the creative teaching principles that appeared in the first book of the Creative Teaching Series. Constantly use these as a guide to evaluate your progress toward becoming a more dynamic, creative teacher.

PRINCIPLES OF CREATIVE TEACHING[1]

1. In creative teaching, something new, different or unique results.
2. In creative teaching, divergent thinking processes are stressed.
3. In creative teaching, motivational tensions are a prerequisite to the creative process. The process serves as a tension-relieving agent.
4. In creative teaching, open-ended situations are utilized.
5. In creative teaching, there comes a time when the teacher withdraws and children face the unknown themselves.
6. In creative teaching, the outcomes are unpredictable.
7. In creative teaching, conditions are set which make possible preconscious thinking.
8. Creative teaching means that students are encouraged to generate and develop their own ideas.

1. James A. Smith, *Setting Conditions for Creative Teaching in the Elementary School* (Boston: Allyn and Bacon, Inc., 1966). These eighteen creative principles are the main headings of paragraphs found on pages 157–162.

9. In creative teaching, differences, uniqueness, individuality, originality are stressed and rewarded.
10. In creative teaching, the process is as important as the product.
11. In creative teaching, certain conditions must be set to permit creativity to appear.
12. In creative teaching, teaching is "success" rather than "failure" oriented.
13. In creative teaching, provision is made to learn knowledge and skills but provision is also made to apply these in new problem-solving situations.
14. In creative teaching, self-initiated learning is encouraged.
15. In creative teaching, skills of constructive criticism and evaluation skills are developed.
16. In creative teaching, ideas and objects are manipulated and explored.
17. Creative teaching employs democratic processes.
18. In creative teaching, methods are used which are unique to the development of creativity.

RULES TO FOLLOW IN STIMULATING CREATIVE WORK

In interviewing and observing teachers who have been successful in developing creative ability, we have found that they generally follow certain patterns of behavior which we have translated into rules and outlined below to assist you:

1. Stress that the children don't copy.
2. Tell them to do something that is original and unique from what the others produce.
3. Do not evaluate except on the above two points.
4. Do not make changes in the children's work except in spelling, grammar, or where there is some danger involved.

INQUIRY DISCUSSIONS: A SPECIAL TECHNIQUE

Inquiry discussions (or invitations to inquiry) are lessons inviting students to inquire through discussion of a science problem. A typical one presents a problem and invites the students to devise experiments, make hypotheses, interpret data, draw conclusions from data, and understand some of the factors involved in the problem. The primary purpose of the discussion is to show students the kinds of processes used in scientific inquiry by involving them in thinking as a scientist does. It is not the goal of an inquiry discussion to cover subject matter except incidentally.

The information provided in an inquiry discussion may be based on some actual scientific investigation with part of the story left out for the students to fill in. Inquiry discussion should be first used in the upper elementary grades and should start with very simple information. More complex discussion such as the outlining of controlled experiments or interpretation of complex data may be started in junior high and progress to a high level of sophistication in high school and college.

How to Structure an Inquiry Discussion

The instructor presents an inquiry discussion as follows:

1. The teacher gives the students background information about a scientific problem. Only part of the information may be presented at first and the children are asked questions.
2. He invites the students to react to the information given.
3. He occasionally may ask diagnostic questions to call attention to some factor involved in the problem. Through them the teacher helps the students discover something they may have overlooked.
4. He does not answer questions except by asking another question or giving additional information.
5. After some discussion, more information may be given so that the students have more to go by in discussion of the problem.

Designing an Invitation to Inquire

Outlined below are suggested steps to follow in writing your own invitations:

1. Decide what aspects of scientific investigation you wish to teach, i.e., designing an experiment, hypothesizing, inferring, learning about experimental error.
2. Decide what subject matter area you will use. This will usually be related to the unit under study.
3. Select the concepts and principles you want the students to learn and list questions to ask about the problem. Keep the questions relatively divergent so the students will have more opportunities to invent and be original.
4. Write a problem related to your objectives. The ideas may come from a science book or from research reported in the paper or a science journal.
5. Write the inquiry discussion in a series of steps. Insert in different sections additional information to help the child progress in depth into the topic and methods of the research.

Note the examples given in the following sections and try some of them. Then be experimental and create your own. By so doing you are bound to have fun and gain important insights in ways to give students opportunities to be creative.

Examples of the Invitation to Inquire

Phototropism (Upper Elementary Level)

Teacher's Note:	Plants may be stimulated by light to react. This phenomenon is called phototropism.
To the student:	Mary brought a geranium plant to class. John noticed the plant didn't appear to grow normally.
(Inferring)	What do you think he noticed? (Student discussion)
Teacher's Note:	The above question requires students to make inferences. Note in the rest of this discussion that the mental processes required of the student are placed in the margin.
To the student:	John noticed that the plant leaned.
(Inferring)	Why do you think it leaned? (Student discussion)
To the student:	Someone later noticed there was something different about the leaves.
(Inferring)	What do you think was different about the leaves?
(Inferring)	What would you ask Mary about this plant?
To the student:	After some time, one of the boys asked where Mary had this plant at home.
(Inferring)	Where do you think she had the plant?
To the student:	She replied that she had it near the window.
(Inferring)	What does this suggest about why the plant leaned? (Student discussion)
Designing an experiment:	How would you design an experiment to show what caused the plant to lean? (Student discussion)
(Hypothesizing)	How do you think the plant will appear after two weeks? (Student discusssion)
(Hypothesizing)	What do you think would happen if you turned the plant half way around every day? (Student discussion)
Designing an experiment:	What would you do to find out?

Geothermal Reservoirs (Junior High Level)

To the student:	Geothermal reservoirs are naturally occurring pools of hot water beneath the earth's surface. The hot water is released from wells drilled sev-

eral thousand feet beneath the earth's surface into these reservoirs. This source of energy has been used by Iceland, Italy, Japan, New Zealand, and California to produce steam to power turbines to make electrical power. Fossil fuels, such as oil and gas, and nuclear fuels present far greater pollution problems than do geothermal sources. The need for increased electrical power is becoming crucial as our population and industry increase. The search is on therefore to find good geothermal resources. Dr. Robert W. Rex, director of a University of California geothermal project, hypothesized that California's Imperial Valley would be a desirable source of this power.

(Inferring)   Knowing what you do about geology, what reasons would you give for agreeing with Dr. Rex?

To the student: Geothermal reservoirs are usually associated with certain geological formations as indicated in Figure 8-1.

(Inferring)   What geologic features are associated with the reservoirs?

(Hypothesizing) Where in the world and Unitd States would you expect to find these features?

(Hypothesizing) Where would be the least likely places you would expect to find these reservoirs in the United States?

Designing an investigation: How do you think Dr. Rex verified that the Imperial Valley would be a good source?

(Inferring)   What other problems do you think are associated with obtaining and using geothermal power?

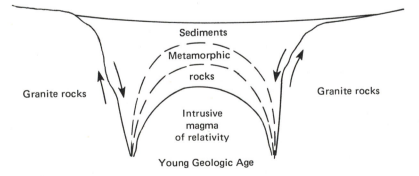

FIGURE 8-1. *Geological formation. (Adapted from diagram produced by the Pure Oil Company.)*

Teacher's Note :   Some of the problems could be: a high level of
brine in the water; subsidence of the surface if
water and steam are continually withdrawn
from the reservoirs; geothermal power cannot
be increased rapidly for sudden peak needs of
electrical power; and some of the best possible
sites are on government lands.

Symbiosis (Upper Elementary Level)

Teacher's Note :   Symbiosis is the living together of two organisms
where it is mutually advantageous. Stress that
there are many examples of organisms mutually
helping each other.

To the student :   Some biologists were studying the effects of
plants on each other when placed in the same
environment. They used soil containing many
simple plants. Among the plants were several
kinds of green algae and relatively colorless
fungi. Since most plants get their food from the
process of photosynthesis, which requires the
presence of chlorophyll (a green pigment), how
could the fungi stay alive?

(Inferring)   What do you suspect might be in the environment which produces food for the fungi?

(Inferring)   What might the environment contain to do this?

To the student :   The biologists analyzed the soil and found dead
organic matter from decaying plants present.

(Inferring)   What relationship might there be between fungi
and dead organic matter?

(Inferring)   What evidence is there that we use dead organic
matter to stay alive?

Designing an   What would you do to prove or disprove that
experiment :   fungi use dead matter?

To the student :   The biologists collected some sand. They placed
it in an oven and heated it at a very high temperature for several hours until all of the
organic matter had been burned. They then
placed spores from fungi and some fungus
plants on the sand and watered them. The fungi
soon died. However, a few of one type of fungus
survived.

(Inferring)   What can you conclude from this experiment?

To the student :   The scientists then got an idea for an experiment.

Designing an   What experiment would you do when confronted
experiment :   with this type of information?

To the student :   The biologists removed the algae from the

	environment of the fungi but watered and cared for them both.
(Inferring)	What do you suspect happened to the algae? The fungi?
To the student:	The biologists found the algae were able to live without the fungi as long as they were protected and had a lot of moisture. They could not, however, live under the rough environmental conditions similar to those under which they existed in the presence of the fungi.
(Inferring)	What do you conclude from this information? How were the algae beneficial to the fungi? What evidence is there that the fungi were beneficial to the algae? In what way?
To the student:	The condition in which two or more organisms live in close association for the benefit of each other is called "symbiosis."
(Inferring)	Why is the above association of a fungus and an alga an example of symbiosis? What are some other examples of symbiosis?
Teacher's Note:	Termites have small protozoa in their digestive tract capable of digesting wood. A termite not having these protozoa will starve. This is another example of symbiosis. Look in a biology text for other examples of symbiosis and read these to your class.

Erosion (Upper Elementary Level)

To the student:	A farmer bought a piece of land having a big sandy hill on it. When he bought it, the climate was dry and little erosion occurred. But during the spring heavy rains came.
(Inferring)	What do you think happened to the sandy hill?
To the student:	The rains caused the hill to become very eroded. Gullies developed and in the lower part of the hill there were large deposits of sandy mud.
(Inferring)	Why do you think this happened?
To the student:	During the summer the farmer decided to do something to try to prevent erosion the following spring.
(Hypothesizing)	What do you think he did?
To the student:	He planted the area with grass and clover seed. Across the gullies he piled rocks to make small dams and filled the gullies as best he could.
(Inferring)	Why do you think these were wise practices?
To the student:	A few years later the farmer decided to farm the hill.

(Inferring)   What precaution should he take in farming this
                      area?
Teacher's Note: He should be certain to use contour plowing so
                      that the ridges made by the plow will move
                      around the hill rather than straight up and down
                      it. The ridges will help to prevent water runoff.
                      He should also rotate crops to insure the soil
                      doesn't become depleted and should use other
                      soil conservation practices.

Air Pressure (Upper Elementary Level)

Teacher's Note: The following discussion can easily be done as
                      a demonstration. Part of it may have to be done
                      solely by discussion because of limitations in
                      equipment. This activity illustrates the principles
                      that volume and pressure in gases increase with
                      temperature. It also shows how temperature,
                      pressure, and volume are interrelated.
To the student: A scientist blew up a balloon and placed it inside
                      a bell jar. (A bell jar is a large thick jar that can
                      be placed over a vacuum pump and have the air
                      pumped out of it.) The scientist began to pump
                      the air out.
(Hypothesizing)   What do you think will happen to the balloon?
                      Why?
Teacher's Note: The balloon will become larger. Under normal
                      conditions there is about 14.7 pounds of pres-
                      sure per square inch pushing against the bal-
                      loon; however, inside the balloon there is also air
                      pushing against it. When the pressure from the
                      outside is reduced by pumping air out of the jar,
                      the pressure inside the balloon has less to re-
                      strain its expansion and the balloon therefore
                      enlarges.
To the student: The scientist next removed the balloon from the
                      jar and with a grease pencil made two dots on
                      the face of the balloon about two inches apart.
                      He replaced the balloon in the jar and repeated
                      what he had done before. This time he noted,
                      however, the difference on the pressure gauge as
                      the distance between the dots on the balloon
                      changed.
(Inferring)   What do you think he found?
(Hypothesizing)   How would you change a balloon's volume with-
                      out using vacuum pumps or changing the
                      quantity of air in it?
Teacher's Note: The spots on the balloon would increase in dis-
                      tance from each other as the pressure in the jar

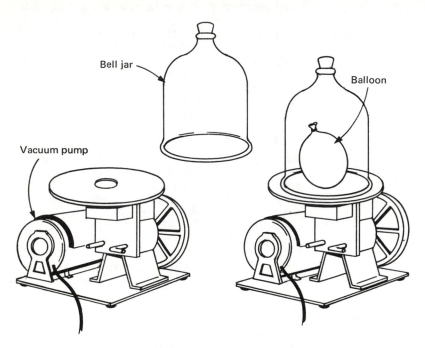

FIGURE 8-2. *A vacuum pump.*

decreased. If a balloon is placed near a heat source or taken to a higher altitude, it will expand. The heating of the gas in the balloon would cause this. The higher the altitude, the less atmospheric pressure pushing on the outside of the balloon, thus the more it would expand.

To the student: The scientist next placed the balloon in an oven which he very slowly heated. At intervals he opened the oven, recorded the temperature, and measured the size of the balloon and the distance between the dots.

(Inferring) What do you think he found?

(Inferring) What do you think happened to the balloon as it got hotter?

(Inferring) How would you make a balloon smaller?

To the student: The scientist next placed his balloon in ice water in a bucket and completely submerged it.

(Inferring) What do you think happened to it?

To the student: After a few minutes he recorded the temperature of the water and the distance between the spots.

(Inferring)   What would happen to the distance between the dots?

Teacher's Note: It is suggested students actually determine the distance of the dots and the size of the balloon placed in the oven and in the cold water.

Measuring: How should you measure the distance between the dots?

Measuring: How would you measure the size of the balloon?

Teacher's Note: The circumference of the balloon and the distance between the dots can be measured by a tape measure. After students have made these measurements for the expanding balloon in the oven and the contracting balloon in the cold water, have them plot this information on two graphs.

Graphing: How could we plot this information on a graph?

Graphing: Why would it be good to plot it on a graph?

Teacher's Note: If time doesn't allow, plot a graph and show there is a direct relationship between temperature and volume as shown in Figure 8-3.

(Inferring)   What can you conclude from the graph?

(Hypothesizing)   If you were to send a weather balloon up high in the atmosphere where the temperature is cold, what do you think would happen to the balloon?

(Hypothesizing)   What effect will the sun's rays have on the balloon?

Designing an experiment: How would you find out?

INVENTING OR IMPROVISING

One way to stimulate creative involvement of students is to present possibilities for them to make inventions.

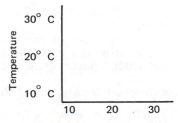

FIGURE 8-3. *Relationship between temperature and volume.*

Myers and Torrance[2] and Sidney J. Parnes[3] have outlined techniques for helping individuals become more divergent in their thinking. These authors suggest presenting an object and having students think of ways to modify it. Examples of questions that might be used:

What if it were made:

1. bigger?
2. smaller?
3. of different material?
4. by combining it with something else?
5. more esthetically pleasing, i.e., using different colors?
6. with altered parts or position?
7. with something added?
8. with something taken away?
9. of different textures?

Following are examples of things to use with the above questions:

1. coffee cans and other tin cans	9. peanut butter jars
2. oatmeal box	10. paper clips
3. clothes hangers	11. nails
4. fishing reel	12. clothespins
5. spools	13. egg cartons
6. toy drums	14. wood blocks
7. milk cartons	15. newspapers
8. rubber bands	16. bones

Examples of Invention Problems

In invention activities, the students are presented with a problem requiring the production of some invention or given something and asked to make it better or give other uses for the object. Some examples that might be done on an elementary level:

1. How can a better balance be made than the simple board often found in science kits?
2. What other uses can you make of tin cans, milk cartons, peanut butter jars, paper clips, or clothes hangers?
3. How would you construct something to show the effects of friction?
4. How would you construct a tall tower out of straw?

2. R. E. Myers and E. Paul Torrance, *Can You Imagine* (Boston: Ginn & Co., 1965).
3. Sidney J. Parnes, *Student Workbook for Creative Problem Solving Courses* (Buffalo: The University Press, State University of New York, 1963), p. 35.

5. What use can used batteries serve?
6. Other than for drinking to what use can a plastic cup be put?
7. How would you construct something using common objects to indicate some scientific discovery?

How would you combine the following objects to make something useful, while using as many as possible?

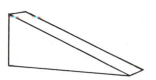

Inclined plane

Wedges

Straws

Pulleys

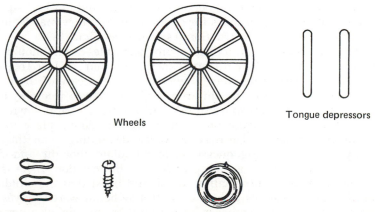

Wheels

Tongue depressors

Rubber bands   Screw

Masking tape

FIGURE 8-4.   *Combining unrelated objects.*

COUNTERINTUITIVE OR DISCREPANT EVENTS

Much has been said thus far about the importance of problem solving in creative activity. It has also been stated that the degree of creative involvement depends upon the attitude of the teacher and the nature of the problem. More sophisticated problems require more creative responses. One technique to motivate and involve children in solving problems with a high degree of creativity is to use a discrepant or counterintuitive event. These two terms have been used interchangeably by science educators and refer to the same type of activity. A counterintuitive event is the presentation of phenomena counter to what a person intuitively thinks is likely. For example, if a bar magnet is suspended by a string and another bar magnet is brought near it without touching it, the suspended magnet will turn. If the experimenter flips the magnet he is holding and brings it close to the suspended magnet again, the latter will now turn in the opposite direction. To children this discovery goes against what they intuitively believe should happen. It appears almost like magic to them.

Counterintuitive events catch the attention of children through sheer wonderment. Their eyes grow larger, they make sounds to express their amazement, and questioning and discussion follow at a rapid pace. These events can be used in a number of ways. They may serve to stimulate further experimentation, as a demonstration activity, or to provide a situation for the evolution of many problems. They have been used in films and in film loops to represent inquiring episodes for children. In fact they may be used in almost any type of instructional science technique.

The presentation of a discrepant scientific event should be followed by discussion, further experimentation, or just free exploration to determine other phenomena. In the case of the magnet mentioned above, the children might engage in free play and find out that magnets move in other directions (up and down) as well. The teacher should not explain what is taking place in an event of this nature. He may, however, depending upon the activity, ask penetrating questions to stimulate thought and discovery, or may act as a source of limited information. If he is to act as a source of information, he should insist that the children phrase their questions to him so they may be answered by yes or no. He should give no other information than this. Below are some examples of counterintuitive events. These examples of discrepant events are given for illustrative reasons; you should try to look for others as well. When you discover a phenomenon in science which might serve as a discrepant event, write it down on a card and keep a file of these for future reference.

Examples of Counterintuitive Events

1. A nonwaxed paper cup is one-tenth filled with water and is heated by a candle placed under it. Although the flame of the candle is directly below the cup, it does not burn.

(*Teacher's Note:* The paper cup does not burn because as the water is heated, the warm water in the cup rises carrying away this energy. Cold water then falls to the bottom to replace the warm water. This process, called "convection of hot water rising and cold water falling," keeps the temperature at the bottom of the cup below the point where the paper would burn. When all the water boils away, the cup will burn because there is little transfer of heat energy away from the bottom of the cup.)

2. Two sealed bottles of liquid are placed in plastic bags in the freezer of a refrigerator and left for twenty-four hours. When the bags are taken out the next day, one of the bottles is broken and the other is not.

(*Teacher's Note:* One of these bottles is filled with water and the other with alcohol but the children don't know this. The alcohol didn't freeze because it freezes at a much lower temperature than water. The bottle with water in it froze and broke because when water is changed to ice it expands.)

3. Hamsters are active at night and sleep mainly during the day.

(*Teacher's Note:* This should be discussed from the viewpoint of adaptation and survival. What advantages does the hamster have by being active at night?)

4. An ice cube is held in the lower part of a test tube by some steel wool that has been pushed into the tube just above it. The tube is almost filled with water. The water in the test tube is heated with a burner above the steel wool for some time. The ice cube, however, doesn't appear to melt.

(*Teacher's Note:* Warm water rises and cold water falls or stays at the bottom. The water at the point where it is being heated is continually rising and being replaced by colder water from the surfaces. There is little circulation, however, between the colder water near the ice cube and the water heated above it, because cold water will not rise over warm water. This is another example of convection.)

5. A snail slides over a razor blade without being cut.

(*Teacher's Note:* A snail secretes a slimy material that helps protect it from the possibility of being injured by sharp surfaces as it glides over these.)

6. A wagon is pulled with a ball in it. When the wagon starts, the ball goes to the back of the wagon; when the wagon stops, it moves forward.

(*Teacher's Note:* These are examples of inertia. The law of inertia states: A body at rest tends to stay at rest, and a body in motion tends to continue moving at the same rate and in the same direction.)

7. Water flows from a tap slowly and is deviated from its normal fall when a comb charged with static electricity is brought near it. A charged comb picks up small pieces of paper, flour, dirt.

(*Teacher's Note:* This shows the electrical nature of matter. When you rub a comb, it becomes negatively charged. When it is placed next to the flowing water, the negative charge forces some of the electrons away from the side of the water nearest the comb leaving its side positively charged. Since unlike electrical charges are attracted, the water flow which is near the comb and which is positive, is attracted to the negatively charged comb.)

8. A bucket or glass of water is swung overhead without the water falling out of the bucket.

(*Teacher's Note:* This is another example of inertia.)

9. Use phenolphthalein solution, acids and bases, and other indicators to show chemical solutions will change color by the addition of an acid or a base to them.

(*Teacher's Note:* Phenolphthalein is used by scientists as an indicator of the presence of an acid. In acid solution it appears pink to red while in neutral solution (pure distilled water) and basic solution, it is colorless.)

10. Show the leaning tower of Pisa and ask why it doesn't fall. When will it fall? Use a milk carton, a string, and a weight attached to the string (plumb line). Insert a nail at about the center of the milk carton, attach the plumb line and let it drop so that it swings freely and doesn't hit the table. Have the children determine with these materials at what angle the tower will fall and why.

(*Teacher's Note:* When the weight at the end of the plumb line hangs beyond the base of the carton, it will fall over. This is due to the fact that tipping the tower lowers its center of gravity, making it unstable. The weight of the upper tower acting downward causes it to fall.)

11. Tie a piece of string to a paper clip and suspend the clip in midair by placing it near a magnet held above it.

(*Teacher's Note:* The magnetic field acts on the paper clip keeping it suspended in midair.)

12. Place an 8″ by 10″ piece of paper to your lips. Hold each side of the paper by one hand using the thumb and the forefinger. Roll the paper toward the lips and blow across it.

(*Teacher's Note:* The paper will rise because a moving stream of air above the paper exerts less pressure than the air pressure beneath the paper.)

13. Place a jar over one end of a magnet and pick up iron filings with the magnet.

(*Teacher's Note:* A magnetic field will pass through glass.)

14. Fill a jar or a flask with water, cover it with a card or filter paper, and invert it. The water stays in the jar.

(*Teacher's Note:* The water stays in the jar because of the adhesive forces between the card, water, and jar.)

15. Place a piece of paper under a glass. Pull the paper out quickly. The glass doesn't move.

(*Teacher's Note:* This is another example of inertia.)

16. Light a crumpled waxed drinking straw. Drop the burning straw into a milk bottle. Place a shelled, hard-boiled egg over the milk bottle.

(*Teacher's Note:* The egg is pushed into the bottle by the outside pressure. The burning straw causes the air in the bottle to expand and escape from it. When the egg is placed on the bottle, the burned straw goes out. The air, as a consequence, cools and condenses. Since there is now less air in the jar exerting less air pressure than outside the bottle, the egg goes into the bottle.)

17. Puncture three holes at various heights in a large juice can. When the can is filled with water, the water sprays out at different distances.

(*Teacher's Note:* It flows the farthest out from the hole near the bottom because water pressure increases with depth.)

Inquiry Development Technique

Dr. Richard Suchman has developed an inquiry approach that involves presenting a counterintuitive event and then asking students to construct an explanation or theory as to why it happened.[4] In his approach the following rules are followed:

1. The questions should be phrased by the students so that the instructor just has to answer yes or no.
2. Once recognized by the instructor, the student may ask as many questions as he wants before yielding to another student.
3. The instructor does not answer yes or no to statements of theories, or to questions asking the teacher's approval of a theory.
4. Individual students can test any theory at any time.
5. Students can call a conference to confer with other students without the presence of the teacher.
6. Students can work with any investigative materials any time they feel it necessary.

An example of how a portion of this type of procedure might be done in class is as follows.

The instructor sets up a demonstration involving three 100 cc graduates. Before class he pours 50 cc of water into one of the graduates and into another 50 cc of alcohol. In front of the students he pours the 50 cc of water and 50 cc of alcohol into the third graduate. He asks students to come up to the desk and observe accurately how much liquid there is in the third graduate. The students will make varying measurements but all will probably observe less than 100 cc. He asks the students to return to their desks and explains the six Suchman rules for the inquiry game they are going to play. The inquiry discussion begins. Part of the discussion might progress as follows:

Student:	Did some of the liquid spill when you poured it?
Teacher:	No
Student:	Is the reason there is less in the third graduate due to the liquid evaporating?
Teacher:	No
Student:	Are both liquids the same?
Teacher:	No
Student:	Is one liquid kerosene?
Teacher:	No

4. J. R. Suchman, *Inquiry Development Program: Developing Inquiry* (Chicago: Science Research Associates, 1966).

Student: Is one liquid alcohol?
Teacher: Yes
Student: Do these liquids behave this way usually when com-
            bined?
Teacher: Yes
Student: Does the way they act have something to do with
            how their molecules move?
Teacher: Yes

This approach can be used with any counterintuitive event. Turn to pages 239–241 and select a counterintuitive event. Try the technique using it with one of your own classes. Think up some counterintuitive events yourself and use this method. The first time you use Suchman's method you will probably have some difficulty. This is because you have to learn to act differently than is your normal teaching behavior. But after a few experiences you will become relatively sophisticated at it and have considerable fun with your class.

Suchman has provided sixty-six physical science problems, twenty-five presented in films, and twenty-nine using a special teacher demonstration kit as an aid to teachers. This material together with a resource book and teacher's guide are commercially available from Science Research Associates. They generally work best with the upper elementary and junior high school student.

Film Loops

There are presently on the market many science film loops available for use with an 8mm projector. Film loops may be shown to an entire class, in small groups, or by individuals. If the teacher wishes to use them for class discussion, she may show a portion of the loop, stop the projector by pushing a button, and then ask the class what they think will happen next in the film. For example, a film loop might show some dishes on a table. A man comes along and begins to pull the tablecloth. The teacher would stop the projector and ask: "What do you think will happen to the dishes and why?" After some discussion, she may project more of the film and stop it again to ask other inquiring types of questions.

Some producers of film loops have made them showing counterintuitive events. Commercial producers of film loops have also made many noninquiry verification or observational types of loops. These can, however, be modified so that they give more opportunities for students to inquire and be creative. On an individual basis students can observe a film loop and answer questions written by the teacher on a worksheet. If the students fail to obtain the information they need the first time, they can play the loop through until they are able to answer all the questions on the answer sheet.

A worksheet prepared for a film loop used in the eighth grade is shown below:

Film Loop: Paramecium

Part 1—Structure and Function

1. How does the shape of this animal seem to be adapted to its surroundings?
2. What can you tell from the movement of the water surrounding the paramecium? Does this seem to be related to the structures on the outside of the animal?
3. Describe the action of the vacuoles shown in the film. What function does this action suggest?
4. How does the shape of the paramecium change? What does this suggest about the membrane surrounding the animal?
5. Observe the movement of the materials inside the animal. How would you describe this movement? How does the movement vary in different areas? How would you explain this difference?
6. How are the cilia arranged on the surface of the animal? How does this arrangement suggest the paramecium is able to move?
7. How do food vacuoles seem to form?
8. How would you go about slowing down the motion of the paramecia so that you could observe them better?
9. If you wanted to speed up the movement and internal reactions of the animal, what would you do?
10. What experiment would you do to determine whether paramecia respond to different stimuli? What stimuli would you subject them to?

Video Recorders

Video tape recorders can also be used with children to involve them in creative activity. For example, when children give a science demonstration or perform some experiment in class, this activity can be taped. The children involved in the activity might be asked later to view the tape and suggest ways to improve their demonstration or experiment or to suggest other activities or experiments related to the material they recorded. At other times, they might be asked to suggest some experiment to tape to show other classes or parent groups. The production and development of such a science video program by the children can be used in itself as an opportunity for creative enterprise.

Thirty-five-millimeter Photographic Slides

A 35mm photograph can be used to involve children in creative activity. A photograph of a discrepant event should preferably be used in this technique. For example, a picture of a fault, or an unconformity in geology, might be shown by projecting a 35mm slide to the class as a whole, to a small group, or to an individual. If the class views the slide, the teacher can lead a discussion about it. If an individual is allowed to use a viewer to look at the slide on his own, a worksheet should be provided with questions that are likely to allow him to respond creatively.

Instead of a discrepant event, a picture or some apparatus used to demonstrate a science principle might be shown and questions asked about it. If the class doesn't discover the function of the apparatus, it could be explained. The instructor might then tell the children that the apparatus is not available and that they are to suggest ways the same principle might be demonstrated in class by using home-made equipment.

The Polaroid Camera

With a Polaroid camera, take a picture of a counterintuitive science activity. For example: Fill a flask with water, and place a small file card over the top. Take a picture of the apparatus, then quickly invert the jar. The card will remain against the top of the flask and the water will not pour out. Have someone take a picture of the inverted flask and card while you hold the flask. Paste the first picture on a card and write the following question on it: "What do you think will happen to the water in the flask and the card when the flask is turned over?" This question should be followed by a statement telling the students to go on to the next picture card after they have finished writing their answers on a piece of paper. Paste the second picture on a card. Write beneath the picture: "Why do you think the water stays in the jar?"

A series of similar activities can be prepared in this manner and the pictures placed in a shoe box for the children to examine as they choose.

PICTORIAL RIDDLES

A pictorial riddle presents scientific information on poster board, the blackboard, or on a transparency. These drawings, or pictures, are used as a center of discussion when the teacher asks the class what they suggest to them. In answering questions about the diagrams the children become involved in such scientific processes as observing, classifying, formulating hypotheses, defining or changing variables, and interpreting data and making conclusions.

Two general formats can be used in constructing riddles. One type illustrates a situation under normal conditions; the other illustrates a discrepant event. For example, a pictorial riddle might have a picture of two children teeter-tottering. They are both in balance. If they are the same size and about the same distance from the pivot point, or fulcrum, this would be expected. A picture depicting a discrepant event, on the other hand, might show a large boy being held up on one end of a teeter-totter by a small boy on the other end. The teacher would hold the first diagram up to the class and ask why the boys are in that position. The children will probably give only a few answers. With the second diagram, she might ask how the situation it illustrates is possible. There are more than twenty answers to this question. Because of greater motivation and the chances for multiple responses, the second type of riddle (illustrating a discrepant event) provides more oportunities for children to be creative.

A good type of question to use initially in showing a riddle or projecting a transparency onto a screen is: "What are all the things you could ask about this picture?" This type of question gives children numerous chances to be creative. In the process of discussing the riddles, the children may suggest problems for study. They should be encouraged to devise and perform experiments to solve these problems.

The construction of pictorial riddles by children can also be used as a creative activity. Showing these by overhead projection to the rest of the class will motivate others to want to create similar riddles.

How to Prepare Riddles

Listed below are a few suggestions to follow in making and giving pictorial riddles:
1. Decide what it is you wish to teach. You may want to use a riddle to introduce a unit or evaluate the understanding of information children have learned.
2. Attempt to make the riddle so that it will give greater chances for creative responses. This can be done if a counterintuitive event is shown.
3. If possible, draw the riddle on the transparency and project it. This allows for greater visibility and attracts attention.
4. Ask the class: "What are all the things you can ask about this picture?" Outline some other questions you might like to ask the class during the discussion.
5. Ask divergent questions having a number of possible "yes" responses. Do not ask convergent questions such as those that only require a yes or no answer.
6. If possibilities for experimentation arise from the discussion, encourage the pupils to experiment.
7. Suggest that the children make riddles themselves.
8. Start a file and maintain a collection of riddles. After giving a riddle, evaluate its use and the types of questions that arose in the discussion. Make note of these for future use.
9. Whenever you see a picture or get an idea for a riddle, place a notation about it in your file.
10. From time to time evaluate the riddles, keeping those that seem to elicit the most creative responses and discarding those that don't.

Two formats can be used to construct riddles (see page 248).

Before and After Riddles

Dr. Alan McCormack in his doctoral dissertation has suggested combining pictorial riddles in the form of a "before" and "after" presentation.[5] In this approach the students are shown pictures or diagrams of a counterintuitive nature. The pictures depict some phenomenon before and after it has been manipulated. The students are then asked to make inferences as to what caused the

5. Alan J. McCormack, "The Effect of Selected Teaching Methods on Creative Thinking, Self-Evaluation, and Achievement of Students Enrolled in an Elementary Science Education Methods Course" (unpublished Ed.D. dissertation, University of Northern Colorado, 1969).

Normal Conditions

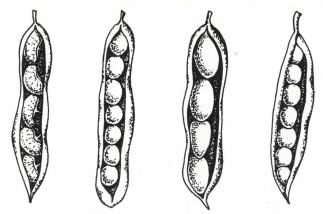

What are all the things you could ask about this picture?
What makes these pods different? How are they similar?
How have other pods you have seen varied?
What do you think causes these differences?
*If you were going to grow the most desirable pods, what would
 they be like? Why?*

FIGURE 8-5.

Teacher Manipulated Conditions

14,000 feet

12,000 feet
above sea level

What are all the things you can ask about this picture?
Why isn't this a true representation of nature?
Where do trees grow on mountains in the United States?
*What conditions are needed for trees to grow? (Note that
 the instructor purposely drew the mountain showing no
 timberline to see if students would recognize the abnormal.)*

FIGURE 8-6.

What would you ask about this picture?
What are all the ways that this rock could be moved?
What are all the natural ways this rock could have been brought
  to this place?

FIGURE 8-7.

Plastic
bucket of
water

What questions can you ask about this diagram?
Why does the water stay in the bucket as the child swings it?
What would happen if the child were to swing the bucket faster?
What would happen if the child were to swing it slower?
How is the motion of the plastic bucket of water related to
  how satellites move about the earth?

FIGURE 8-8.

What things can you ask about these planets?
If you were going to make a visit to these planets what prepar-
*   ations would you have to make?*
Which of the planets would you want to visit first and why?
Which of these planets would be easiest to visit and why?
(NASA Photo)

FIGURE 8-9.

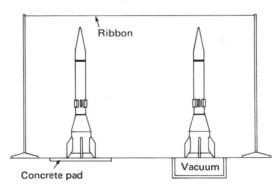

What would you ask about this picture?
Which rocket would break through the ribbon first? Why?
Why do you think one rocket sits on a concrete pad while the other is
*   supported with its exhausts opening into a huge vacuum chamber?*
From which rocket would the gas escape the most rapidly? Why?
What does the escape of gas have to do with the motion of the rocket?
What other questions can you ask about rockets?

FIGURE 8-10.

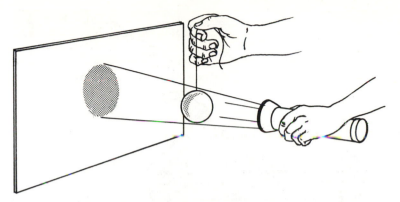

What can be done to change the shadow?
What would you need to do to make a huge shadow of yourself?
How would you find out?

FIGURE 8-11.

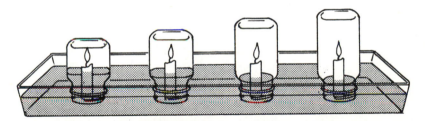

Burning (oxidation): What could you ask about the diagram above?
If the candle lengths were changed what difference would it make?
What would happen if larger bottles, thicker or thinner, longer or
* shorter candles were used? How would you find out?*

FIGURE 8-12.

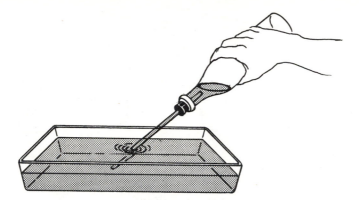

*Air pressure and heat: What could you ask about the diagram above?
How could the water be made to go down the tube from the pop bottle?
How could the water be made to rise more in the pop bottle? What
could be done to change the speed at which the liquid moved up the
tube into the bottle?*

FIGURE 8-13.

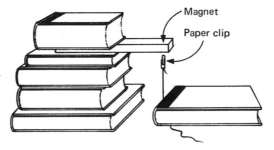

*Magnetism: What questions could you ask about the diagram above?
What would happen if the string were shortened?
What would happen if the metallic paper clip were replaced with a
piece of plastic?*

FIGURE 8-14.

*Distribution of mass: What questions would you ask about the
    diagram above?*
Why is the boy deep in the snow and not the girl?
*If the skis were shorter would it make any difference in how
    the girl stood in the snow?*
*If you were going to design something to help the girl and boy
    move across the snow faster, what would it be? Why?*

FIGURE 8-15.

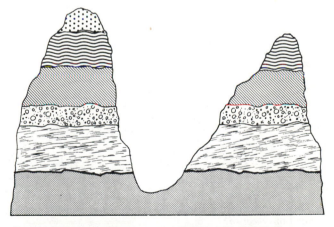

Erosion: What questions can you ask about this diagram?
How could this have happened?
How did this structure look at one time?
What do you think will happen to this formation in the future?
How would you explain the differences in the layers?
What could have caused the great cuts between the peaks?
How would you prove your ideas to another person?

FIGURE 8-16.

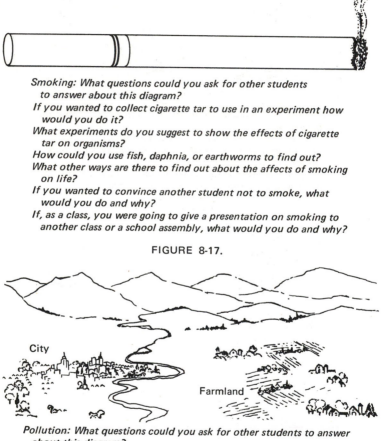

Smoking: What questions could you ask for other students to answer about this diagram?

If you wanted to collect cigarette tar to use in an experiment how would you do it?

What experiments do you suggest to show the effects of cigarette tar on organisms?

How could you use fish, daphnia, or earthworms to find out?

What other ways are there to find out about the affects of smoking on life?

If you wanted to convince another student not to smoke, what would you do and why?

If, as a class, you were going to give a presentation on smoking to another class or a school assembly, what would you do and why?

FIGURE 8-17.

Pollution: What questions could you ask for other students to answer about this diagram?

If this stream were polluted what do you think would be the causes?

Where would the pollution be the least and where the most?

What would you do to correct the pollution?

How would you determine whether the stream was polluted?

How would you use fish to determine this?

What ways would you use chemical tests, microscopes, or light to determine this?

FIGURE 8-18.

What do you think will happen to the eggs?
What is needed for this to happen?
How long would it take for these eggs to hatch compared
  to chicken, turkey, or duck eggs?
How would you find out?
If some of the eggs don't hatch what might be some of
  the reasons?
What would we need to hatch an egg in our classroom?

FIGURE 8-19.

Structure and function: What questions can you ask about these pictures?

What are the advantages and disadvantages of the different beaks and feet?

What would happen if the beaks and feet above were made: smaller, larger, stronger, weaker?

If you were going to design a bird well adapted to survive in your neighborhood, what would it look like and be able to do?

FIGURE 8-20.

This field is going to be converted to a housing development.
What are all the changes that will occur in the environment
  as a result?
What will happen to the kinds of life found in the field?
What types of pollution will occur?
How could the pollution be reduced?

FIGURE 8-21.

What can you ask about this picture?
Where is this arch located?
Why can't you see the city around the arch?
Why can you see the upper but not the lower part of the arch?
What causes pollution?
What should be done to reduce pollution?
How can we all help to reduce pollution?
What effect does air pollution have on life?
What experiments could be done to find this out?

FIGURE 8-22.

What questions can you ask about the cans in this pond?
What will these cans do to the pond?
What hazards do the cans present?
What benefits might they serve if any?
If you were going to try to get people not to throw cans in rivers
    or ponds, what would you do and how would you know if it worked?
What things could you make from these cans?

FIGURE 8-23.

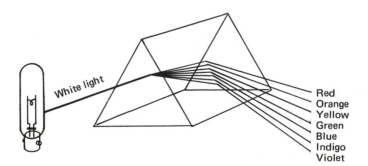

What questions can you ask about this picture?
What did the prism do to the light?
What does this tell you about white light?
In what ways could a prism be used?
If you were given three or four prisms what would you do with them?
What other things will produce a spectrum like a prism?

FIGURE 8-24.

Each of these are arks:

None of these are arks:

Which of these are arks? Why?

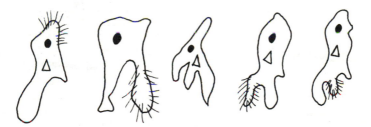

If you were going to draw some arks, what would they look like and why?

FIGURE 8-25.

BEFORE	?	AFTER

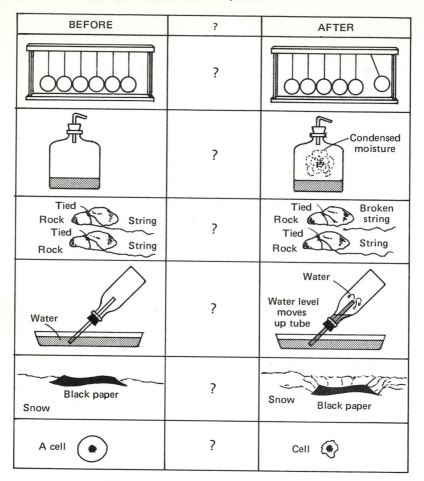

FIGURE 8-26. *Before and after riddles.*

"after" situation. Figure 8-26 shows some examples of this type of riddle.

Encourage Students to Make Their Own Riddles

After students have seen several examples of your riddles they should be encouraged to prepare, either individually or in groups, some of their own science riddles for the class. These should be given in front of the class by the students who prepared them.

Cartoon types of riddles is particularly good for class discussions. Students should therefore be encouraged to draw or use cartoons as much as possible. The creation of a cartoon obviously elicits more creative ability than the use of one that is available in print.

At the beginning, or after a riddle has been presented, the class should be invited to name the riddle. The name, however, should not give away the purpose of the riddle.

HOW WOULD YOU DRAW DIAGRAMS TO SHOW . . .

Scientific Principles or Theories

Preparing diagrams to explain a scientific principle or theory can provide students with opportunities for creative enterprise. In this procedure the following phrase is used: "How would you draw diagrams to show . . . ?" This is followed by what it is that you want the students to illustrate. For example: "How would you draw diagrams to show mechanical advantage?" Other examples are:

1. Cells are basic structures of life
2. Stimulus-response
3. Good nutrition
4. Molecular theory of matter
5. Organisms cause disease
6. Solubility
7. Reflection
8. Evolution
9. Photosynthesis
10. Mass
11. Adaptation
12. Environment affects organisms
13. Organisms affect environment

Inventions

Another approach in using diagrams is to have students invent something. Can you draw a diagram to show:

1. an improved safety designed car
2. a better adapted plant
3. a better adapted animal
4. an improved human body
5. a better bike
6. a better roller skate
7. an improved clothes hanger

HOW WOULD YOU RELATE WORDS?

In the upper elementary junior high school levels students might be given either lists of words or sets containing two or three words and asked to relate them. The words may involve some science subject matter, science processes, or history. It is suggested that in student discussions the instructor ask students to start with relating three words. After several students do this, encourage students to relate as many of the words as possible. Examples of how these are constructed are shown below:

Relating of Science Processes

To the student: Choose any three of the following and construct a sentence indicating how they are related:

Hypothesizing	Observing
Problem	Classifying
Inferring	Comparing
Interpreting data	Quantifying
Theorizing	Experimenting
Measuring	

Relating Science Subject Matter

To the student: Choose any three of the following and construct a sentence indicating how they are related:

Ecology	Community
Biome	Energy
Succession	Food web
Ecosystem	Population density
Balanced	Distribution
Food chain	

Relating Science History

To the student: Choose any three of the following and construct a sentence indicating how they are related:

Germ	Pasteur
Bacteria	Koch
Disease	Leeuwenhoek
Antiseptic	Vaccine
Smallpox	Rabies

Word lists may also be used as a basis for having students write stories. Students would be given the lists and asked to write stories using all of the words.

BRAINSTORMING

The use of brainstorming is suggested by Alex Osborn for stimulating fluency and flexibility of ideas.[6] Although the technique is generally recommended for small groups, it also has relevance for the individual since a person can brainstorm himself.

The technique usually involves several individuals—four to six are suggested. They are presented with a problem and asked to think of as many creative ideas as possible. Members of the group must abide by four rules:

1. No criticism of the ideas is allowed.
2. Productive ideas should be stressed.
3. Offering ideas that are built on previously suggested ones is encouraged.
4. Wild ideas are encouraged.

Below are some examples of problems that might be used in brainstorming.

1. How can we determine whether air pollution is increasing?
2. How can we reduce the drug problem?
3. How could we increase the efficiency of a bicycle, roller skate, wagon, wheelbarrow, scooter?
4. How would you make an inexpensive balance?
5. How would you determine the degree of pollution of a stream?
6. How would you make a paper cup more desirable?
7. What uses can be made of popcorn other than for food?

ENVIRONMENTAL ACTIVITIES FOR INVOLVEMENT OUTSIDE CLASS

There is material available from a variety of sources to stimulate environmental activity. One such example is found in an ESCP project. The Earth Science Curriculum Project Environmental Studies has produced materials to help students become more aware of their surroundings. They believe their investigations will lead to helping students become more aware of themselves and helping to give them opportunities to develop many of their talents. The materials consist of a series of teaching lessons

6. Alex F. Osborn, *Applied Imagination* (New York: Charles Scribner's Sons, 1953).

placed on cards. The "actions" outlined on these cards involve the use of Polaroid cameras, magazines, frosted acetate, tracing paper, masking tape, pens, pencils, brushes, fingerpaints, aerial photos of the school area, maps, string, meter sticks, counting devices, and tape recorders. A typical assignment has students use a tape recorder to record sounds such as: "sounds you like and dislike; morning, day, and night sounds."

Write to ES, Box 1559, Boulder, Colorado 80302, to obtain further information about these materials and others in production. Use them as guides for some of the things you might do in your own school environment. Some additional suggestions which use the environmental approach for creative development are outlined below:

1. Give students a Polaroid camera and ask them to:
   a. Take a picture of something they think looks abnormal in their environment.
   b. Prepare a series of pictures to indicate how they are becoming better people through involvement in their school and environment.
   c. Prepare a picture depicting a scientific problem.
   d. Take a picture illustrating progress, pollution, concern for fellow man, social implications of scientific development.
2. Create some artistic or photographic work illustrating the application of some scientific principle.
3. Photograph a pollution area and then try to improve it while applying good ecological principles. Successive photographs should be made to illustrate the results of the change and suggestions for further improvement.
4. Suggest ways to make some part of your school more esthetically pleasing, modify the area as suggested, and then evaluate its effect on students.

SYSTEMS ANALYSIS APPROACH

Systems analysis is an industrial technique of analyzing a production system and planning the sequence of all things involved in producing an object or accomplishing some objective. Analyzing problems using systems analysis provides opportunities for students to utilize their cognitive analytical and creative talents. Part of the sequence of how such an approach might be presented in a classroom is given below in two examples.

Example I. Problem: (The teacher reads this part to the class.)

FIGURE 8-27. *Photography—choosing the subject, taking the picture, developing, and printing—has elements of "magic" for the child, thus encouraging observation, discovery, and creative thought. (Photo by Lee Youngblood)*

It is decided to build a rocket to go to the moon. You have been hired to be director of the project. As director you can order anything you want from me in the form of people and material. You must, however, describe what it is you want and in the proper sequence. What is it that you want first?

Students generally will reply they want workers. They don't think of the fact that the director will need an office, office furniture, and a secretary first. If this is the case you might ask them if they are sure they want what they first described. Or ask—Where do you want these workers delivered? When the students ask for something you say—All right, now you have these goods or workers. You should ask the class whether or not they agree that the material requested is the best thing to order next. Usually an extensive discussion follows. At some point also ask—What effect will the above discussions have on polluting the environment?

Example II. Problem: You want to produce a film depicting the need for improving some condition in the community. What should you do first and what other things should be done in sequence after this?

PREPARING A SCIENCE FOLDER

Encourage pupils to make a science folder or notebook. Included in it should be photographs they take, stories and plays they write, pictures, diagrams, experiments, cartoons, or riddles. They should also include things that depict their feelings and demonstrate creative talent or how their views of science have changed through the year. They might also prepare a list of science problems that they have originated. From time to time, the instructor should ask members of the class to get their folders, go over their problems, and select ones they would like most to study. The class should then discuss all the problems and decide which to study.

STORIES TO STIMULATE CREATIVITY

Plays and stories about scientific discoveries can be used to stimulate creative activity:

1. Read or tell a class about some scientific discovery.
2. After the scientific problem in it has been outlined, relative to the discovery, stop and ask the students what hypotheses they would make about it.
3. Discuss these and then describe the hypothesis the scientist made.
4. Next have the students write or tell how they would go about solving the problem.
5. Discuss their ideas in class and go on to finish the story. At the conclusion of the story, ask the students to evaluate their hypotheses and research designs with those the scientist made.
6. Discuss the strengths and weaknesses of the students' proposals. Emphasize that although many students differed from the scientist's approach they did have good ideas and some of them could be worth testing.
7. Compliment the students whose ideas seemed especially promising.

Outlined below are some specific questions and techniques you might use.

1. If you were this scientist what would you do next?
2. Of the ideas presented by various members of our class, which appear to be the best and why?

3. If you were the scientist at this point, how do you think you would feel about what you are doing?
4. What is creative about what this scientist has done up to this point?

WRITING A PLAY ILLUSTRATING SCIENTIFIC DISCOVERY

A class can also be encouraged to write a play or story showing science as process. The framework for these can be similar to those found in detective and science fiction stories or actual scientific investigations. Before the students write the stories, the teacher can discuss how the methods of science and criminal investigation are similar. He could read some examples of both types of investigations and have the student make comparisons. It is desirable to have pupils write about some discovery they have made or some problem they will be working on during the time they will be writing. With this approach the students are more likely to analyze their work and make hypotheses about the problem they are trying to solve. This assignment provides creative opportunities for them to learn about science while learning communication as well. Integrating the learning of science as a process with writing a play provides for greater development of talent and makes learning more relevant and pleasurable.

MAKE AND COLLECT CARTOONS DEPICTING SCIENTIFIC PRINCIPLES

Encourage students to prepare or collect cartoons illustrating some scientific principle or a poor understanding of one. The production of these should be shared with the class and other members encouraged to suggest how the drawings, diagrams, or captions could be improved. An example of two cartoons are given below that might be used with primary children. The principles illustrated in the cartoons should also be discussed.

MAKE STICK FIGURES INDICATING SOME SCIENCE CONCEPT

Encourage students to prepare stick or straw figures to illustrate some scientific principle or idea. For example, they might make

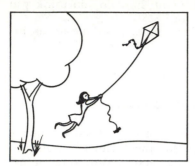 

"The kite is pulling me up in the sky."   *"The leaves are flying south for the winter."*

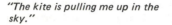

FIGURE 8-28.

figures to show levers, streamlining, effects of gravity, how magnetic forces operate, or the construction of buildings, bridges, and the human body to illustrate points of stress.

PREPARE SCIENCE COLLAGES

Have students prepare their own collages illustrating science concepts. These might include such topics as the need for control of: pollution, population, erosion, drugs, smoking, the conservation of forest lands, and the development of good nutrition.

IDENTIFY HIDDEN OBJECTS

Students may be encouraged to identify hidden objects in a picture or collage, or apply what they have learned to a new object. For example, students may be given a collage and asked to indicate on it where weathering, erosion, or faults have occurred: In the case of identifying parts of an object, they first might study simple machines and then be given an egg beater or pencil sharpener and asked to locate as many machines as possible on it.

CREATIVELY FILL THE SPACES

Have students creatively use several spaces on a paper describing their impressions or feelings about a topic (have them enlarge and use diagram below). Ask: How would you use these spaces to show how animals vary in the ways they live?

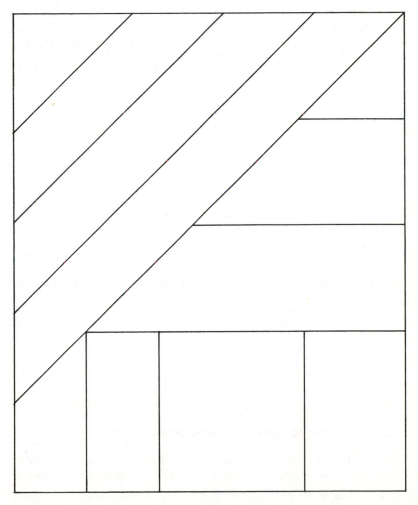

FIGURE 8-29.

ADDITIONAL CREATIVE SUGGESTIONS:

1. Have children complete a story, i.e., you might give them some ecological situation and have them finish it. These stories can be used as a basis for class discussion.
2. Build something unique, i.e., have them build something using as many simple machines as possible that do something. You might give them a large piece of cardboard, tape by which to attach the machine, and wedges, levers, wheels, pulleys, and inclined planes.
3. Play "Here's the answer, what is the question?" i.e., "The dirt goes into the river. What are the questions you can ask?"
4. Play "I am," i.e., "I am a magnet, what are all the things I can do, or how many ways can you use me to do something unique?"
5. Play, "Why visit?" i.e., "Why visit an observatory, planetarium, museum, a field, a sidewalk area, Colorado, California?"
6. *Play Fluency and Flexibility Games.* Give the children a problem and ask them to come up with as many ideas as possible relative to it, i.e., to list as many problems as they can think of that they might have with a wagon. List the many uses of a wheel. List all the ways they can think of to reduce pollution.
7. Have the children write their own science book.
8. Make their own original science bumper stickers.
9. Build a scientific model of something out of plaster of Paris, i.e., an ecosystem.
10. Construct a new animal using physical parts of other animals and describe its adaptive advantages.
11. For the above, make up names of new animals which are combinations of other animals' parts, i.e., a monkdog, a lizturt.
12. Prepare their own flower by combining parts of several plants.
13. Convey some scientific concept or principle out of pieces of wood.
14. Use egg cartons in some way to illustrate some scientific concept.
15. Keep a science diary.

USE OF A GRID TO FORCE CREATIVE PRODUCTION

Zwicky has outlined an approach to free individuals to make creative relationships.[7] Essentially he has suggested a grid in

7. J. E. Arnold, *Useful Creative Techniques: A Sourcebook for Creative Thinking* (New York: Charles Scribner's Sons, 1962), p. 255.

TABLE 1.   HOW CAN YOU AFFECT THE WAY A
BALL BOUNCES?

| Characteristics of the Ball | *Other Than Ball Characteristics* | | | |
	Air Resistance	Bouncing Surface	Temperature	Forces Applied
Size				
Weight				
Surface				
Material				
Shape				

which variables related to a problem are placed on different axes. A simplified example of how this might be used is shown in Table 1. The student writes in his hypotheses in spaces provided. This approach involves the following steps:

1. Identify a problem.
2. Identify two series of variables. The example above involves the ball's variables and variables in the environment.
3. Have the students write in the squares provided what they think will happen when the variables are combined.
4. After the students do this there should be class discussion and, if possible, experiments performed to see if their hypotheses were correct.
5. In the upper elementary and middle school, students should be encouraged to construct some grids of their own problems. The motivated, science-oriented individual is most likely to be challenged by this type of activity.

HOW TO USE EXPERIMENTS CREATIVELY

An Experiment Usually Has a Control

To provide maximum opportunity for creative growth, students should have the opportunity to experiment, to make discoveries, and to solve problems. An experiment may differ from other methods of investigation (such as observing or classifying) because in experimenting, one or more variables—such as temperature, pressure, time, distance, or light intensity—must be controlled. Most experiments require a "control," which is primarily used to make comparisons. Perhaps a student wanted to test the effects of fertilizer on bean plants. He planted some beans in cartons and fertilized them. They grew well. He concluded that the fertilizer helped them grow. However, he had no way of knowing whether the beans would have grown well without fertilizer. If he had fertilized some bean plants and not others, he could have compared the fertilized ones with the unfertilized controls and noted the difference. His conclusions, as a result, would have been more valid for the bean plants under observation, particularly if several samples had been used. Most experiments performed in the elementary school usually concern the control of only one variable at a time while those in the secondary school may involve multiple variables.

Experiments Are Used to Solve Problems

Outlining a procedure to solve a problem experimentally requires originality on the part of the student. When problems arise in class, have the students describe how they would go about solving them experimentally. There will probably be several views on how each problem might be solved. Encourage discussion of these, and if the students cannot agree on one procedure have the groups supporting different approaches attack the problem in different ways. After the students have collected data and drawn conclusions, it is a good practice to have them report their findings to the class. The class can then discuss the information and draw conclusions. After the students have completed an experiment, they should be asked what they would do to improve their experimental procedure if they were to repeat it.

Make Experiments Open-ended

Most experiments provide opportunities for further investigations. If they do, they are called "open-ended" experiments because their conclusions do not end the possibilities for further investigation. At the completion of one experiment the teacher should ask if there are any possibilities for other experimentation. In this way the pupils are encouraged to identify problems. This is very desirable because defining a problem is a valid scientific behavior providing rich opportunities for students to be creative.

Avoid "Cookbook" Experiments

Many experiments written in science texts or teacher guides are cookbook in nature. This means the student goes through them in a series of steps as though he were following a recipe in a cookbook. Cookbook methods are not scientific methods. When does a scientist ever have a list of steps prescribed for him to perform in solving a problem? For example, where is the list of steps to follow in finding a cure for cancer?

Part of being scientific means outlining an experimental procedure. In a cookbook situation the experimental procedure is already outlined for the student. When they are included in the instructional materials, the teacher should attempt to make them more inquiring. One way to do this is to change the form of the experiment by presenting the problem to the class before they come across it in their reading. The teacher should ask the class how they would solve it. When they have outlined a plan of action, they can be encouraged to carry it out. The teacher tries to make the experimental situation inquiry-oriented so students can experience what it means to act scientifically.

GUIDE CHILDREN TOWARD DISCOVERING OPEN-ENDED POSSIBILITIES IN AN EXPERIMENT

In every experimental situation there are factors—variables— which influence the outcome of the experiment. In testing the effects of light on plants for instance, the following class situation might occur.

Bean plants are growing in milk cartons half filled with soil. Some plants have been covered with black paper so no light can enter while others have been left uncovered and placed where they will receive light. After a few days, the students compare the plants grown in the light with those grown in the dark (the control plants). They conclude that plants need light in order to grow. In so doing they have learned something about the effect of one factor in a plant's environment.

There are, however, other factors that affect plant growth. The teacher can open doors by encouraging students to be aware of them. He could make the experiment open-ended by asking a few simple questions: What other things might affect the growth of plants? What experiments would you do to find out if these factors affect plant growth? If the students have difficuly suggesting factors influencing growth, the teacher can ask more direct questions: How might the temperature or water affect the growth of plants? How can we find out? How will plants grow in water? How about soil, what influence does it have? The children would then outline experimental procedures to verify their hypotheses.

By making students aware of factors involved in an experimental situation, the teacher:

1. Enables them to see the open-ended possibilities in all experimentation.
2. Encourages them to make more than one test.
3. Cautions them not to overgeneralize on scant evidence.
4. Indicates the difficulties in isolating a single variable.

This knowledge can be of considerable benefit in helping students develop creative ideas. They see, as a result of learning about factors, that there are an infinite number of creative opportunities in scientific investigation. They learn perhaps for the first time the creative nature of the scientific enterprise. The primary teacher can contribute immeasurably to this end if she provides very simple activities so the children can learn the influence of one factor. She will need to give considerably more guidance and direction than teachers in upper grades when the children set up and carry out experiments. The development of an understanding by primary grade children of how factors are involved in experimentation provides a wonderful foundation in the later grades for creating more sophisticated and varied types of experiments. Teachers of the upper grades can elicit from students with this background a greater number of creative responses.

Some factors that may be involved in any experiment are listed below to guide you in asking questions which make students cognizant of the open-ended aspects of a problem. As students experience situations where these factors are operating and as they become more aware of them, they increase in their ability to originate problems and demonstrate their creative ability.

Number and Types of Reactants

Light—the type of light, color, and the intensity
Sound—type and intensity
Humidity
Type and abundance of food supply
Gases and other chemicals in the environment
Pressure

Motion
Magnetic field
Electrical field
Electricity
Gravitational field
pH—how acidic or basic are the conditions present
Temperature

STEPS TO FOLLOW IN HELPING STUDENTS EXPERIMENT

To encourage students to become involved in experimentation have them:

1. Describe how they would individually go about solving a problem experimentally. Before any experiment, ask the students the following question: "If you were going to solve this problem, what would you do?" By so asking you give the class the opportunity to *design an experiment.* There will probably be several views on how each problem might be solved.
2. As a group have them discuss how they might solve the problem. If the students cannot agree on one procedure, have the groups supporting different approaches attack the problem in different ways.
3. Perform experiments.
4. Collect data.
5. Draw conclusions.
6. Report findings to the class.
7. Discuss the information obtained from all the groups.
8. Evaluate their experimental procedures. In the upper elementary, junior, and senior high school, students should be asked to evaluate their procedures because in the process they might come up with a new synthesis of problem solving procedures. The evaluative question, "If you were going to design an experiment to obtain better data, what would you do?" allows for more creative responses by students.

CHANGING A COOKBOOK EXPERIMENT TO MAKE IT MORE CREATIVE

The experiment below is presented in its original cookbook form. The sections following contain suggestions for changing this and other experiments to provide for more creative possibilities and open-endedness.

Cookbook Example (Upper Elementary Grades)

Experiment:
How the skin protects the body against infection.

Materials:
Four apples, some soil, a needle, adhesive tape, antiseptics (such as alcohol, iodine, or merthiolate).

Procedure:
Obtain four apples. Mark two of the apples "The Control" and put them aside. Make a circle about an inch in diameter with marking pencil on the other two apples. Take a needle and stick its tip into some soil. Plunge the tip of the contaminated needle into the middle of the marked circles on the apples to a depth of about one-eighth of an inch. Sterilize one apple by placing an antiseptic on the place where the needle broke the skin. Place a piece of adhesive tape over this hole. Observe the apples over several days.

Procedure to Stress Open-endedness and Creativity Using the Same Activity

Before the students do an experiment the teacher should discuss its problem with them. She might ask: (Inquiry Discussion) "What happens when you get a break in your skin? Why should you put disinfectant on it and cover it? What experiments might be done to show what happens when the skin is cut? How would you use apples in an experiment to show what happens? What experiment would you perform to determine whether a disinfectant is effective in preventing infection?" The teacher would then allow the students to set up their experiments, make observations over several days, collect data, and draw conclusions. After they have had ample time to do this, she would ask the following questions:

What did you conclude from your experiments?
How could you have improved your experimental procedure?
What possibilities for other experiments do you see? (If there is no response from the students she could continue.)
What effect did the temperature have on decay caused by the infection?
What other factors might affect the rate of decay?
How could you find this out?
How do disinfectants vary in providing protection against infection?

How would you find out?
Besides infection, what other things may affect the appearance
of the apple?

Cookbook Example (Lower and Middle Elementary)

Experiment:
Tropisms in Plants

Teacher's Note:
Plants react to various stimuli occurring in their environment.
The word "tropism" in Greek means "to turn." A tropism in a
plant is the process of its moving or turning in response to an
external stimulus.

Materials:
Shoe box, corn seeds, petri dishes or plastic transparent dishes
with tops.

Procedure:
Place some corn seeds in the bottom of a petri dish. Over the
seeds pack moist absorbent paper tightly and then place the
cover on the petri dish. Stand the dish upon its edge and, after
germination, observe the direction of root growth. When the roots
have developed partially, turn the plate so the opposite is down.
Several days later observe what happens and report your conclusions.

Procedure to Stress Open-endedness and Creativity
Using the Same Activity

In the inquiry discussion before the students start the lesson, the
teacher could ask: What do seeds need in order to sprout? (hypothesizing), Which way do roots grow? (summarizing), How
could you devise an experiment to try to confuse the roots of a
sprouting seed? (designing an experiment). Allow the students
to carry out their experiments.

If some students don't have any ideas, ask them to help you
carry out your experiment. Ask: What do you think about sprouting some seeds and then turning them so the roots will be up and
the leaves down? How could you prepare these seeds so they would
be clearly visible sprouting? What about control? What should
the control be?

Place six seeds in the bottom of each of two petri or plastic
dishes. Place wet paper toweling tightly over them and cover.

Tape the covers to the dishes. Stand both dishes on their sides. After germination observe and record root growth. When the roots have partially developed, turn one of the dishes so roots are pointing upward. Allow it to stand for several days. Ask: What do you think will happen to these roots?

After several days have the students observe and record their observations. Ask:

What do you conclude from your experiments?
How could you have improved your experimental procedure?
What possibilities are there for other experiments?
How would other plants respond to similar conditions?
How would you find out?
What would the presence of light do to root growth?
How would you find out?
What would the color of light have to do with growth?
What other factors would affect root growth?

Cookbook Example (Middle Elementary)

Experiment:
The effect of different wavelengths of light (the color of light) on plant growth.

Materials:
Bean plants—four each in small milk cartons, one for each group of two to four children. Colored transparent wrap—red, green, blue, and white.

Procedure:
Obtain four bean plants in cartons, wrap each plant with a double layer of color wrap using a different color for each plant. Place where the plants will receive sunlight and observe over several days. Report your conclusions.

Procedure to Stress Open-endedness and Creativity
Using the Same Activity

Before the students begin the activity ask:

What do plants need in order to live?
If they don't mention light, ask: What effect does light have on growth?
How could you find this out?
What effect does different colored light have on growth?
How could you find this out?

TABLE 2.   THE EFFECT OF LIGHT WAVELENGTH ON
PLANT GROWTH

Plants grown in	Size of plant	Condition of leaves	Condition of stem	Amount of chlorophyll
Normal light				
Darkness				
Red light				
Blue light				
Green light				

What experiments could you do with bean plants to find answers
to these questions?
What factors other than light affect the growth of the plants?
How would you find out?
How about the lack of light? What would you do to find out its
effect?
How about water, mineral, herbicides? What experiments could
you do to determine their effect on plants?

Young children may have difficulty keeping records of what
happened in the experiments. Ask: How should you keep a record
of what happens in the experiments? Stress the importance of
accurate observation in science and of keeping good records of
these observations.

An example of one approach they might use is shown in Table 2.
However, if students have different methods let them use theirs
even if they are unsophisticated. This will offer a good opportunity
at the end of the experiment to discuss which method of recording
the data was best. By so doing, your young investigators should
learn the importance of planning an experimental procedure,
including how to collect data before the experiment is carried out.
If artificial light is used, the bulb wattage on both the white and
colored wrap should be constant. This would eliminate one more
variable.

DEMONSTRATION AS A MEANS TO DISCOVERY

Children should be as actively involved as possible in learning
science if they are to manifest their creative potential. For this

reason experimentation by children is the most desirable of all instructional methods in science teaching. However, sometimes individual experimenting is not possible because of lack of equipment, poor facilities, safety reasons, or time. In these instances an instructor will have to resort to a demonstration. The same principles of encouraging pupil involvement should, nevertheless, operate. The more chances children have to interact during the demonstration, the more opportunities there will be for them to show originality and inventiveness.

Furthermore, when children discover alternate views presented by their classmates they get insights into their own egocentric outlooks in solving problems. As a result, they are more likely to learn to look for and devise multiple hypotheses and solutions requiring greater creative investment. In the interaction of ideas between various members of the class during discussion, the demonstration provides many opportunities for creative thinking.

Demonstration can be used to advantage to introduce or conclude a unit. In introducing a unit, the open-endedness of the problem should be stressed and children encouraged to identify other problems that arise from it. The techniques for having children discover the open-ended characteristics of the problem in the demonstration are the same as those suggested on pages 273–274 for experiments. Essentially they are to have the pupils recognize what factors are directly involved in the demonstrations and to suggest the modification of these or the manipulation of some other factor. The experimental design will thereby have to be modified accordingly.

A demonstration at the conclusion of a unit can be used to help children integrate and discover interrelations and applications of the information they have learned. The open-endedness of the demonstration should be stressed to show scientific investigation is unending.

A demonstration for creative purposes should generally follow a pattern similar to that of an inquiry discussion. A demonstration, however, has an advantage over discussion because it may present a counterintuitive activity drawing children's attention. This is particularly true when the demonstration is a counterintuitive event. If the event is presented as a problem-solving situation, it gives children many chances to be creative in devising solutions. For the manifestation of creative activity, this type of demonstration is preferred over observation or validating information.

PROCEDURE FOR SELECTING AND PRESENTING
A CREATIVE DEMONSTRATION

Following are some suggestions to consider in selecting and presenting a demonstration to inspire creative activity:

1. Decide what it is you wish to teach. Subject matter and creative objectives may be included.
2. Determine the advantages of a demonstration over other methods of instruction in attaining these objectives.
3. Select, if possible, a counterintuitive event to contribute to the objectives. For ideas for these events, consult curriculum guides or one of the various sourcebooks in the Appendix.
4. Collect the materials and equipment needed for the demonstration.
5. Use a surprise technique in starting the demonstration. This may be done by keeping all the materials in a closed box and bringing them out of the box at the beginning of the lesson.
6. When all the equipment is visible on the demonstration table, ask the children how they think the equipment might be used. This gives them opportunity for creative thinking.
7. Present the demonstration. Have the children perform or assist in the demonstration as much as possible.
8. Attempt to give few if any answers related to the demonstration. When questioned, reply by phrasing a question to guide the children. For example, in a demonstration where children see a large and heavy weight being balanced on a teeter-totter (a lever) the children might say: "The light weight is farther back on the board than the heavy weight, and that makes it possible to hold up the heavy weight, doesn't it?" The teacher should not answer yes, but instead should say: "How would you prove it? Do you think the heavy weight could be held up only one way?" These questions might be followed by others. He might also lead the demonstration into an experimental situation by passing out levers and weights and letting the pupils experiment to find answers. If some individuals appear to be suffering from lack of direction, he could guide them by saying: "How can the heavy weight be held up by the light weight? What difference would moving the weight back and forth make?" By asking questions as guides, the teaching does not rob the pupils of the opportunity to discover and be creative.
9. At the conclusion of a demonstration, ask the class: What have you learned from the demonstration? From this demonstration, what other ideas for experiments did you get? If you were going to give this demonstration to another class, how

would you change it or the equipment to make it more exciting to see, or to better show what you have learned?

EXAMPLES OF CREATIVE DEMONSTRATION LESSONS

Demonstration: Characteristics of Minerals

Concepts:
Minerals can be identified by color, cleavage, hardness, specific gravity, and luster. Different minerals combined make rocks.

Materials:
Several sets of different minerals.

Procedure:
1) Place several minerals on the table at the beginning of class. Divide the class into six groups. Give each group a set of minerals. Have the children determine how the minerals are similar and dissimilar. Encourage them to devise a scheme so that they could determine, if given some other minerals, whether they were the same or not. 2) After they have had time to do this, ask: What characteristics did you outline in your scheme for identifying minerals?

> (*Teacher's Note:* Write these on the board. (They should come up with some of the following: crystal form, cleavage, hardness, specific gravity, color, and luster. Point out that all of the minerals you gave them were specimens of minerals and are naturally occurring substances found in the earth's crust. They all have one or more of the above characteristics in common.)

3) Give the children rocks containing some of the minerals they just looked at. Ask: Can you discover in these rocks any of the minerals you have just studied? What do you think is the difference between rocks and minerals?

> (*Teacher's Note:* If the children don't discover this difference, explain that minerals make up rocks. The amount of mineral in a rock may vary and determines what type of rock it is.)

Demonstration: Magnets and Magnetic Fields

Concepts:
Around every magnet there is a magnetic field that can attract or repel objects having magnetic properties. Each magnet has two

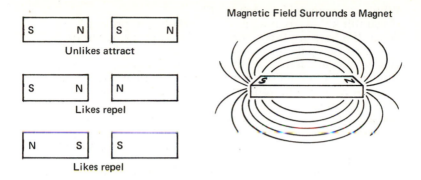

The Interaction Between Bar Magnets

FIGURE 8-30.   *Magnets and magnetic fields.*

poles, north and south. Like magnetic poles (two souths or two norths) repel. Unlike magnetic poles attract.

Materials:
Two round, rod-like magnets.
Two bar magnets.
String.
A stand to support a freely suspended magnet.

Procedure:
1) Place the two round, rod-like magnets on a table or on an overhead projector. Bring one of them close to the other in a lengthwise manner. The magnets will either attract or repel each one. Flip one magnet so the poles of the magnets are opposite to what they were before. Bring one magnet close to the other magnet again. Ask: What did you observe? Who can explain why it happened? When one of the rods was repulsed, where was the other rod? How can something be repulsed if nothing is touching it? (If the children think you have magnets, ask them how they would prove the objects you have are magnets.) 2) Take a bar magnet, tie a piece of string around it, and suspend it from a ring stand or chair so that it can move freely. Bring another bar magnet close to it. Flip the bar magnet you are holding so that the poles are opposite to what they were. Bring it again close to the suspended magnet. Ask:

What did you observe?
Why did it happen?

What are the metal bars made of?

If you think they are magnets, how would you prove it?

When the bars are brought close to each other, when do they first start to repulse or attract each other?

How would you determine the strength of a group of magnets?

How would you hold something up in the air without touching it?

In what way would you use magnets to make some interesting types of toys?

What would happen to a needle suspended on a cork in water if magnets were brought close to them?

What evidence is there that both ends of a magnet are not the same?

How would you show that there is an area around the magnet (called the magnetic field) that can attract or repulse objects which are magnetic?

How would you determine if objects are magnetic?

Demonstration: Bread Mold

Concepts:

Bread mold is a type of fungus.

Fungi reproduce by spores.

Fungi need moisture and a food source in order to grow and develop.

Materials:

Bread. Plastic wrap.

Procedure:

1) The teacher could start with some questions: Where does mold come from? How does it get started? How would you prevent something from becoming moldy? How would you grow a mold colony? 2) Use the suggestions of the children to produce a mold colony. If they don't have any, do the following activity. 3) Take two pieces of bread. Place one in a dry dish. Dampen the other and allow to stand for an hour or two uncovered. Then place it in a plastic bag so that it stays moist. Place the bag where it won't receive much light. Have the children observe it each day until there is a sizable growth on it. (Make sure the flour from which the bread was made was not treated to prevent mold.) Ask:

What have you observed about the bread?

Why did it happen?

Why didn't mold grow on the bread kept in the dish?

What does mold need in order to grow?
How do you think the mold gets started?
What are the little heads on the mold?
What did they look like?

4) Have the children look at the mold through hand lenses or microscopes. If possible, mash one of the black spores from the mold on a glass slide and let the children look through a microscope to see if they can see the spores. Explain that each of the spores is capable of reproducing a new mold plant that may completely spread out over a whole slice of bread. Ask: What experiments can we do to make the mold grow faster? Allow the children to set up and carry out their experiments.

> (*Teacher's Note:* Mold generally grows best where there is ample food, warmth, and dark. If the children really become interested in their studies, you might use or adapt part of the Elementary Science Study unit called *Microgardening.* It offers many opportunities for pupils to work with fungi.)

Demonstration: Effects of Chemicals on Organism (Nicotine)

Concepts:
Animals other than fish live in an aquatic environment. Chemicals in the environment can affect animal behavior. Nicotine is a poisonous chemical. Polluting chemicals in rivers and streams are undesirable.

Materials:
Water, pipette or nose dropper, two glass dishes.
Planaria,[8] daphnia, brine shrimp, earthworms, slugs, or snails.
Nicotine or a liquid obtained from boiling cigarettes in water, and other chemicals such as alcohol, coffee, tea, and detergents.

Procedure:
Prepare the following just before the children begin their science study. Do not let the children see you put the nicotine solution in one of the dishes. 1) Place water in two dishes (25 ml). 2) Place a planaria in each of the dishes, using a pipette to pick them up. Other animals may be substituted for the planaria as suggested above. 3) With a clean pipette put five drops of nicotine or cigarette tar solution from boiled cigarettes into one of the dishes.

8. Planaria may be found under rocks in streams, in the spring. They may be baited by submerging a piece of raw liver tied in cheesecloth and attached to a string so as not to float away.

4) Place the dishes where children can observe them. If you have an overhead projector, place the dishes on it. If possible, make several similar setups so the children can look at them in small groups. Use a stereoscopic microscope for better observation if there is one around. The teacher will allow the children to observe the animals for awhile and then could ask:

What did you notice about the way the worms acted?
How long did this last?
What do you suspect caused the planaria in the two dishes to act differently?
How could you show this? (If the children don't suggest chemicals as an answer, the teacher might guide them with the following questions.)
What effect would chemicals have on the worms?
How could you find out?
What chemicals would you use?
What would happen if the amount of chemical used was different?
How would you devise an experiment to show this accurately?
What would you do to find out if the chemical is a stimulant or depressant? (Terms should be defined for children in careful vocabulary development.)
Why do you think pollution of our streams is undesirable?

Demonstration: Regeneration

Concept:
Animals are capable of regenerating parts of their bodies.

Materials:
Live planaria, flatworms. (These can be obtained either from a biological supply house or from local streams in the spring. To catch them obtain some fresh liver, wrap it in gauze, and tie it with a long string. Place the gauze and liver under water on the edge of a stream and leave it for a day or two. The planaria will be attracted to it. Be sure to secure the gauze so that it won't float away. Encourage your students to gather the planaria on a field trip if possible.) Three petri dishes or transparent plastic dishes with covers, hand lenses, razor blades, teasing needles, microscope, pond water, eye dropper, and microscopic slides.

Procedure:
1) Place all the planaria in a large jar containing pond water from the place where they were taken. 2) Pass the planaria out to the children to examine with a hand lens or microscope. The teacher

can spark a preliminary discussion with the following types of questions:

How do the planaria move?

How do the animals react when disturbed by a current of water?

What other factors are they sensitive to?

Which ones might we study? (Some might be temperature, light, sound, and a small electric current from a battery.)

What is complex and what is simple about the flatworm? (Explain that biologists believe they are relatively simple organisms.)

What do you think would happen if the worms were cut in half?

3) Fill three petri dishes half full of pond water. Mark one dish "front end," another "back end," and the third "middle pieces." Place a drop of water on a glass slide and put a planaria in the water on the slide. After the animal has stopped making erratic movements, use a single-edged razor blade to cut the body into three equal parts by making the cuts across to the long axis of the body. Place the pieces in three dishes. Repeat the operation on six to ten animals. Have the children examine the animal every other day and make sketches showing the growth in each portion of the planaria. Remove and record the number of dead pieces every day. Ask the children:

What changes did you note about the worms?

How do the final developed worms compare with normal planaria?

How many pieces formed a whole animal?

How do other animals compare in regenerating missing body parts? Explain. (If you live close to the sea, attempt to find a starfish that has lost one of the parts of its stars and is regrowing it. Dry and preserve the starfish for future demonstrations.)

What other experiments would you like to do with planaria?

(*Teacher's Note:* Planaria are photonegative. Therefore, keep them as much as possible in the dark below a temperature of 35° Centigrade. Change the pond water frequently with fresh pond water. Once a week, feed them bits of hard-boiled egg. After several hours remove the excess food with an eye dropper. Endeavor to keep the water from becoming foul. With these methods they can be kept for an indefinite period. As they get larger they will automatically reproduce by fragmentation.)

Demonstration: Animals Respond to Stimuli

Concepts:
An earthworm has a simple nervous system. It reacts to stimuli. It may be attracted to a favorable stimulus or repulsed by unfavorable stimuli. (Other organisms such as snails, slugs, mealworms, or flatworms may be substituted for earthworms.)

Materials:
Overhead projector, three transparent dishes (plastic or glass), clear pond water.
5 cc of colored Karo syrup, bits of liver (for flatworms only), 5 cc of vinegar, one piece of black paper.

Procedure:
1) Place pond water in three transparent dishes and put an earthworm in each. 2) Place the dishes containing the worms on the overhead projector. Allow the children to observe their movements. Question the children:

What do you notice about their movements?
How are they able to move in this way?
How could you find out?
How would you react if you were placed on a large overhead projector like the worms?
How would you determine what stimuli these animals will respond to? (Define stimulus as being something that excites an organism. They may be stimulated by a loud sound, for example.)

3) Place one large drop of the colored Karo syrup in front of one of the earthworms. Initially, don't tell the children the names of the substances you placed in the dishes. Ask: What do you observe about the motion of the worm? How is it stimulated, positively or negatively? If you are not sure, what do you suggest should be done in order to make sure? 4) Using the second earthworm, put the dish on the overhead projector. Place a drop of vinegar in front of the worm. Ask: What do you observe? How can you explain the difference in its reactions compared to the first worm? 5) Put the third dish on the projector. Place a bit of hamburger or liver in front of the worm. Ask: What do you observe? 6) Place black paper between the light source and half of one side of a dish and observe. Further questions the teacher might ask are:

What can you conclude?
What conclusions can you make about the worms' ability to respond to stimuli in the environment?

What procedures would you suggest to investigate worms further? What other factors might affect them? (If no suggestions are forthcoming the teacher might ask the following.)

How would you find out if they are sensitive to temperature changes?

How would you test them to see if they are sensitive to electricity? (A small dry cell battery might be used to do this type of experiment.)

SUMMARY

Evidence from psychology indicates the greater involvement of the student the greater learning. Piaget has indicated that all learning is based on experience and he has said that nothing is learned unless it is discovered by the student. Educators aware of this research have emphasized the importance of student involvement.

The activity movement which made its greatest impact in the elementary school program has particular relevance in elementary school science. Science activities for elementary and secondary school students are integral components of a sound science program. It is interesting to note the term "laboratory activity" has become synonymous with the functional or "doing" aspect of the program even in the elementary school. At all grade levels the action of a school's science program takes place in the laboratory situation. Here students hear, smell, touch, see, build, observe, think, explore, discover, fail, and succeed. Here is firsthand experience. No other teaching method can provide all this—not books, films, lectures, nor demonstrations. Indeed there is some question whether we can use the term "science" at all apart from experimental investigation.

Every school system has its own course of study indicating the selection of content and learning activities for science. These are as different as the systems they serve, but across the nation the science program has the general aim of aiding students to understand (1) the nature of science and its interrelationships; (2) the organized information about himself and the world around him—what it is made of, how it looks, the forces that cause things to happen; (3) principles or generalizations based on this information; (4) learning how to discover methods of working that have proved successful in getting dependable answers to questions; (5) information about what scientists do. These general aims allow the teacher wide latitude for providing activities having creativity at their core.

SUGGESTED ACTIVITIES TO INCREASE UNDERSTANDING
OF INFORMATION GIVEN IN THIS CHAPTER

1. Prepare two inquiry discussions.

2. Outline five types of activities that would provide opportunities for children to be inventive.

3. Look through some activity type science texts or sourcebooks and list as many examples of counterintuitive events as time allows.

4. Prepare two examples of pictorial riddles illustrating some scientific principle.

5. Prepare several pictorial riddles illustrating some counterintuitive event and requiring creative responses. Write below the riddle how a creative response is required.

6. Design a play or an episode illustrating some science historical event or the discovery of some scientific principle, but have it unfinished for the students to complete.

7. Write an experiment requiring creative responses.

8. Write several questions aiding students to look for open-ended possibilities.

9. Write two demonstrations requiring creative responses. Describe why you think your demonstrations give students opportunities to be creative. Be as specific as possible in your analysis of the demonstration.

10. Describe some creative artistic assignment that would involve students in thinking about science.

11. Construct several science collages.

12. Outline some other ways you would involve students creatively.

CHAPTER IX

Conclusion

Thus invention, scientific thinking, and aesthetic creation do have in common a facility for the rearranging of previously experienced elements into new configurations. When Sandburg says that "the fog creeps in on little cat feet," and a child calls eraser scraps "mistake dust," and a painter shows the four sides of a barn at once, and a writer speaks of something as being as "relentless as a taximeter," and a man converts a runner into a wheel, and a Newton sees the analogy between apples and planets, there is manifest an activity of mind that seems to be of the same weave despite the differences of coloration.

H. BROUDY

The dynamic influence of science and technology in shaping contemporary society is well recognized by the science educator. For the first time in history man is faced with an ecological crisis of such magnitude that his very existence is threatened. The implications are clear. It has given the teacher great concern for developing curricula that is relevant to our times and our survival. The factors which diminish the quality of life such as overpopulation, pollution, mismanagement of natural resources, and prejudice, to mention a few, are only surface symptoms. The underlying causes are more complex but point directly to the individual and his sense of values. Science then must be taught in the creative context of value process learning focused on basic problems of social and biological significance. New educational models will be required to provide science learnings applicable to a world of accelerating change and sharpened to improve the human condition.

Great strides have been made in curricular improvements. To a greater degree than ever, the process approach in science teaching has received national acceptance and is being widely implemented. Discovery teaching and inquiry training is becoming integral to science programs. Educational technology is bringing the dream of individualizing instruction closer to reality.

In the foreseeable future provision for meeting individual differences may well become the norm rather than the exception. This, perhaps, is the most innovative and significant prospect for fostering the creative potential in children.

Many other efforts to effect needed changes in science study are being made by local, state, and national teachers' groups, science organizations, universities, and several government agencies. Industry, museums, and foundations are cooperating with schools to provide study and for older children on-the-job opportunities with scientists during the summer and on Saturdays. Under a visiting scientist program in physics sponsored by the NSP, outstanding men of science visit schools and talk personally with the students and teachers.

Career and occupational education now has a high priority in federal programs. A model developed by the Department of Health, Education, and Welfare indicates that career awareness should begin in K-6, career exploration should continue through junior high school and the senior high school student should begin to enter the world of work at the entry level jobs. Beyond high school are opportunities for training in technical institutions and professional work in colleges and universities.

Coincident with the new knowledge and the accelerated effort to keep our science classes abreast of the times is the pressing need for modern teaching equipment and materials—items such as laboratory furniture, apparatus, supplies, projectors, recorders, films, tapes, models, and books. In addition to basic equipment and apparatus needed to teach classes in science, natural areas near the school should be utilized for field work wherever possible. Many schools are providing special work areas such as observatories, planetariums, weather stations, museums, special projects rooms, and space for growing and observing animals and plants.

Good elementary school creative science teaching can be accomplished with basic equipment, but it should be appropriate to the age of the pupils and the task at hand. Water, electrical outlets, audio-visual materials, bulletin boards, and storage space are essential. The classroom should have a variety of science books on several reading levels, and the school library should be able to supply reference books and a good selection of supplementary readings for science. A laboratory situation is needed—and the classroom may become just that. Although much progress is being made, only a relatively small portion of the schools yet have the laboratory facilities they feel they need.

The unique tools of science—the instruments and equipment—help the child investigators use their senses to better advantage. The telescope and the microscope, for example, help them see things which they would not be able to see with the naked eye. Scientific apparatus and equipment, audio-visual devices and materials, books, curriculum guides, and extraclass activities are all used to build science experiences—creatively—around the solving of real problems in the pupil's environment. All these experiences are useful in everyday living and build a foundation for further study. A planned sequence from kindergarten through grade twelve and beyond seeks to bring about a smooth transition from the elementary school to junior high and into the senior high school, and from there to college. But at each level creativity should be the focus of concern.

Wide experimentation in teacher training in the use of multimedia education is also taking place. New uses for television, radio, computer technology, printed materials, and a systems approach to teacher and learning are being demonstrated. The training complex is an invention designed to facilitate cooperation between colleges and the schools in improving the pre-service and in-service training of teachers and other school personnel. It is designed to bridge the gap between theory and practice by the use of appropriate protocol and training materials, the teaching of a repertoire of methods, the provision of controlled experience with children and specific practicum experience, related to both the needs of the teacher and the school and community situation in which he is likely to work. Projects underway show promise of improved teacher training.

New terms, such as differentiated staffing, performance based teaching, auxiliary staff, and accountability connote changes in the schools and attempts to meet the diversity of demands upon the schools.

Many school systems are quite advanced in implementing innovative practices to affect positive change, others have come part of the way, and some have yet to make the start. Yet there are some fundamental questions that curriculum planners are grappling with, which, when answered, will make a difference in the creative teaching of science: What learnings are significant for *all* children growing up in a rapidly changing, ecologically deteriorating, technological society? What science learnings are significant? How do we choose those that are imperative to the development of literacy in science for every individual? What is this literacy that enables a person to participate continuously in the intellectual life of his times, take his full share of responsibility in making enlightened social decisions, and find and develop his own creative potential?

Whatever the curriculum changes are to be, who will implement them? We have noted the widespread effort at local, state, and national levels, but the persons most directly responsible for the quality of the science instruction are the teachers. Learning creative science involves much more than modern facilities, equipment, books, and courses of study. These matter little if teachers are unprepared, indifferent, and overworked. Beginning teachers, teachers new to the school, and teachers lacking sufficient science background need help; and the school must provide a variety of ways to help them improve, keep up to date, experiment with new methods, and find the best activities for helping children learn science so as to raise their creativity quotient.

The single most important characteristic of a creative science program is a creative teacher. How can you tell a creative teacher? For want of a better barometer, try gauging the interest, the purpose, the enthusiasm, the inquiry, the problem solving, and the cheerful self-discipline of the students. The effect of the teaching can very often be detected by such observation. An essential role of the teacher is to help the child perform creatively; to discover facts and relationships for himself; to make him resourceful and self-reliant; to develop in him a love for learning and how to learn; to insure an environment in which independent thinking is revered; and, finally, to train him in the use of intuition and imagination. The teacher insures purpose in science activity and sees that the activity leads into other avenues of learning and creative activity.

The teacher also has a moral responsibility in that students must understand the tremendous destructive power of science as well as its promise of a better life for all mankind. The teacher is in a position somewhat akin to the old hermit in an old story sometimes called "Dead or Alive."

> The wise old hermit lived in the woods outside a small midwestern town.
> The wisdom of this man was widely known throughout the community—so much so that many of the young men in the town spent a good deal of their time trying to disprove his wisdom so that all the world would know "he's not so smart after all" (like some scoffers of science we know).

One day, two young men sitting on the bank of the river were indulging in their favorite sport—looking for a way to trick the hermit and thus end this legend of his wisdom.

Suddenly one of the young men reached out and trapped a sparrow that had perched on the limb above his head. "I know how we can outfox the hermit," he said.

"We'll go to the hermit's cave and I'll hide the sparrow cupped in my hands so that he can't see it. I'll ask him, 'What have I in my hands?' If he is able to tell me that it is a bird, I'll then ask him, 'Is it dead or alive?' If he says it is alive, I'll squash my hands and the bird will be dead. If he says it's dead, I'll open my hands and let the sparrow fly away."

Hurrying through the woods, they soon came to the hermit's cave.

"Old man," cried the tormentor, "what have I in my hands?" The old man looked at him thoughtfully and then answered him, "A bird, my son." "Tell me, old man, is it dead or alive?" For a long time the old man just looked at the boys and then he answered, very slowly, very deliberately, "It's up to you, my son, it's in your hands."

Throughout the country today over one million elementary school teachers have in their hands the power to guide the education of our future citizens, in this science-based, problem-riddled world. It's up to you, they are in your hands!

Selected Bibliography

Creative Teaching

Allstrom, Elizabeth. *You Can Teach Creatively*. Nashville: Abingdon Press, 1970.

Animal Welfare Institute. *Humane Biology Projects*. The Institute, 22 E. 17th St., New York, N.Y., 1960.

Barret, Raymond E. *Build-It-Yourself Science Laboratory*. Garden City, N.Y.: Doubleday & Company, 1963.

Brehm, Shirley A. *A Teacher's Handbook for Study Outside the Classroom*. Columbus, Ohio: Charles E. Merrill Publishing Co., 1969.

Carin, Arthur and Sund, Robert B. *Teaching Science Through Discovery*. 2d ed. Columbus, Ohio: Charles E. Merrill Publishing Co., 1970.

Carr, Albert B. *The Black Box*. Englewood Cliffs, N.J.: Prentice-Hall, 1969.

Combs, Arthur W., et al. *Helping Relationships*. Boston: Allyn and Bacon, 1971.

Compton, A. H. "Case Histories of Creativity: Creativity in Science." In *Nature of Creative Thinking*. New York: Industrial Relations Institute, 1953.

Goldstein, Philip. *How To Do an Experiment*. New York: Harcourt, Brace & World, 1957.

Ideas for Science Projects. National Science Teachers Association, 1201 Sixteenth Street, N.W., Washington, D.C., 1963.

Kuslan, Louis I. and Stone, A. Harris. *Readings on Teaching Children Science*. Belmont, Calif.: Wadsworth Publishing Co., 1969.

Kuslan, Louis I. and Stone, A. Harris. *Teaching Children Science: An Inquiry Approach*. Belmont, Calif.: Wadsworth Publishing Co., 1968.

Kansdown, Brenda, et al. *Teaching Elementary Science Through Discovery and Colloquim*. New York: Harcourt Brace Jovanovich, 1971.

McGavack, John and LaSalle, Donald P. *Guppies, Bubbles and Vibrating Objects: A Creative Approach to the Teaching of Science to Very Young Children.* New York: John Day Co., 1969.

McGavack, John, Jr., and LaSalle, Donald P. *Crystals, Insects, and Unknown Objects.* New York: John Day Co., 1971.

Merrick, Paul D. *The Shell Game.* Webster Groves, Mo.: Webster College, 1966.

Moore, Shirley, ed. *Science Projects Handbook.* Science Service, 1719 North Street, N.W., Washington, D.C., 1960.

Piltz, Albert and Gruver, William. *Science Kits,* U.S. Office of Education OE 29049, Bulletin 1963, no. 30, 1963.

Schmidt, Victor E. and Rockcastle, Verne N. *Teaching Science with Everyday Things.* New York: McGraw-Hill, 1968.

Smith, James A. *Setting Conditions for Creative Teaching in the Elementary School.* Boston: Allyn and Bacon, 1966.

Staff, Bella Vista School. *Creative Vistas.* Bella Vista School, Jordan School District, Salt Lake City, Utah, 1971.

Sund, R. and Bybee, R. *Becoming a Better Science Teacher.* Columbus, Ohio: Charles E. Merrill Publishing Co., 1973.

Thier, Herbert D. *Teaching Elementary School Science, A Laboratory Approach,* Lexington, Mass.: D. C. Heath and Co., 1970.

Torrance, E. Paul and Myers, R. E. *Creative Learning and Teaching.* Dodd, Mead & Co., 1970.

Torrance, E. Paul. *Encouraging Creativity in the Classroom.* Dubuque, Iowa: William C. Brown & Co., 1970.

Wilt, M. Elizabeth. *Creativity in the Elementary School.* New York: Appleton-Century-Crofts, 1959.

General Books on Creativity

Bearly, Molly. *The Teaching of Young Children, Some Applications of Piaget's Learning Theory,* New York: Schocken Books, 1970.

Cropley, A. J. *Creativity.* New York: Humanities Press, 1968.

Davis, G. A. and Scott, J. A. *Training Creative Thinking.* New York: Holt, Rinehart and Winston, 1971.

Getzels, J. W. and Jackson, P. W. *Creativity and Intelligence: Exploration with Gifted Students.* New York: John Wiley & Sons, 1962.

Ghiselin, B. *The Creative Process: A Symposium.* Berkeley, Calif.: University of California Press, 1952.

Gorman, Richard M. *Discovering Piaget, A Guide for Teachers.* Charles E. Merrill Publishing Co., 1972.

Gowan, John C. *Development of the Creative Individual*. San Diego: Robert R. Knapp, 1971.

Guilford, J. P. *Intelligence, Creativity and Their Educational Implications*. San Diego: Robert R. Knapp, 1968.

Heist, Paul, ed. *Creative College Students: An Unmet Challenge*. San Francisco: Jossey-Bass, 1968.

Maier, Norman R. *Problem Solving and Creativity in Individuals*. Belmont, Calif.: Brooks/Cole Publishing Co., 1970.

Maslow, Abraham H. *Toward a Psychology of Being*, 2nd Ed. New York: Van Nostrand Reinhold Co., 1968.

Osborn, Alex F. *Applied Imagination*. New York: Charles Scribner's Sons, 1953.

Piltz, Albert. *To Strengthen Science Education* (tape-filmstrip). U.S. Office of Education. Distributed by Creative Arts Studio, Washington, D.C., 1963.

Piltz, Albert. *Science for the Eight to Twelves*. Association for Childhood Education International, Bulletin 13-A. Washington, D.C., 1964.

Sharp, Evelyn. *Thinking Is Child's Play*. New York: E. P. Dutton & Co., 1969.

Shouksmith, George. *Intelligence, Creativity and Cognitive Style*. New York: John Wiley & Sons, 1971.

Taylor, Calvin. *Talent and Education: Present Status and Future Directions*. Papers presented at 1958 Institute on Gifted Children, University of Minnesota Press, Minneapolis, 1960.

Taylor, Calvin, ed. *Creativity Progress and Potential*. New York: McGraw-Hill, 1964.

Taylor, Calvin, ed. *Widening Horizons in Creativity*. New York: John Wiley & Sons, 1965.

Taylor, Calvin, ed. *Instructional Media and Creativity*. New York: John Wiley & Sons, 1966.

Taylor, Calvin, ed. *Climate for Creativity*. Elmsford, N.Y.: Pergamon Press, 1970.

Wadsworth, Barry J. *Piaget's Theory of Cognitive Development*. New York: David McKay Co., 1972.

Wall, Janet, and Summerlin, Lee. *Standardized Science Tests: "A Descriptive Listing."* National Science Teachers Association, Washington, D.C., 1973.

Articles Concerned with Creativity

Anderson, H. H. *Creativity and Its Cultivation*. New York: Harper, 1959. Addresses presented at the Interdisciplinary Symposia on Creativity, Michigan State University, East Lansing, Mich.

Blough, G. O. "Some Observations and Reflections about Science Teaching in the Elementary School." *Science and Children* (December 1971), pp. 9–10.

Bybee, R. and McCormack, Alan. "Applying Piaget's Theory." *Science and Children* (December 1970), pp. 14–17.

Chittenden, E. A. "Piaget and Elementary Science." *Science and Children* (December 1970), pp. 9–14.

De Roche, E. F. "Some Creative Activities in Elementary Science." *Catholic School Journal* (December 1967), pp. 54–55.

Dewing, K., and Taft R., "Some Characteristics of the Parents of Creative Twelve-Year-Olds. *Journal of Personality* (March 1973), pp. 71–85.

Feldhusen, J. F. et al. "Teaching Creative Thinking." *Elementary School Journal* (October 1969), pp. 48–53.

Gibson, J. E. "Test Your Creativity." *Science Digest* (September 1970), pp. 23–24.

Griffith, C. "Environmental Studies, A Curriculum for People." *Science and Children* (January–February 1972), pp. 18–21.

Krippner, S. "Ten Commandments That Block Creativity." *Educational Digest* (January 1968), pp. 23–26.

Maltzman, I. "On the Training of Originality." *Psychological Review* (July 1960), pp. 229–242.

Mary Anthony, Sister. "Science Spurs Creativity." *Catholic School Journal* (September 1965), pp. 58–59.

Mason, M. "Creativity in Our Schools." Interview with Arnold Toynbee by Margaret Mason. *The Instructor* (April 1968), pp. 21, 132.

McCormack, A. J. and Doi, G. "Creativity Is a Bunch of Junk." *Science and Children* (September 1972), pp. 9–12.

Piltz, A. and Berson, M. P. "Head Start to Discovery." *Science and Children* (December 1965), pp. 6–9.

Rensulli, J. S. "Talent Potential in Minority Group Students." *Exceptional Child* (March 1973), pp. 437–144.

Row, Mary Budd. "Science, Silence, and Sanctions." *Science and Children* (March 1969), pp. 11–13.

Rubin, L. "Creativeness in the Classroom." *Journal of Secondary Education* 38 (March 1963), pp. 188–189.

Tamir, Israel P. "Understanding the process of Science Curricula." *Journal of Research in Science Teaching*, vol. 9, no. 3 (1972), pp. 239–245.

Samples, R. E. "Nature and Creativity." *Science and Children* (November 1969), pp. 9–10.

Samples, R. E. "Karis Handicap—The Impediment of Creativity." *Saturday Review*, July 15, 1967, pp. 56–57, 71.

Taylor, Calvin. "Creativity and the Classroom." *Science and Children* (May 1964).

Taylor, Calvin. "Talent Awareness Training." *The Instructor* (May 1969), pp. 61–68.

Taylor, Calvin. "Be Talent Developers." *N.E.A. Journal* (December 1968), pp. 67–69.

Torrance, E. P. "Comparative Studies of Creativity in Children." *Educational Leadership* (November 1969), pp. 146–148.

Torrance, E. P. "Rewarding Creative Thinking." *The Gifted Child Quarterly* (Winter 1961), p. 116.

Wayman, J., "Creative Child: What You Can Do." *Teacher* (March 1973), pp. 26–28.

Reports on Creativity

Education of the Gifted and Talented. Vols. I and II. Report to the Congress of the United States. U.S. Commissioner of Education, Pursuant to P.L. 91-230, Sec., 806, D.H.E.W., 1971.

Sourcebooks for Teachers

Eighth Report of the Information Clearinghouse on New Science and Mathematics Curricula. College Park: Science Teaching Center, University of Maryland, 1972.

Hone, E., Joseph, A., et al. *A Sourcebook for Elementary Science.* New York: Harcourt, Brace & World, 1971.

Piltz, Albert. *Science Equipment and Materials for Elementary Schools.* U.S. Government Office of Education OE 29029. Bulletin 1961, no. 28, 1963.

_____. *Extending Children's Early Science Interests.* Booklet no. 51. Chicago: F. E. Compton Co., 1958.

Roloff, Joan G., *There Is No Away.* Readings and Language Activities in Ecology. Beverly Hills: Glencoe Press, 1971.

Sund, Robert B., Tillery, Bill W., Trowbridge, Leslie W. *Elementary Science Discovery Lessons: The Earth Sciences.* Boston: Allyn and Bacon, 1970.

Sund, Robert B., Tillery, Bill W., Trowbridge, Leslie W. *Elementary Science Discovery Lessons: The Physical Sciences.* Boston: Allyn and Bacon, 1970.

Sund, Robert, Tillery, Bill W., Trowbridge, Leslie W. *Elementary Science Discovery Lessons: The Biological Sciences.* Boston: Allyn and Bacon, 1970.

Middle and Secondary School Level

Joseph, A., Brandwein, P. et al. *A Sourcebook for the Physical Sciences.* New York: Harcourt, Brace & World, 1961.

Morholt, E., Brandwein, P., and Joseph, A. *A Sourcebook for the Biological Sciences.* New York: Harcourt, Brace & World, 1966.

Bureau of Secondary Curriculum Development, New York State Education Department. *The General Science Handbooks,* Parts I, II, III. Albany, 1961.

United Nations Educational, Scientific and Cultural Organization. *UNESCO Sourcebook for Science Teaching.* Paris, 1956.

Heller, R. *Geology and Earth Sciences Sourcebook for Elementary and Secondary Schools.* Prepared under guidance of the American Geological Institute. New York: Holt, Rinehart and Winston, 1962.

Neuberger, Hans, and Nicholas, George. *Manual of Lecture Demonstrations, Laboratory Experiments, and Observational Equipment for Teaching Elementary Meteorology in Schools and Colleges.* The Mineral Industries Experiment Station, College of Mineral Industries. University Park, Pa.: Pennsylvania State University, 1962.

Understanding Environmental Education. A Collection of Readings in Environmental Awareness. U.S.O.E., HEW, Washington, D.C., 1970.

HOW TO DO IT SERIES
of the
National Science Teachers Association,
201 Sixteenth Street N.W.,
Washington, D.C. 20036

How to Plan and Organize Team Teaching in Elementary School Science
(471-14594) L. Jean York (35¢)

How to Teach Measurements in Elementary School Science
(471-14580) Neal J Holmes and Joseph J. Snoble (35¢)

How to Use Behavioral Objectives in Science Instruction
(471-14596) John J. Koran, Jr., Earl J. Montague, and Gene E. Hall (35¢)

How to Provide for Safety in the Science Laboratory
(471-14576) James R. Irving (35¢)

How to Use an Oscilloscope
(471-14572) Morris R. Lerner ($1.00)

How to Use Photography as a Science Teaching Aid
(471-14560) Herman H. Kirkpatrick (35¢)

How to Evaluate Science Learning in the Elementary School
(471-14564) Paul E. Blackwood and T. R. Porter (35¢)

How to Care for Living Things in the Classroom
(471-14288) Grace K. Platt (35¢)

How to Record and Use Data . . . in the Elementary School Science
(471-14292) Mary Clare Petty (35¢)

How to Investigate the Environment in the City: Air and Water
(471-14630) David C. Cox (50¢)

How to Individualize Science Instruction in the Elementary School
(471-14294) Theodore W. Munch (35¢)

How to Read the Natural Landscape in Forests and Fields
(471-14618) Millard C. Davis (50¢)

How to Present Audible Multi-imagery in Environmental Ecological Education
(471-14614) Pascal L. Trohanis (50¢)

How to Study the Earth From Space
(471-14624) Robert E. Boyer (50¢)

How to Handle Radioisotopes Safely
(471-14616) John W. Sulcoski and Grafton D. Chase ($1.00)

How to Tell What's Underground
(471-14640) Rolland B. Bartholomew ($1.00)

Measures of Creativity

There are several psychological tests to measure creativity. Unfortunately for the elementary teacher most of these are for grades seven and beyond. If you desire a complete list of these for children as well as adults, write to Educational Testing Service, Test Collection Department, Princeton, New Jersey 08540 and ask for their publication entitled "Measures of Creativity."

The creativity tests available for the elementary level are listed below:

Christensen, Paul B. *Consequence Test.* Sheridan Psychological Services, Inc., 10481 Santa Monica Boulevard, West Los Angeles, California 90025. Grades 7–16. Tests ideational fluency and originality. 1958.

Shaefer, Charles E. *Creativity Attitude Survey.* Psychologists and Educators, Inc. Suite 212, 211 West State Street, Jacksonville, Illinois 62650. Grades 4–6. Determines openness, desire for novelty, confidence in own ideas, theoretical and aesthetic orientation, and appreciation of fantasy. 1971.

Davis, Gary A. et al. *Attitude Questionnaire.* Wisconsin Research and Development Center for Cognitive Learning, University of Wisconsin, Madison, Wisconsin. Grades 7–8. Determines feelings of the individual about creativity in general. 1969.

Davis, Gary A., et al. *Hanger Problem.* Source same as above. Grades 7–8. The subjects are asked to give as many ways as possible for using a wire coat hanger. 1969.

Davis, Gary A., et al. *Hot Dog Problem.* Source same as above. Grades 7–8. Subject is told he is going to open a hot dog stand and is asked to propose as many as possible new and different types of hot dogs he would have. Test measures originality and practicality. 1969.

Shaefer, Charles E. *Similes Test.* Source same as above. Measures poetic expression creativity. Grades 4–16. 1963.

INDEX

Activities:
  different, 105
  encouraging, 103–104
  environmental education, 263–
    264
  family, 72
Adapting Science Materials for
    the Blind (ASMB), 168–171
Administrators, 36, 221–223
Arts, adjunct to science creativ-
    ity, 108
ASMB (*see* Adapting Science
    Materials for the Blind)
Authoritarianism, 48

Behavior, experience and, 46
Biological Science Curriculum
    Study (BSCS), 131
Blackwood, Paul, 4–7
Blough, Glenn O., 1
Books, science-related, 71 (*see
    also* Textbooks)
Brainstorming, 111–112, 263
Broudy, H., 291
Bruner, Jerome S., 129
Buckley, Helen, 57, 58–61

Career awareness, 292
Cartoons, 267
Checklists:
  environmental education, 84
  parental role, 72–73
Chemical Bond Approach,
    (CBA), 131
Chemical Education Material
    Study (CHEM), 131
Choices, for students, 104–105
Classroom, science room com-
    pared, 121–123
Cognitive development:
  individual differences, 43–44
  Piaget's stages of, 39–43

Collages, 268
Community:
  libraries, 95–96
  role of, 74–75
  science museums, 96–97
Conceptually Oriented Program
    in Elementary Sciences
    (COPES), 178–186
Concrete operational stage, cog-
    nitive development, 41, 43
Conditions, creative learning, 51–
    54
Continuing education, 118
  Project In-step, 201–205
Copernicus, Nicolaus, 10
COPES (*see* Conceptually Ori-
    ented Program in Ele-
    mentary Science)
Counterintuitive events, 238–246
"Covering," learning distin-
    guished from, 57
Creative teaching:
  drug education, 91–94
  environmental education, 75–
    90
  factors, 116–126
  principles, 226–227
  programs, 129–206
  science generally, 97–112
Creativity, scientific:
  attributes, 7–10
  defined, 4–7
  development activities, 26–
    35, 100–112
  environmental influence, 46–
    51
  failure to encourage, 20–22
  fostering, 66–67, 100–112
  and intelligence, 18–20
  parents' role, 48–51
  and science education, 10–11
  in teachers, 106–107

Culturally deprived children, 75
Curiosity:
  satisfaction of, 70
  stimulating, 102–103
Curriculum revision, 119, 129–
  132, 206, 208–223, 275–279

Darwin, Charles, 10, 48–49
Demonstration technique, 279–
  289
  selection, 281–282
Descriptions, scientists and, 5–6
Development:
  cognitive, 39–44
  school role, 97–112
  theory for creative, 55–57
Diagram technique, 261
Discovery approach, 55–57
Discovery charts, use of, 110–111
Discovery lessons, 111
Discrepant events, 238–246
Discussion technique, inquiry,
  227–235
Drug education:
  creative teaching of, 91–94
  defined, 91

Earth Science Curriculum Project
  (ESCP), 131, 263
Ecology, 77–78 (see also En-
  vironmental education)
Ecosystem, 77–78
Edison, Thomas A., 106
Ehrlich, Paul, 106
Eisner, Elliot W., 7, 9
Elementary Science Project
  (ESP), 177
Elementary Science Study (ESS),
  132–148
Elementary and Secondary Edu-
  cation Act, Title I, 75
Emotional stability, and creativ-
  ity, 9
Engineers, as a resource, 94–95
Environment:
  classroom/science room, 121–
  123
  and mental development, 46–
  51, 100
  role of home, 69–74
Environmental education:
  activities, 263–264

creative teaching of, 75–90
  instructional aids, 84–87
  program, 195–201
  sources, 88–89
  teaching guide, 79–83
  wilderness areas, 89–90
Environmental Education Act of
  1970, 76–77
ESP (see Elementary Science
  Project)
ESS (see Elementary Science
  Study)
Evaluation:
  ASMB, 171
  COPES, 182–184
  ESS, 146
  Individualized Science, 190–
  191
  materials, 219–220
  MINNEMAST, 174–176
  Model Educational Program in
  Ecology, 200
  Project In-step, 205
  Science—A Process Approach,
  153–154
  SCIS, 166
  self-analysis by teacher, 120
  SFTS, 195
Experience(s):
  and behavior determination,
  46
  enriching, 45–51, 71–72
  failure as, 106
  first-hand, 108
  parental role, 71–72
Experiments, 271–273
  controls, 271–272
  encouraging participation,
  103–104
  revision of, 275–279
Explanations, scientists and, 6

Failure, as positive experience,
  106
Fairs, 74–75
Feynman, Richard P., 49–51
Film loops, 243–244
Finkelstein, Leonard B., 21
Formal operational stage, cogni-
  tive development, 41–42, 43
Fox, 10
Furniture, science, 123

Gagné, Robert M., 55, 56
Galilei, Galileo, 10, 47–48
Getzels, J. W., 9
Government role:
   culturally deprived children, 75
   curriculum revision, 130
   environmental education, 76–77
Grid, use of, 270–271
Guilford, J. P., 8

Haeckel, Ernst, 77
Harvard Project Physics (HPP), 130
Hawkins, David, 26–34, 97–98, 99
Hess, Robert D., 46
Hidden objects, 268
Hilgard, Ernest, 111
Hippocrates, 3
Hogan, Nathan, 19
Home, role of, 69–74

Independence, creativity and, 9–10, 100–101, 103
Individual differences, cognitive development, 43–44
Individualized instruction, 44
Individualized Science, 186–191
Innovation, environmental education as vehicle, 79
Inquiry approach, 55–57 and choices, 104–105
   counterintuitive events, 242–243
   discussion technique, 227–235
   encouraging, 103
Instructional aids, 243–246
   environmental education, 84–87
Instrumentation, role of, 10–11
Intelligence, creativity and, 18–20
Interest groups, 102
Invention technique, 235–237
IPI Science (see Individualized Science)

Jackson, P. W., 9
Johnson, Philip G., 218

Kits, science, 108–110, 123–124
Kneller, George F., 225
Knowledge:
   authoritarian basis, 48
   product/process, 14–15, 131

Laboratories, mobile, 124
Laboratory equipment, 123–126, 292–293
Learning, creative:
   conditions for, 51–54, 97–100
   "covering" distinguished from, 57
   example, 53–54
Leeuwenhoek, Antonius van, 7
Liaison groups, professional, 95
Library, as resource, 95–96
"The Little Boy" (Buckley), 58–61
Lockard, J. David, 132

McCormack, Alan, 247
MacKennon, Donald, 19
Materials:
   ASMB, 169–170
   COPES. 180–181
   ESCP, 263–264
   ESS, 134–145
   evaluation of, 219–220
   homemade and inexpensive, 125–126
   Individualized Science, 188–190
   laboratory, 123–126, 292–293
   MINNEMAST, 173
   Model Educational Program in Ecology, 199
   Project In-step, 202–204
   Science—A Process Approach, 151
   SCIS, 159–163
   SFTS, 194
   workshops for, 119
Materials, sources:
   environmental education, 88–89
   self-enrichment reading, 117–118
"Messing About in Science" (Hawkins), 26–34

Methods:
ASMB, 169
COPES, 180
ESS, 134
Individualized Science, 188
MINNEMAST, 172
Model Educational Program in
Ecology, 199
Project In-step, 202
questioning, 61–64
Science—A Process Approach,
151
SCIS, 158
SFTS, 194
MINNEMAST (see Minnesota
Mathematics and Science
Teaching Project)
Minnesota Mathematics and Sci-
ence Teaching Project
(MINNEMAST), 172–177
Model Educational Program in
Ecology, 195–201
Motivation, 64–66
Muller-Willis, Lydia, 177
Museums, science, 96–97
Myers, R. E., 236

National Commission on Mari-
huana and Drug Abuse, 91–
94
National Science Foundation, ed-
ucation programs, 118
National Society for the Study of
Education 46th Yearbook,
99–100
Newton, Isaac, 10
Nichols, Dr., 147–148
Nonconformity, 100–101
Nutrition education, 93

Older children, as resource, 107–
108
Open-endedness, experiments,
272, 273–275
Osborn, Alex, 263

Parents, role of, 48–51, 69–74
Parnes, Sidney J., 236
Pasteur, Louis, 8
Peer pressure, creativity inhibited
by, 21
Perseverance, 105–106

Personality traits, creativity and,
9–10
Physical Science Study Commit-
tee (PSSC), 129–130
Piaget, Jean, 39, 102, 177
Piaget's theory, cognitive develop-
ment, 39–43
implications, 44–45
Plays, writing of, 267
Points of view, recognizing differ-
ent, 102
Polaroid camera, 245–246
Predictions:
scientists and, 6
stimulation through, 108
Preoperational stage, cognitive
development, 40–41, 42
Problem-solving, 64–66, 238
experiments, 272
recognition of ability in, 102
Programs, 129–206
ASMB, 168–171
COPES, 178–186
ESP, 177
ESS, 132–148
Individualized Science, 186–
191
MINNEMAST, 172–177
Model Educational Program in
Ecology, 195–201
Project In-step, 201–205
Science—A Process Approach,
148–155
SCIS, 156–168
SFTS, 192–195
Project In-step, 201–205
Publicity, science programs:
ASMB, 171
COPES, 184–185
ESS, 146–147
Individualized Science, 191
MINNEMAST, 176
Science—A Process Approach,
154
SCIS, 166–167
SFTS, 195

Questioning:
divergent, 206, 236
stimulation by, 61–64

Reading ability, 20
  emphasis upon, 70
Reading programs, for teachers, 117–118
Reform, educational:
  curriculum, 119, 129–132, 206, 208–223
  environmental education as vehicle for, 79
  experiments, 275–279
  textbooks, 208–209
Reinforcement:
  of perseverance, 105–106
  by positive recognition, 101
Riddles, pictorial, 246–261
  before and after, 247
Riesman, David, 9
Roe, Anne, 19, 20
Rushing project work, 103

Salk, Jonas, 103
Scholastic tradition, influence of, 14–15
Schools:
  and community, 74–75, 108
  and creative development, 97–112
  emphasis on verbal skills, 20–21, 70
  and home, 73
Science:
  creative discipline, 1–2, 5–6
  defined, 5
  role of, 3–4
  and superstition, 2–3
  teaching trends, 218–219
Science—A Process Approach, 148–155
Science Curriculum Improvement Study (SCIS), 156–168
Science folders, 266
Science for the Seventies (SFTS), 192–195
Science nights, 108
Scientific creativity:
  attributes, 7–10
  defined, 4–7
  environmental influence, 46–51
  failure to encourage, 20–22
  fostering, 66–67

  and intelligence, 18–20
  parents' role, 48–51
Scientists:
  characteristics of creative, 7–10
  as a resource, 94–95
SCIS (see Science Curriculum Improvement Study)
Self-improvement, teachers, 117–120
Sensory-motor stage, cognitive development, 40, 42
SFTS (see Science for the Seventies)
Slides, 35mm, 245
Sources, materials:
  curriculum revision, 132
  drug education, 94
  environmental education, 88–89
  self-enrichment reading, 117–118
Space-filling activity, 269
Sputnik, 129
Stevenson, Adlai, 69
Stick figures, 267–268
Stories, 266–267
Structuring, excessive, 23–26
Suchman, J. Richard, 25, 242–243
Superstitions, and science, 2–3
Surprise box, use of, 110
Systems analysis approach, 264–265

Talented children, interaction, 102
Talents, diversity of human, 15–18
Taylor, Calvin, 16–17, 20, 131, 208
Teacher(s):
  creativity in, 106–107
  device-oriented, 35
  failure to recognize creativity, 22–23
  insecurity of, 21–22
  role in creative learning, 54, 57–61, 97–112, 116–120, 274
  self-improvement, 117–120

Teacher preparation:
  COPES, 182
  ESS, 146
  Individualized Science, 190
  MINNEMAST, 174
  Model Educational Program in
    Ecology, 200
  Project In-step, 205
  Science—A Process Approach,
    152–153
  SCIS, 164–166
  SFTS, 195
Teacher's Guide (Santee School
  District), 79–83
Team teaching, 119–120, 221
Team work, 103
Textbooks:
  revision, 208–209
  selection criteria, 210–217
  use, 25, 209–210

Torrance, E. Paul, 18–19, 21, 45,
  105, 131, 236

U.S. Office of Education, 75

Verbal skills, overemphasized,
  20–21
Video recorders, 120, 244–245

Wallach, Michael A., 19
White, Burton L., 46
Wilderness areas, environmental
  education and, 89–90
Words, relating, 261–262
Workshops, new materials, 119

Zirbes, Laura, 116
Zwicky, 270